Strategic Nursing Management

Power and Responsibility in a New Era

Judith F. Garner, RN, BSN, MSN
Executive Director
Medical and Heart Programs
Presbyterian Hospital
Albuquerque, New Mexico

Howard L. Smith, PhD
Professor
Anderson School of Management
University of New Mexico
Albuquerque, New Mexico

Neill F. Piland, Dr PH
Director
Health Services Research and Education Division
Lovelace Medical Foundation
Albuquerque, New Mexico

AN ASPEN PUBLICATION®
Aspen Publishers, Inc.
Rockville, Maryland
1990

Library of Congress Cataloging-in-Publication Data

Garner, Judith F.
Strategic nursing management : power and responsibility in a new era /
Judith F. Garner, Howard L. Smith, Neill F. Piland.
p. cm.
Includes bibliographical references.
ISBN: 0-8342-0147-X
1. Nursing services—Administration. I. Smith, Howard L.
II. Piland, Neill Finnes. III. Title.
[DNLM: 1. Administrative Personnel. 2. Nursing—organization &
administration. 3. Power (Psychology). WY 105 G234s]
RT89.G36 1990
362.1'73'068—dc20
DNLM/DLC
for Library of Congress
90-89
CIP

Aspen Publishers, Inc., grants permission for photocopying for limited
personal or internal use. This consent does not extend to other kinds of
copying, such as copying for general distribution, for advertising or
promotional purposes, for creating new collective works, or for resale. For
information, address Aspen Publishers, Inc., Permissions Department,
1600 Research Boulevard, Rockville, Maryland 20850.

Editorial Services: Lorna Perkins

Library of Congress Catalog Card Number: 90-89
ISBN: 0-8342-0147-X

Printed in the United States of America

1 2 3 4 5

To Dr. Borje O. Saxberg, a true scholar and gentleman whose ideas helped form this book.

Table of Contents

Preface

A new age confronts nurses and the nursing profession. This new age is best exemplified by several fundamental shifts in the health care environment. Competition, prospective payment, investor-owned and corporate organizations, multi-institutional alliances, and retrenchment have dramatically altered health care organizations' objectives, policies, and cultures. Like other contributors in the service delivery process, nursing now confronts a more intense set of expectations as a result of these pressures. Additionally, the nursing profession is grappling with numerous concerns about the role of nurses. Collaborative practice, increasing acuity, primary nursing, career ladders, recruitment, retention and turnover, satisfaction, remuneration, and other issues are unsettling to those in the profession.

The nursing profession is challenged to resolve these conflicting pressures as they affect nursing departments, programs, and staff members. In daily service delivery this challenge falls to nurse managers. They ultimately deal with the stress accompanying the changing health care environment. Nursing staff look to them for direction, for protection from adverse factors affecting nursing care, and for inspirational leadership. This is a reasonable expectation because many nurses want to concentrate on what they do best: delivering high-quality patient care.

Nevertheless, several consistently appearing symptoms (e.g., staff turnover, budget overruns, low morale, and stable rather than advancing productivity) suggest that nurse managers are not entirely prepared to meet this challenge. The situation has prompted this book's publication. The bottom line is that nurse managers must develop and fine tune their managerial skills in responding to a complex environment and set of problems if they expect to improve patient care delivery and attainment of organizational objectives.

Nurse managers need to cultivate a management perspective that is strategic in orientation. Historically, they have followed a narrow vision of managing that focuses primarily on nursing operations and supervisory responsibilities. For many this management approach will continue, but more are being asked to participate in budgeting, personnel scheduling, program planning, patient care, and financial and strategic-level decisions. Nurse managers may be unprepared to respond to these new expectations because of the lack of proper managerial training.

Additionally, the profession has traditionally been delegated limited authority and responsibility by top health care administrators. Consequently, the extent to which nurses can adopt an active managerial style is constrained. As a result, nurse managers usually have an operations management or supervisory perspective. They seldom have nurtured (or received nurturing to develop) a strategic viewpoint. In this new age, nurse managers have more opportunities to experience substantial changes in their power and responsibilities than ever before.

The trends described above are exemplified by varying terminologies surrounding nurses in management positions. Traditionally, nurses have been involved in nursing administration. Administration, as opposed to management, implies a much narrower and maintenance-oriented posture than management. Today, nurse managers are increasingly found in organizational positions exemplifying this broader role. Nonetheless, the profession could respond more quickly to its new opportunities and expectations than it does at present. A managerial orientation among nurse managers is needed by health care organizations that suddenly have begun to operate in a businesslike manner.

Nursing and health care organizations require a vibrant, dynamic, creative, risk-taking, visionary, customer-driven, committed-to-excellence view of management. Nurse managers are discovering that they are challenged to cultivate a strategic and decisive orientation to function effectively in this new health care environment. The common denominators for success are skills development and a confident, results-oriented approach to managing. The purpose of this book is to help nurse managers hone their skills, management styles, and applications to nursing services. In this respect, the text (1) identifies skills and strategies needed by nurse managers in the new age of nursing; (2) provides specific educational, training, and reference material for cultivating these skills and management styles; (3) outlines viable methods for implementing the strategies; (4) delineates how these strategies can help nursing programs reach distinction; (5) effectively prepares nurse managers in these competencies for the new environment; (6) outlines a vision of nurse management for the 1990s and beyond; and (7) assists the nursing profession in moving toward an enlightened view of managing.

Chapter 1

The New Age for Nursing Administration

Many unsettling changes are occurring in the health care field that profoundly influence how health services are organized, financed, and delivered. These changes and their manifestations are significant to all nursing and health professionals. The changes have produced a climate of uncertainty and pessimism about the future. As a result, these revolutionary changes have met with passive resistance, resignation, and occasionally outright confrontation on the part of nurses—consequences that are not totally unanticipated. Like other health care sector workers, nurses are striving to protect themselves and patient care from undesired change due to factors over which they have limited or no control.

Change also implies the ability to capitalize on opportunities; however, this chapter analyzes the opportunities for nurses and nurse managers that result from transformations occurring in health care. The purpose of this chapter is to examine the changing health care environment from a nursing perspective. Central to this analysis is understanding why nurse managers need improved skills, vision, and ability to lead nurses and the nursing profession toward a new age. Nurse managers stand at the brink of vastly enlarged power and responsibility. Nevertheless, it is uncertain whether nurse managers are prepared to develop skills, attitudes, and competencies that will allow them to capitalize on these opportunities.

PRESSURES FOR A RESTRUCTURED HEALTH SYSTEM

What are the changing role expectations for nurse managers? How can nurse managers play a crucial part in resolving problems caused by the transition underway in the health system? In answering these questions it is essential that the major trends stimulating change in the health system be defined and analyzed. Of particular interest are the pressures illustrated in

1

Figure 1-1. Competition and entrepreneurialism, prospective payment, medical technology, corporate growth, changing public values, and diminished control by physicians are stimulating a metamorphosis in health care. These factors usher in a new age, which represents an environment filled with threats and opportunities for nurses and nurse managers.[1] It is uncertain whether or not nurse managers are prepared to rise to the occasion in effectively managing the expanded power and responsibility before them.

The primary point implied by Figure 1-1 is the opportunity for nurse managers to become more involved in resolving nursing and organizational problems.[2] Health care organizations need an active, visionary, and capable response from nurses and nurse managers to the pressures noted in Figure 1-1. Without such a response, health care organizations will encounter great difficulty in controlling costs, maintaining patient care quality, achieving fiscal solvency, meeting competition, or providing a satisfying context for work. Nurses will also be unable to fulfill effectively their patient care and personal goals. To a great extent this means that nurse managers must develop a broad vision of their power and managerial responsibilities. An additional consideration is the extent to which variations in performance by nursing services are felt throughout the organization.

These factors suggest that nurse managers will continue to be challenged to adopt an organization-wide or strategic perspective. This opportunity may never come again. A vibrant role undertaken by nurses implies more than just token representation in, or assignment to, nurse management positions. Instead, nurses can contribute in an active, leading manner that provides inspirational direction for other health professionals and the entire organization.

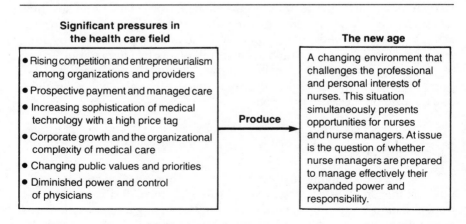

Figure 1-1 An Overview of the Pressures Responsible for a Restructured Health System

Competition

Competition among all health providers is an intense pressure upsetting the health field.[3] There are many visible manifestations of heightened market activity. First, proliferation of incentive-driven reimbursement policies such as prospective pricing and prepayment have introduced a broad range of economic motives and have stimulated competition. For example, because hospitals have more incentive to discharge patients early under prospective payment, greater competition has arisen in home health care. Second, market behaviors have become more overt and aggressive. This is best exemplified by trends in health care marketing. Providers (e.g., physicians) and organizations (e.g., hospitals) have vastly expanded their promotional efforts. Advertising, once regarded as unthinkable, is becoming commonplace. Third, corporations are expanding their involvement in the health field. Most noticeable is the growth of investor-owned organizations. This has intensified the debate over the ethics of profit and the tradeoffs with quality of care.

Competition is not a new or unknown phenomenon in the health care field or nursing. All the so-called market forces mentioned above have existed in the health field in one form or another, although they were often subtle or hidden. Now, competition is much more visible and recognizable. For example, increasing numbers of nurse entrepreneurs are starting successful nursing businesses. From a health system perspective there are both disadvantages and advantages accompanying increased competition and entrepreneurial activity. A central concern is that by introducing powerful market-oriented competition the care delivery process and behavior of providers may be significantly altered. Conversely, advocates suggest that competition instills efficiency and serves as a preferable alternative to regulation. Both perspectives offer compelling arguments.

Health professionals may become increasingly sensitive to costly mistakes in patient care due to a growing emphasis on economic results. For example, nurse practitioners may raise their productivity to the point that they minimize time when diagnosing patients' complaints. They may not make correct diagnoses, design a prudent treatment plan, or assuage patients' concerns. Similarly, health care organizations may be tempted to introduce savings in care delivery (e.g., by terminating services) primarily to increase profits, to stabilize fiscal solvency, or to improve market position. Additionally, the amenity level of patient care may be compromised (e.g., by reducing patient perquisites and services) to raise profits. Finally, hospital advertising to raise admissions may be undertaken in bad taste, thereby denigrating the nobility of health care delivery.

An optimistic view of competition suggests that long-run positive results will occur from competition. Higher-quality care coupled with more efficient pricing, wiser investment decisions, adoption of growth strategies, and cost containment are all possibilities in a reformed health care system. Competition could provide enough motivation to make an otherwise inefficient marketplace much more efficient.

An illustration of market forces at work is the so-called oversupply (actually a maldistribution) of physicians.[4] An oversupply improves the medical staff recruitment power of health care corporations. There is more competition in the health care system for fewer clinical positions, particularly those at the most prestigious and desirable institutions. Consequently, there are more degrees of freedom for health care organizations when choosing medical staff members. Physicians can be selected who have a demonstrated ability to provide quality care and to present low malpractice risks. Medical staff members could also be identified who have demonstrated the ability to control medical practice costs.

Hospitals, health maintenance organizations (HMOs), group practices, and other health delivery organizations are now able to select the best clinicians available rather than merely filling medical staff slots. In effect, the marketplace is reversing many traditional assumptions about provider-organization relationships. The prognosis for the future is a more market-driven relationship between physicians and organizations. This may introduce interesting alterations in professional perquisites. For example, physician reward systems (i.e., salary, benefits, and nonmonetary amenities) are expected to stabilize gradually. In some communities, health care organizations will not be bargaining for physician services; physicians will be pursuing organizational affiliations and medical staff privileges.

An oversupply implies decreased independence and freedom of choice for physicians. Mobility will be associated with the ability to achieve corporate or organizational goals, including the provision of high-quality care at low cost and the capacity to build market share through a growing patient base. Physicians who are unable to achieve these goals will become more dependent on the organizations in which they practice. They will be less able to transfer from one medical staff to another. Even if they are not liabilities (i.e., if they are able to avoid malpractice suits and excessive costs when providing services), their independence may still be undermined. Health care organizations will simply have a greater choice in the pool of all physicians.

Finally, an oversupply of physicians implies higher reliance on health care organizations' competitive efforts. Few solo practitioners can survive in a competitive environment unless they offer a distinctive product or service in terms of quality care, productivity, or price (i.e., unless they have the ability to provide a low-cost, but medically sound, service). Therefore, many solo practitioners are being driven out of individual practice into group practices or other medical organizations that have sufficient resources for a vibrant competitive effort. Concurrently, physicians who already belong to group practices are becoming more dependent on their organizations to market medical services.

The competitive forces confronting physicians have a distinct analog in nursing, but the situation is reversed for nurses.[5,6] An undersupply of (or, alternatively, a sharply increased demand for) skilled nurses appears to exist in the health care delivery system. Actually, the nursing shortage problem is attributed to numerous factors such as insufficient wages, changing personal goals among registered nurses, working conditions, and role conflicts. Whatever the causal factors, it is apparent that many nurses are choosing to leave nursing and to remain out of the nursing labor force.[7] This phenomenon has produced distinct labor market reactions by hospitals and other health providers. A new willingness on the part of health care institutions to pay higher wages, to expand benefits, to improve career ladders, to cultivate collaborative practice, and to experiment with innovative solutions reflects a response to the market and competition.

Many of the constraints faced by physicians (discussed above) are reversed for nurses. As the comparative analysis given in Table 1-1 suggests, competition in health care is causing revolutionary changes for professional providers. Competition can simultaneously be good and bad; its value depends on the perspective being applied. For the short run, nurses appear to benefit from higher competition for their services. Physicians appear to be losing ground as a result of competition at the professional and organizational levels.

Table 1-1 Competition's Impact on Physicians and Nurses

Physicians	*Nurses*
Emphasis on productivity and efficient practice; more stringent expectations and control surrounding medical practice	Emphasis on productivity and efficient practice; adoption of practice models (e.g., primary nursing) that are more professionally satisfying to nurses
Competition for clinical positions; less opportunity to select practice of choice	High availability of clinical positions; more opportunity to select practice of choice, and more opportunities outside hospitals
Lower mobility and autonomy	Higher mobility and autonomy
Stabilizing or slowly evolving range of benefits and perquisites	Expanding range of benefits and perquisites
Reliance on organizations to market services and to fund practice (e.g., group practice)	Decreasing reliance on organizations

Prospective Payment and Managed Care

Directly coinciding with more intense health care competition are changes in reimbursement practices by third-party insurers. There have been, and will continue to be, significant revisions in reimbursement policy involving prospective payment (or pricing), capitation payment, and managed care. Hospital payments were the first to be altered, but it is the continuing evolution of reimbursement that has major implications for the delivery of health care services. Hospitals, nursing homes, home health agencies, and other organizational providers are experiencing prospective payment systems. A number of proposals have surfaced, including physician payments under the prospective payment mechanism. In sum, health care services will be constrained by prospective payments. Nursing services will be forced to participate in the increasingly austere environment confronting health care organizations.[8]

The trend toward prospective payment is unlikely to deviate in the future as a result of cost pressures. Providers are being told in advance what payments will be made for services rendered. Providers must then keep service costs below payment rates if an annual operating surplus or profit margin is to be attained. When the costs of service rise above the prospective prices, a loss is incurred. Yearly performance is a matter of summing the respective gains and losses that determine financial solvency. Enough fiscal periods showing a loss could result in bankruptcy.

Prospective pricing establishes new incentives for health care providers to control costs and to enhance revenues. Management of cost control and productivity is fundamental for survival. Prospective pricing introduces a unique, incentive-based approach to regulation in the health services field. Nevertheless, it is uncertain that health care organizations or professionals fully understand the implications of the incentives. The primary issue is how to trade off patient services for fiscal solvency, a balance that many medical and nursing professionals are uncomfortable making. Intertwined with this imperative for revised operating practices are regulatory policies and clinical traditions. Regulations are gradually restricting the capacity of clinicians to operate autonomously, free from control by organizational, governmental, and professional entities.

Physicians may attempt to alter the mix of patients whom they serve from Medicare or Medicaid to commercial carriers and private payers. Prospective payment has become a widespread phenomenon that limits this strategy. Alternatively, physicians may monitor proposed percentage increases in fees paid by managed care plans to formulate timely reactions (e.g., by retaining or dropping patients with these reimbursement policies). These strategies enable physicians to adjust the economic inputs and outputs from their practices, but their options are rapidly becoming limited as more payers adopt prospective pricing incentives. Hospitals did not behave any differently from physicians in responding to Medicare's diagnosis-related groups (DRGs). In the initial stages of Medicare DRGs, hospitals evaluated each DRG to determine which were economic winners and which were losers. Those DRGs generating more costs than revenues were minimized and even deleted from hospitals' ranges of services. This strategy has become less feasible because Medicare has the ability to control payment margins.

These reactions do not necessarily indicate sensitivity to the larger issue accompanying prospective pricing. The crucial issue is the amount of control established by the third-party payers. Before prospective pricing, third-party insurers had little influence over the costs and service patterns of providers. Now, prospective payment provides insurers the ability to control service delivery efforts throughout the health services sector. The ability to determine when prospective payments for hospital or physician services will be changed (e.g., increased to account for inflation) is a main point of contention, yet most providers overlook this fact because they have become so caught up in the details of prospective payment. Medicare could freeze hospital reimbursement across 470 different DRGs. This is powerful control because the third party limits the revenue-producing capability of providers.

Medical Technology

Technology and its proliferation is another factor affecting the distribution of power in the health field. Technology eventually affects the relationship between providers and health care organizations. New technology has been effective in raising standards of care while introducing economies of operation through higher productivity. Regardless of the quality and productivity implications, many developments in medical technology are enormously expensive and normally best utilized in large-scale operations. Further complicating these relationships is the recognition that regulation has traditionally determined where and by whom medical technology (e.g., computed axial tomography scanners) will be acquired.

Technological equipment has historically been centered in hospitals. Medical technology normally requires ready access to large amounts of capital and numerous highly skilled personnel. Technology is productively used in many hospitals because a large number of practitioners have access to it for diagnosis and treatment purposes. Additionally, the expense of new equipment is rapidly amortized in hospitals. Hospitals develop revenue streams that ensure capital for replacing and adding new technology, but these benefits have worked against individual practitioners. Increasingly, sophisticated medical technology requires specialized training. Specialty eventually creates barriers to primary care physicians and other clinical personnel to using the technology.

Small providers (e.g., solo practitioners, partnerships, and group practices) are increasingly unable to compete with larger health care organizations because of limited capital resources and the inability to support sophisticated equipment. Given the capital, maintenance, and staff support requirements of new medical technology, it is likely that the dilemma will continue. For example, it is predicted that by the 1990s there will be a shortage of credit to finance the $193 billion of capital needed for hospital facilities or equipment.[9] More power will shift into the hands of successful health care organizations that are capable of financing medical technology for their clinicians. Large multispecialty group practices, HMOs, and multi-institutional health care chains have the best prognosis for coping with the technological revolution in medicine.

Organizational Complexity

The use of nurse managers appears to be an appropriate mechanism for resolving nursing problems in the health field that are due to the growing organizational complexity of the system.[10] Whether the problem is regulation, reimbursement, multi-institutional arrangements, or corporate involvement, the health care system is much more organizationally complex today than ever before. This complexity has shifted control of health care services toward organizations and away from individuals. Additionally, the nursing and medical professions are losing control because many professionals cannot or will not devote attention to retaining control; they want to practice medicine or nursing. A recent survey of nursing directors in magnet hospitals and faculty directors of the National League of Nursing indicated that nursing practice is the primary nursing issue today.[11] Use of the nurse manager is viewed as a promising means by which the nursing profession can retain control over its future and instill some rationality into an otherwise disagreeable set of circumstances.

Health care is no longer a service that can be effectively delivered by independent individuals. Teams of specialists backed by highly functional support systems dominate the delivery process. Primary nursing is an excellent example of an organizational system orchestrated by nurses and shown to have merit over traditional care patterns.[12-14] Such approaches are expensive to create and operate and difficult to assemble and maintain, however. Additionally, they require skilled management expertise to control operations and utilization. Medical care has been driven to a perturbing point. Primary care is highly constrained. Referral is commonplace. Independence is seldom viable. Primary care nurses and physicians are increasingly interdependent and linked to specialists.

Group practices and other organizational forms are surfacing as effective means for addressing the complexity of medical care, but these group arrangements and organizational systems cannot derive efficiency from the informal relationships and professional networks that characterize traditional medical practice. The implication for physicians and nurses is threatened professional autonomy. Organizational systems are not based on a nurturing vision for nursing and medical practitioners.

In some respects it can still be argued that physicians are the main integrators of care in the health system. Although the physician is implicitly the leader of a collaborative team, the team is far more powerful than any of its individual members. Physicians now have an entirely different posture with respect to this team than they did in the past. Fifty years ago the solo practitioner functioned without team assistance as a healer in society. Today, the health care team can provide quality and cost-effective care only when deployed with the backing of a substantial and skilled organization. Nursing care is an excellent case in point. Nurses are able to make many decisions that once were considered the sole domain of physicians. Patient care cannot function effectively by relying solely on physicians to make decisions. A team approach is needed.

Nurse managers may not be able to influence significantly the growing complexity of the health care system; but this does not imply that they should relinquish their advocacy. Nurse managers can contribute in many meaningful ways to the overall structure and process of their organizations. Nurse managers can assist in formulating productive structures that organize nursing to deliver high-quality care. Every team needs a leader, and nurse managers should help nursing staff realize that the team is a collaborative group of individuals. Reliance on traditional beliefs about physicians as all-knowing leaders only prevents the development of a collaborative and hence productive team. In sum, nurse managers can set the tone for how nurses are perceived by the remainder of the organization.[15]

Prospective payment also creates an organizational imperative that dominates the health care system and influences clinicians. Prospective pricing and managed care function best in organizational systems because the scope of activity is expanded, extensive coordination is necessary, and disciplined specialization is essential. This is well illustrated by Medicare's prospective payment system, which covers more than 470 different diagnosis categories. With a payment system that complex, sophisticated data management systems are needed to accumulate, aggregate, and analyze data. Such systems facilitate making decisions about responding to payment rates and planning for the future impact of prospective pricing. Managed information and sophisticated technical analysis improve organizational decisions and policies.

The organizational imperatives accompanying prospective payment are clearly evident in HMOs. The key elements of an effective HMO program include quality control, exact costing of services and products, cost-effective facility development, precise personnel management, and competitive strategic management. These ingredients will not materialize without purposeful integration. The effort must be organized. To achieve this, HMOs attempt to minimize conflicts of interest among organizational constituents (e.g., professional personnel, facilities operations, and marketing effort). In effect, HMOs must reinforce commitment to the overall organization and develop an atmosphere of teamwork. Subunits (e.g., nursing) are encouraged to suboptimize their interests in promoting the entire organization.

Changing Public Values

Prospective payment is consistent with trends in the public mood that favor cost consciousness.[16] Although there has been considerable discussion about the impact of prospective payment on providers and third-party payers, the effect on health consumers has been understated. Consumers have observed that an increasing proportion of their earnings is being allocated to health expenditures. Additionally, poverty jeopardizes health insurance coverage.[17] Even with health insurance coverage, it is difficult to avoid rising costs. Employers have tended to push rising health costs back on employees. The culmination of these trends is a desire for less costly health care by the public not only in terms of health insurance premiums and acute care treatment but also in the preventive aspects as well.

Coupled with this changing public mood is a growing distrust of the health care system. There is a lingering suspicion (perhaps related to physician incomes and profits by pharmaceutical companies) that the health care system is self-serving despite its assurances that it serves the public interest. In addition to the cost consciousness accompanying prospective payment, there seems to be a more favorable attitude toward illness prevention today. Commitment to exercise, nutrition awareness, and prevention of substance abuse suggest a popular belief that costly disease episodes can be avoided.

The healthy lifestyle interest of society affects the demand for pathology-oriented health care services. Health professions are not structured (or positioned) to facilitate this new approach to living. Medicine is generally episodic and disease oriented. Consequently, physicians and other providers are unable to envision how they can optimally integrate healthy living with medical care. Generally speaking, by training they do not respond well to preventive medicine. Furthermore, the delivery of preventive medicine is both professionally and economically unrewarding for practitioners compared with pathology-based health care.

Diminished Power and Control of Physicians

Accompanying the progressive changes in the health system is the breakdown of physician domination and control. Physicians perceive an impending and real loss of power and control. This reaction is to be anticipated. Like any professional group enjoying certain perquisites, physicians are reluctant to forego these privileges. Consequently, the medical profession often reacts to the restructuring of the health system with blocking, stalling, and defensive tactics aimed at legislative, regulatory, judicial, economic, and public policies.

The intensity of the medical profession's reaction to a restructured health system is governed by physician commitment to the traditions that define medical care. Among these are autonomy, professional control, solo medical practice, and fee-for-service entrepreneurialism. These customs and beliefs have produced a powerful profession and, taken together, have become a primary obstacle to change. With intense commitment there is conflict as the profession experiences pressures to change radically over a short period of time.

Both individually and collectively, physicians have been free of most restraints on their practices. For example, quality of care regulation has typically been managed by the profession without external control. Autonomy is also evident in the laissez-faire management of physicians by hospitals, medical groups, and other large organizational health care providers. The relationship between physician and organization has characteristically underscored the independence of the physician. Both physicians and organizations have maintained their own agendas. Health care organizations have cautiously avoided encroaching on the autonomy of physicians.

Professional control has been maintained in the belief that physicians are the authorities best able to assess peer performance. This belief continues in the medical profession. Legally mandated use of physicians in policy or top administrative positions of governmental health services (e.g., state and local health departments) illustrates professional control. There is no a priori reason why a state or local health department needs to be managed by a physician, but this privilege (and similar ones) has ostensibly been created by extensive professional control.

Solo medical practice is one of the strongest underpinnings of the medical profession. Physicians are educated with the assumption that they will eventually initiate their own practices. This assumption has created the somewhat romantic perception in the profession that individual practitioners are the basis of a viable health care system. Associated with this belief is membership in and support of a powerful professional association (i.e., the American Medical Association). The sanctity of solo practice is viewed as being conducive to maintaining professional integrity.

Solo practice is related to another physician-oriented custom: fee-for-service entrepreneurialism. Fee-for-service is the prevailing method by which physicians have been paid for their services. The fee-for-service mechanism helps sustain the entrepreneurialism of solo practice. It also permits a convenient contractual relationship between the physician and institutional providers, particularly hospitals. The profile that emerges is one of the solo practice physician maintaining autonomy and professional control aided by fee-for-service reimbursement.

The demise of these traditions suggests one definitive conclusion: The medical profession is losing control of health care delivery. Supports, norms, traditions, privileges, and values are rapidly disintegrating or evaporating, and physicians are in a predicament because of their intense socialization to these customs. Not only do they personally experience a tremendous amount of anxiety and conflict, but they are also fundamentally unprepared to respond through new value strategies or tactics. In many respects, this creates a high degree of alienation because practitioners have limited impact on the entire system and because the medical profession has lost the ability to moderate, much less control, the entire process.

IMPLICATIONS FOR NURSE MANAGERS

What are the implications of a restructured health system for nurse managers? The answer to this question is most easily ascertained by examining Figure 1-2. As this diagram suggests, concurrent with the health system revolution has been a dramatic alteration in nursing values. Once content with relatively subservient, following, low-profile, nurturing-oriented, and menial roles, nurses are now demanding a more active and responsible role in patient care. Figure 1-2 indicates that the emerging value system conflicts in many respects with the characteristics of a restructured health system.

Emerging Nursing Values

Nurses are now more concerned about professional clout, recognition, and rewards.[18] They no longer are content to work for compensation that is not commensurate with their education. They now have the professional clout to enforce their demands for higher remuneration, better benefits, and meaningful support. Aided by a shortage of skilled nurses, members of the profession are discovering that they can demand and receive a more extensive

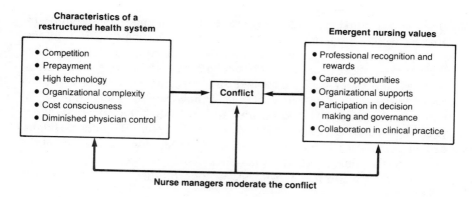

Characteristics of a restructured health system

- Competition
- Prepayment
- High technology
- Organizational complexity
- Cost consciousness
- Diminished physician control

Conflict

Emergent nursing values

- Professional recognition and rewards
- Career opportunities
- Organizational supports
- Participation in decision making and governance
- Collaboration in clinical practice

Nurse managers moderate the conflict

Figure 1-2 Conflict between Emergent Nursing Values and a Restructured Health System

range of benefits. Although its members are still viewed as being undercompensated, nursing is rising in its wage and salary status. These gains are helping diminish the perception that nurses provide all the care for little money while physicians invest little time yet reap all the monetary benefits. For most nurses, however, the issue is much larger than just the amount of a paycheck. They are vitally concerned about the recognition, professional and personal rewards, total compensation package, and intrinsic value involved with being a nurse.

Career opportunities have become an issue for many nurses,[19] but their educational preparation is a continuing debate.[20] A high proportion of nurses want the option of professional advancement to be available. They may not necessarily pursue the opportunities, but they want them to be available should they decide to alter their professional pursuits. Many recognize that unless additional education is received such professional advancements will be difficult to accomplish. Nonetheless, unless the options are viable (e.g., involving revisions in organization or program structures and expansion of managerial positions) and unless resources become available (e.g., through continuing education and management development), nurses may encounter difficulty when expanding their careers.

Nurses are expressing greater interest in and preference for organizations that support high-quality care delivery and patient advocacy.[21] Prospective payment has reduced the slack in organizational budgets. Cost-containment policies in health care organizations ultimately confront care delivery policies.[22] Nurses have observed that health care organizations are not at all reluctant to slash nursing budgets and ancillary staff in meeting fiscal goals.[23] The impression is that cost comes before quality. Furthermore, nurses are being asked to increase their productivity without organizational support.

Consequently, nursing standards are severely threatened. These belt-tightening measures ultimately mean that nurses are bearing the brunt of cost control either through staffing cuts or support reductions. Judging by nurse turnover rates, there needs to be a better balance of demands and resources.

Nurses, like other highly educated and skilled professionals, express a desire to participate in decisions influencing how they complete their assignments. Consequently, as the health care environment changes they are increasingly cognizant of how these changes affect clinical practice. Heightened participation in clinical and administrative decision making is essential to reducing the alienation that results when their views are not solicited. One remedy is to provide nurses with more opportunities to determine their governance.

Nurses also express interest in collaborative patient care rather than dictated patient care. Some nursing authorities have suggested that collaborative practice is a preferred model in which physicians, nurses, and ancillary staff can jointly determine care plans.[24,25] Although truly collaborative practice is more an ideal than an operating reality (because of reimbursement and legal constraints), there remains a distinct impression that effective care is attainable when all providers have input into the care plan. Nurses play a pivotal role in almost any care plan. This fact should be recognized in how nurses' professional insights are incorporated into patient care.

The Conflict of Values

A restructured health system represents an entirely new service delivery context. The past environment was typically noncompetitive and resource rich. This has been replaced with an intense atmosphere and businesslike attitudes. Competition and cost consciousness are now the primary drivers of health care organizations. Whereas quality was a primary focus of health delivery under cost-based reimbursement, greater attention is being given now to the cost implications of service delivery. For many health professions this change in attitudes and values produces a significant reordering of priorities that affects how care is delivered. For example, nurses have observed growing constraints on patient care, particularly in the level of resources allocated to support nursing; ancillary staff members are being cut to improve prospects of attaining budgets; nurse staffing is more constrained; and there are higher expectations for productivity.

At many levels the emerging values held by nurses conflict with the characteristics of a restructured health system. In a time of growing fiscal restraint due to competition, prospective payment, and cost consciousness, nurses are seeking professional fulfillment not only in terms of recognition but also in terms of rewards. Needless to say, many health care organizations do not feel that they can support the investment sought by nurses at this time.

The resource constraints also affect nurses' growing realization that cost control is being derived at their expense. Nurses are being asked to do more with less. They have fewer colleagues to share the workload. They ultimately perform many tasks outside their job descriptions because ancillary staff have already been decreased in belt-tightening measures. Having done so much for so long with so little, it is understandable why nurses are leaving hospitals for other pursuits.

Any organization attempting to establish a lean and trim structure inevitably must delete positions (particularly staff positions) that do not contribute directly to the production of a good or service. This translates into the termination of many positions other than direct patient care that nurses could feasibly fill. Hence interest in the nursing profession in alternatives to traditional clinical or administrative positions ultimately conflicts with the needs of health care organizations. Hospitals and other health providers need nurses in clinical practice; they do not have the surplus resources to support expanded roles.

Nurses have struggled for decades with the domination of physicians over nursing care. Now, as physicians begin to lose control over health delivery because of reimbursement policy changes, a physician surplus, and corporate expansion, paradoxically nurses may not be any better off than before. The primary factor causing this paradox is the growth of large-scale organizations—multi-institutional systems—that determine how health care is delivered. Both nurses and physicians encounter a new constraint on care delivery: the expectations of corporately managed institutions. Although many nurses are interested in sharing clinical control with a team of providers, collaboration is constrained by the needs of efficient and effective health care delivery. Thus both nurses and physicians are discovering that collaborative practice implies a third party: the organization and its goals.

Finally, as Figure 1-2 suggests, participative decision making and self-governance by nurses are also affected by a restructured health system. Consistent with thinking about building corporate cultures devoted to excellence, nurses' participation in organizational governance should lead to better performance. Competitive, cost-conscious, and constrained health care organizations need to involve all personnel in efforts to achieve greater operational efficiency and quality service delivery. Nevertheless, there are limits on how far decentralized decision making and participation can be taken when corporate goals demand specific targets for financial performance.

Nurse Managers and the Conflict

Figure 1-2 implies that nurse managers hold exceptional promise for resolving the conflict between a restructured health system and emerging nursing values. Nurse managers are the primary intermediaries in the conflict. They are in a key position to represent and manage the interests of both organizations and staff nurses, but they can only do this effectively if they understand the issues and concerns of both parties and seek equitable resolutions that reduce the conflict.

For example, nursing departments are being asked to provide more services with fewer staff members. The challenge for nurse managers is to convey the interests of nurses to top management. Simultaneously, staff should be involved in determining innovative solutions. In the negotiation process nurse managers may draw on a wide range of skills, including financial management, promotion (i.e., marketing), operations analysis, and strategic planning, to argue forcefully nursing's case with top management. Nurse managers will also rely on other skills, such as those relating to leadership, motivation, group dynamics, and culture building, in eliciting nurses' commitment to a prudent plan that recognizes organizational constraints.

Neither the organization nor the nursing staff can do the job alone. Furthermore, without competent guidance from nurse managers, something (e.g., esprit de corps or commitment) may be lost in the give-and-take between the two parties. Conflict could escalate under these circumstances. For these reasons, it is imperative that the nursing profession (and organizations) cultivate the development of nurse managers who are capable of moderating the inherent conflict.

OPPORTUNITIES FOR NURSE MANAGERS

The health care system is changing rapidly. The implications are numerous and will influence all health care providers. Few providers will be affected as significantly as nurses, however. Not only do nurses face significant transitions in clinical responsibilities, they also confront decreasing support from organizations in service delivery efforts. The nursing profession is discovering that it needs advocates who responsibly and effectively represent nurse interests.[26]

Nurse managers can play an important role in moderating the perceived impact from these events. Even so, the nursing profession has not acted effectively in presenting and arguing its case. Health care organizations are dominating the health system; the interests of nurses are easily lost in the daily give-and-take of large-scale institutions. Nurses need representatives in positions of authority who can participate in and influence the crucial decisions and issues facing the health system. Nurse managers can minimize the contention between the staff nurse and the organization.

The nursing profession will continue to spend considerable effort in the coming years in defining its role in the new institutional entities shaping the health care field. Unless nurses develop effective means of interfacing with and influencing the evolving organizational structure of the health system, their input may be lost. They need representatives who are comfortable with and capable of working in an organizational context. Nurse managers should be able to provide this representation while adequately protecting the interests of the nursing profession. This representation is crucial because nurses have achieved only limited success in designing and attaining an improved professional environment.

The Prospects for Nurse Managers

Health care organizations are rapidly becoming the most powerful, dominant force in the health care system. Many health care professionals are increasingly at odds with institutional providers. This conflict has significant implications for the nursing profession. As the health care system is increasingly controlled by organizational entities, attention should focus on the dysfunctions developing for health professionals. Are clinicians such as physicians and nurses recognized as important contributors in setting strategic objectives and direction in the health industry? Are mechanisms created by which clinicians' viewpoints are constructively integrated into organizational decision making? As these questions suggest, the relationship between the nursing profession and evolving health care organizations must inevitably be closer. This demands commitment and sharing that exceeds the reciprocity typically found between nurses and health care organizations.

There is a growing opportunity for the entire nursing profession, and particularly nurse managers, to define and fulfill new roles in health care organizations. For nurse managers these roles should center on the increased power and responsibilities that they stand to gain as a result of financial constraints on health care organizations and the continuing shortage of nurses. Nurse managers should exercise judgment that is based on nurses' education and experience and embellished by appropriate education in managerial skills. Meanwhile, nurses at the clinical level can continue to focus on service delivery efforts, for which they are best qualified.

Nurse managers and nurses can adopt more organizationally active and relevant roles in their institutions. Because organizations are dominating the health system, it is vital that nurses become more active in managerial and executive positions that entail responsibility for guiding the health system. The need for nurses to take part in leadership and management responsibilities in health care organizations by nurses can no longer be ignored. Organizations face severe fiscal conditions; nurses must provide leadership to ensure that patient care and professional well-being are maintained. On the other hand, leadership responsibilities have not entirely been appreciated by nurses in the past. In many respects, when nurses became involved in managerial and organizational issues it was because they did not have a strong commitment to nursing practice. Such attitudes did not recognize that there is a crucial, not a token, role for nurses in the management of health care organizations.

Effective integration of nurses into meaningful management positions dictates an appropriate place, an appropriate role, and appropriate authority. It implies that nurses should be chosen for positions that are strategically relevant to leading nurses and the profession. This suggests that nurse managers should be responsible for bringing the nursing staff and the organization together in solving problems. Management positions should be allocated to nurses who are evaluated for their ability to manage rather than their ability to practice nursing. Health care organizations should be selecting their brightest and most articulate nurses, training them to assume management responsibilities, and promoting them in response to demonstrated ability, interest, and commitment.

Obstacles Confronting Nurse Managers

Nurse managers are often ill-prepared for a world in which the basis of power is organizational authority (i.e., the hierarchy of authority). The ability to influence operations and service delivery efforts depends on one's position in the power pyramid. Because of their education, skills, and traditional staff relationships, nurses have not acquired extensive organizational authority or power. The nursing profession could place the authority and control of nurses in a new perspective. The profession could develop leaders—nurse managers—who can fulfill the responsibilities and requirements of organized health care. In delivering high-quality and low-cost health care, organizations can simultaneously control and nurture professional and ancillary staff. This suggests that nurses will need to function in a management control system while expressing advocacy for staff members. Those nursing departments that produce excessive costs, generate patient complaints, or raise malpractice risks must be identified and addressed in the organization's (and the patients') best interests.

Some nurses have eagerly sought positions of leadership and control but often were not adequately prepared to manage when they did attain such positions. Consequently, nurses in general are usually unprepared to communicate with professionally trained managers about their concerns, and they are unable to form these concerns into concepts that are managerially understandable or resolvable. Nurse managers who develop the necessary management skills could serve as an effective intermediary between nurses and organizations.

Nurses can easily understand the serious ramifications of a lack of a common frame of reference. The problem is more serious than appearances suggest, however. Nurses are essentially allocating the management and governance of health care to others. As a result, they are unable to provide meaningful input into policy and strategy formulation in health care organizations. Nurses are inadvertently relinquishing control of nursing care because they are not asked to contribute to or to exercise control over health care organizations. They have little power because they do not mandate or participate actively in policy setting, policy implementation, or strategic management in health care organizations.

It is not surprising that leadership positions in health care corporations are seldom held by nurses. Hospital administrators and other managers trained in business administration generally hold positions of managerial authority in health care organizations. These individuals have a common frame of reference. They are adept at working in an organizational context and are well prepared to work toward the interests of the health care organization. They can communicate effectively with others in the organization. Consequently, they often build on the power that has been delegated to them. In short, they have the skills to function in organizations and the values to make a strong commitment to organizations.

Governing boards of health care organizations are also dominated by professionals other than nurses. It is rare to find nurses represented on a board of directors or trustees. A far more common occurrence is to discover hospital administrators, insurance executives, and business leaders as board members because of their valuable management expertise. They are likely to understand business strategy and the need to respond to a competitive environment. Nurses are, precisely because of their values and education, exceptionally poor selections for such leadership positions. They lack a vision of where health care is headed because of their emphasis on nursing issues. Certainly, nurse managers are responsible for addressing the problems confronting the nursing staff, but health care organizations need their key leaders in governance positions to have a broad understanding of problems, not just nursing issues.

Nurse Managers in a Reorganized Health System

Considering that nurses are generally ill prepared to provide effective management insight for a world of health care that is increasingly dominated by organizations, what is an agenda for the nursing profession during the reorganization of the delivery system? There is little question that the health care system is undergoing a revolution. The crucial issue is how the system will evolve as it seeks to reduce the pressures that it faces. Pivotal to virtually any solution to these pressures are nurses and their leaders. The responsibility rests with nurse managers. If nurse managers cannot function as effective representatives in guiding the emerging health care delivery system, both the nursing profession and organizations may suffer. By integrating nurses into management positions, health care organizations can demonstrate their willingness to work with the profession rather than trying to control it. This could minimize the degree of contention between nurses and health care organizations.

As long as health care organizations lack effective nurse leaders who are able to shape and influence policy, to participate in setting corporate or organizational strategy, and actively to determine strategic decisions, then nursing has a limited power base. This further undermines the already tenuous relationship between nurses and organizations. The uneasy alliance in which nursing and health care organizations have coexisted is deteriorating. Nurses are becoming less content with traditional clinical and middle management positions. Without expanded career ladders for either clinical or managerial jobs, aspirations become stymied. Failure to address successfully the role of nurse managers may develop into an adversarial relationship between nurses and a besieged management.

AN AGENDA FOR NURSE MANAGERS

In the future, nurse managers can support the profession by becoming more involved and skilled in managing organizations. As long as they do not communicate or think in organizationally relevant terms, nurse managers will be minimally effective in furthering nurses' interests in the health care system. Consequently, the nursing profession should reconsider its level of investment and commitment to cultivating nurse managers with organizationally relevant orientations and skills. Nurse managers should be able to span the gap between clinicians and organizations. Given the trends toward corporate and organizational control in health care, nurse managers can help the profession convey its interests to top management. They can also help organizations develop collaborative rather than adversarial relationships with nursing staff members.

In developing strategic management skills, nurse managers can implement a managerial perspective that has often been missing in nursing administration. The desire to make this transition and the capability to do so, however, depend on whether nurse managers supplement their repertoire of skills with appropriate management training. Managerial development does not begin or end with a management degree or training through continuing education. Nurse managers who are interested in the challenges presented by a restructured health system must make a personal commitment to the quest for improved skills. Essential to their development are an understanding of strategic management, a recognition of the complexities in balancing organizational and nursing objectives, and an attempt to move programs, departments, and organizations toward excellence.

As leaders, nurse managers can help divert attention from an impassioned view (in which nursing is the scapegoat for fiscal and competitive forces) toward a new value paradigm that recognizes and effectively addresses the realities confronting the profession. As part of this process, nurse managers and the profession can openly acknowledge the growth of corporate and organizationally dominated health care. What is needed is a constructive acceptance of the increasing organization of medical care. Market forces and reimbursement policies are driving the health system toward corporate, organized health care and multi-institutional systems. Nurse managers can participate in managing the evolution of a health system that builds on, rather than around, nurses.

Figure 1-3 is a visual model of an agenda for developing nurse managers. This model illustrates the steps that are essential to move nurse managers from concept to reality. In essence, Figure 1-3 presents a plan for the survival of the nursing profession and for the removal of contention between nurses and health care organizations. It is not a question of whether nurses work for organizations or whether organizations work for the interests of nurses. Nurses and health care organizations are mutually dependent on one another and should be seeking an equitable collaboration. Reciprocal arrangements can help promote the ends of both, but there is a prerequisite for nurses to

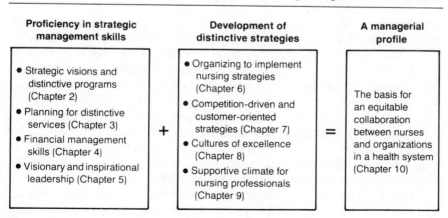

Figure 1-3 An Agenda for Nurse Managers

become actively involved in the strategic management of health care organizations. Only a sharing partnership will function effectively in the future.

Strategic Management Skills

An agenda for nurse managers is predicated on two primary efforts. First, a better understanding of and proficiency in strategic management skills is needed by nurse managers. Nurse managers will be challenged to formulate and plan competitive strategies, notably strategies that incorporate fundamental management concepts (discussed in Chapter 2). Once a vision is articulated, a plan for implementing it can be specified (discussed in Chapter 3).

The constraints confronting the health system mandate solid grounding in financial management skills (discussed in Chapter 4). Although nurse managers should be thoroughly familiar with and competent in all management functions (i.e., marketing, planning, accounting, human resource management, operations management, and financial management), financial management skills are particularly vital when negotiating annual budgets.

Finally, strategic management skills require visionary and inspirational leadership (discussed in Chapter 5). Nurse managers often must combine leadership responsibilities with clinical duties. Under these circumstances it may be difficult to provide the inspirational leadership necessary for nursing services; several guidelines are offered in Chapter 5 that may be useful in this regard. Nurse managers can fulfill both sets of responsibilities while providing quality leadership in motivating nurses toward distinctive service.

Distinctive Strategies

Strategic management involves setting objectives and designing action plans to implement the objectives. Implementation involves the day-to-day operations of a nursing unit, department, or organization. The starting point in effectively implementing strategy is organization. There are many concepts and models of organizing under which nurse managers operate during the course of their careers. In some cases nurse managers may be requested to recommend alternative program structures or designs. In still other situations they may be asked to comment on the fundamental problems in an existing program, work unit, department, or organizational structure. In these situations, they will need a solid understanding of organizing to implement nursing strategies (discussed in Chapter 6).

A leading discovery in management practice is the need to focus squarely on customers. As the health field is finding out, competition is increasingly driving service delivery efforts progressively toward a client or customer orientation. Fundamentally, this trend reflects the market in action. Nurse managers have an especially important role in encouraging nurses to focus on customers, clients, and patients (discussed in Chapter 7). Congruent with a customer orientation is the pursuit of excellence (discussed in Chapter 8). Nurse managers are responsible for recognizing and promoting excellence in their programs and among staff members. The ability to provide a visible model is a fundamental starting point for this process. The process goes beyond simply setting standards as a role model, however; the key to successful performance by health care corporations has been creating a culture centered on excellence.

Nurse managers are also responsible for fostering a supportive climate for nursing professionals. Some nurses express high levels of dissatisfaction with some facets of their jobs while simultaneously indicating satisfaction with other facets. This situation illustrates the fundamental obstacles confronting nurse managers who desire to lead nurses toward higher standards of performance. Several of the problems facing the nursing profession are examined in Chapter 9 relative to alternative strategies that show promise for resolving the inherent dilemmas.

When nurse managers attain proficiency in strategic management skills and begin to develop distinctive strategies for their units, teams, programs, departments, or divisions, then they begin to establish a credible managerial profile. This managerial profile (discussed in Chapter 10) is the basis for an equitable collaboration between nurses and organizations in a restructured health system. By recognizing the value of a distinct image or profile and by achieving it through skills development and strategy building, nurse managers may rightfully attain a more productive leadership role in health care.

NOTES

1. M.M. Mowry and R.A. Korpman, "Hospitals, Nursing and Medicare: The Years Ahead," *Journal of Nursing Administration* 17 (November 1987): 16-22.

2. M.F. Fralic, "The Effective Nurse Executive's Blueprint for Success: If We Can't Do the Job, Our Successors Will!" *Journal of Nursing Administration* 18 (June 1988): 9-12.

3. J.C. Goldsmith, *Can Hospitals Survive? The New Competitive Health Care Market* (Homewood, IL: Dow Jones–Irwin, 1981).

4. P.M. Ellwood and L.K. Ellwein, "Physician Glut Will Force Hospitals To Look Outward," *Hospitals* 55 (1981): 81-82.

5. L.H. Aiken and C.F. Mullinix, "The Nurse Shortage: Myth or Reality?" *New England Journal of Medicine* 317 (3 September 1987): 641-645.

6. J.K. Inglehart. "Problems Facing the Nursing Profession," *New England Journal of Medicine* 317 (3 September 1987): 646-651.

7. P.A. Prescott and S.A. Bowen, "Controlling Nursing Turnover," *Nursing Management* 18 (June 1987): 60-66.

8. J. Lancaster, "1986 and Beyond: Nursing's Future," *Journal of Nursing Administration* 16 (March 1986): 31-37.

9. C. Bradford, G. Caldwell, and J.C. Goldsmith, "The Hospital Capital Crisis," *Harvard Business Review* 60 (September/October 1982): 56-68.

10. A. Levenstein. "Some Basic Concepts for the New Year," *Nursing Management* 16 (December 1985): 42-43.

11. A.L. Urquhart et al., "Perspectives on Nursing Issues and Health Care Trends," *Journal of Nursing Administration* 16 (January 1986): 17-23.

12. K.J. Sellick, S. Russell, and J.L. Beckmann, "Primary Nursing: An Evaluation of Its Effects on Patient Perception of Care and Staff Satisfaction," *International Journal of Nursing Studies* 20 (1983): 265-273.

13. M. Manthey et al., "Primary Nursing: A Return to the Concept of 'My Nurse' and 'My Patient,' " *Nursing Forum* 9 (1970): 65-83.

14. K.S. Hegedus, "Primary Nursing: Evaluation of Professional Nursing Practice," *Nursing Dimensions* 7 (1980): 85-89.

15. J.P. Barrett, "Hospitals Must Change Policies To Recognize RNs as Professionals," *Modern Healthcare*, 13 December 1983, 130-134.

16. J. Daria and S. Moran. "Nursing in the 90s," *Nursing* 15 (December 1985): 26-29.

17. P. Moccia and D.J. Mason, "Poverty Trends: Implications for Nursing," *Nursing Outlook* 34 (January/February 1986): 20-24.

18. L.L. Curtin, "The Decade Ahead: Five Major Issues," *Nursing Management* 14 (October 1983): 9-10.

19. C. Gassert, C. Holt, and K. Pope, "Building a Ladder," *American Journal of Nursing*, 12 October 1982, 1527-1530.

20. M. Gallivan. "Debate Heats up over Two-Tiered Nursing System," *Hospitals*, 60 (5 March 1986): 93-95.

21. T.J. Sullivan et al., "Nursing 2020: A Study of Nursing's Future," *Nursing Outlook* 35 (September/October 1987): 233-235.

22. L. Aiken, "Assuring the Delivery of Quality Patient Care," in *Nursing Resources and the Delivery of Patient Care* (Bethesda, MD: Department of Health and Human Services, National Center for Nursing Research, 1989), NIH publication no. 89-3008, pp. 3-10.

23. C.F. Mullinix, "Research on Influences Affecting Availability of Resources for Patient Care Delivery," in *Nursing Resources and the Delivery of Patient Care* (Bethesda, MD: Department of Health and Human Services, National Center for Nursing Research, 1989), NIH publication no. 89-3008, pp. 11-15.

24. D. Mechanic and L. Aiken, "A Cooperative Agenda for Medicine and Nursing," *The New England Journal of Medicine* 307 (1982): 747-750.

25. C. Ziegfeld and S. Jones, "An Innovative Strategy to Facilitate Nurse-Physician Interaction," *Journal of Continuing Education in Nursing* 18 (March/April 1987): 47-50.

26. Fralic, "The Effective Nurse Executive's Blueprint for Success," 10.

Chapter 2

Strategic Management and Distinctive Nursing Programs

Although more health care organizations are now recognizing the importance of managing their strategic direction, confusion remains about what strategic management actually encompasses. There is a tendency to equate strategic management with strategic planning. While strategic management may include strategic planning, the two concepts are decreasingly synonymous. Strategic management is the less formal and more visionary of the two. Strategic planning usually implies a commitment to defining formally the mission, objectives, and strategies for organizations. Authorities have underscored the importance of preventing strategic planning from becoming a static set of plans.[1] Nonetheless, strategic planning has been associated with direction setting by top managers, corporate planning departments, and boards of directors. In contrast, strategic management incorporates a broader spectrum of organizational members in the process. Strategic management is active, vibrant, changing, and flexible. It requires input into strategic direction from many organizational levels.

As early as 1983, the health care literature was observing that strategic planning and strategic management activities in hospitals are practiced infrequently.[2,3] Consequently, three key direction-setting questions were not being raised in practice: What is the present business, and how is the organization performing? In what direction should the organization be headed? How will it get there? The tendency to drift along in setting organizational direction soon came to an end, however. New competitive and reimbursement pressures brought health care organizations more into line with their corporate counterparts. By 1987 the health care literature had recognized that hospitals face a hostile environment. Hospitals were now seen as needing more sophisticated and aggressive planning systems.[4] As an institutional process, effective planning is based not only on input from external constituents but from internal members as well.[5]

Corporations have reached the point at which the value of a flexible strategic planning system is recognized and supported. Nonetheless, there is some debate as to whether the health care field is rapidly adopting this perspective. Evidence is found on both sides of the argument. Nursing administrators have been encouraged to view strategic planning as a systematic, formal process.[6,7] The benefits of incorporating diverse views from throughout health care organizations including nursing departments are also acknowledged, however.[8] Considering the complex economic forces confronting health care institutions, a flexible strategic management perspective may be more harmonious than a formal approach in setting work unit, department, division, and organizational directions.

DIFFERENTIATING BETWEEN STRATEGY AND OPERATIONS

At what point is an issue strategic or operational? There can be considerable confusion among nurse managers about the differences between strategy-level issues and operating or functional issues. At what point does strategy cross over into operations? A few examples illustrate this ambiguity. When a hospital decides to implement a marketing program for its new thrust into home care, has it entered into a strategic decision or an operational decision? In contrast, are the decisions about which media to use, the consumers to be targeted, the context of the advertising message, and other pertinent marketing issues representative of operating-level decisions? If a psychiatric hospital decides to divest its alcoholism and substance abuse treatment program, has it entered into the realm of strategy, or is programmatic divestiture a fundamental operating decision that is necessary to retain financial solvency? At what point does an issue become strategic rather than operational?

There are several criteria that can be used to differentiate strategic from nonstrategic decisions. Authorities in the strategic management field have identified the standards listed in Table 2-1 to differentiate among decision categories.[9,10] As these criteria suggest, an organization-wide perspective should be adopted rather than a work unit, program, department, or division focus when establishing strategy. This does not imply that strategy is limited to the organization as a whole. Effective strategy must acknowledge the strengths and weaknesses of clinical teams, programs, departments, or divisions that together represent a health care organization. The organization's strategy should be articulated at these specific levels. In short, the interface of subunits in an organization with strategy is constrained by the larger strategy and policy of the organization. The strategic interests of any single unit in an organization should not conflict with the overall organizational strategy.

Table 2-1 Standards Used To Differentiate Strategic from Nonstrategic Decisions

Standard	Illustration
1. Strategic decisions center on macro-organizational issues involving the fit between an organization and its environment	Is a hospital's diversification into home care consistent with market demand, organizational strengths, and competitors' capabilities?
2. Strategic decisions establish guidelines for the configuration and functioning of an organization; structure and administrative processes follow strategy	If the hospital decides to open a home care agency, does it decentralize management control to the agency level and establish accountability mechanisms for a corporate office that facilitates decentralized control?
3. Strategic decisions affect the organization as a whole rather than a specific unit; the implications of strategic decisions influence all organizational units	If the hospital decides to acquire a home health agency, does it consider the secondary costs and benefits that may affect the inpatient portion of the organization? (Capital investment in the home care segment may prevent needed reinvestments in the inpatient segment)
4. Strategic decisions involve most functional activities in an organization; functional activities generally include marketing, human resource management, finance, accounting, operations management, information management, and operating policy	If a hospital decides to introduce its own home care division (with diversified services), has it assessed the financial feasibility and the impact on human resource requirements, information processing capabilities (e.g., the need to devise cost-effective report routing), control (e.g., inventory procurement, maintenance, and replenishment), and marketing potential?

For example, assume that a nurse functioning as program director for senior services at a local health maintenance organization (HMO) has the drive, skill, vision, contacts, and opportunities to make the program regionally famous. The director sets an agenda of services for the program that would substantially improve its standing and reputation over the next 3 years. In some cases, these expectations will exceed the capacity of the HMO to fund program growth. An opportunity to secure a state governmental contract suddenly arises. Simultaneously, a benefactor is willing to provide half the capital needed for new clinic space, equipment, and transportation vehicles. This is an investment that the HMO cannot afford, however. In this situation the strategy of the program conflicts with the strategy of the organization as a whole.

The director of the program should be encouraged to act as an entrepreneur within the constraints of the organization. When department heads and other program leaders lose this entrepreneurial spirit, they may minimize the potential accomplishments of their units. The organization as a whole is less effective unless entrepreneurial spirit emanates from the top echelons. This motivation is much easier to stimulate at operating levels where managers already have vision, establish ambitious goals for their units, and strive to attain progressively higher levels of performance within organizational constraints. In sum, the strategy of any single business unit should be constrained, but not broken, by organizational strategy and available resources.

Further clarification of the differences between strategy and operations is provided in Table 2-2, which identifies seven decision areas surrounding strategy: (1) organizational mission, (2) patient mix, (3) product-service mix, (4) service area, (5) goals and objectives, (6) competitive strategy, and (7) external relationships.[11] This list is not necessarily exhaustive, but for most organizations a decision involving any one of these seven decision areas has a high probability of representing a strategic decision.

Like other managers, nurse managers will adopt a conceptual framework that identifies strategic decisions, explains how these decisions affect the organization, and recommends how decisions should be integrated to maximize organizational or departmental performance. Nurse managers must be able to distinguish between strategy and operations (or tactics) in their daily management activities.[12] For example, strategy (i.e., a plan of action) for a nursing department may involve negotiating a 15 percent budget increase for the next fiscal year. Operations (or tactics) would involve expending the resources associated with the budget increase.

Caution is essential in differentiating between strategic and nonstrategic decisions. It should not be inferred that strategic decisions are important and nonstrategic decisions are unimportant. The issue really distills to allocating scarce resources in terms of time, expertise, talent, and capability.[13] Consistent with this managerial responsibility is the need to reserve time for defining where an organization, program, or department is headed, structuring it to facilitate this progress, responding to changes in the external environment, and establishing a context in which operations can perform smoothly despite changes encountered in the environment.

THE STRATEGIC MANAGEMENT PROCESS

If nurse managers aspire to become better managers and leaders, they must achieve proficiency in strategic management skills, perspective, and vision. Skills refer to the training, education, and experience necessary to operate

Table 2-2 Decision Issues That Differentiate Strategy from Operations

Strategic Decision Set	*Definition*	*Illustration in a Pharmacy*
Basic mission	The primary purposes that the organization is trying to accomplish	1. To provide a diverse selection of high-quality pharmaceuticals at low cost
Patient-customer mix	The organization's customers and primary markets	1. All people of the rural town in which the pharmacy is located, with emphasis on customers referred from local medical groups
Product-service mix	The range of products or services provided to customers	1. Full-service pharmaceuticals with specialty order service in 24 hours
Service area	The geographic area that comprises the markets	1. The community surrounding a rural town with a population of 15,000 people
Goals and objectives	Specific end results for organizational performance toward accomplishing the basic mission	1. To increase sales revenues by 15 percent over the previous fiscal year 2. To increase profits by 5 percent over the previous fiscal year 3. To offer eighty new products
Competitive advantage	Unique characteristics that differentiate an organization from others	1. Records on pharmaceutical use are automated and maintained for every customer 2. Special orders are filled by the next day 3. Low cost is competitive with that of nearest urban market 4. Personalized service is offered
Outside relationships	External events that shape the context for business	1. Major drug chain is analyzing the rural market 2. Primary supplier is being acquired by another large pharmaceutical firm 3. Local medical groups are beginning to offer discount drugs

Source: Adapted from "Limiting the Scope of Strategy: A Decision Based Approach" by R.C. Shirley, *Academy of Management Review*, Vol. 7, pp. 262–268, with permission of Academy of Management, © 1982.

effectively at the strategic level. Perspective refers to a view of how skills should be implemented. Vision implies the ability to foresee the directions that an organization and industry will take. Vision also suggests an understanding of where an organization should be directed in view of impending industry changes. Consequently, vision is interpreted in the perspective of strategic management and the implementation of pertinent skills.

According to Thompson and Strickland,[14] strategic management includes

> the process of defining business purpose and setting objectives, deciding which business to enter, to continue in, and to get out of, formulating and implementing a viable strategic plan, monitoring performance and results, and all of the subactivities that these entail.

Nurse managers must consider cultivating skills that are based on the strategic management concept if they intend to contribute to an organization's direction. Strategic management is not just a pertinent activity at top management levels.

Many health care administrators have opportunities to influence the strategic plan of a corporation.[15] This ability to affect strategic direction increases as one moves up the organizational hierarchy. Nonetheless, low-level managers can provide invaluable input into the strategic plan. For example, a nursing department may participate in the pilot test of a nursing home's attempt to capture a larger share of a target market (e.g., designated socioeconomic group patients). If a nurse manager is assigned responsibility to develop and test the program, a unique opportunity to influence top-level decisions has been encountered.

Attention to the strategic management process at low management levels is inversely proportional to the size of an organization. Extremely large organizations are more likely to have differentiated between strategy and operations. They generally have specific staff to assist top management with strategic planning. The result is more consistent attention to strategic issues. Managers in medium and small health care organizations are usually immersed in operations management issues. They recognize the priority of strategic management, but they invariably attend to current crises first. There is a tendency to think that strategic planning can wait until existing problems are settled. Actually, the precise opposite is desired. Short-run gains seldom outweigh long-run performance. Managers of medium and small organizations do not have the staff to relieve them of operations issues or to assist them in strategic planning, however.

In sum, it is important to recognize that although nurse managers need to develop skills in strategic management and related strategic planning activities it is possible that the skills will only be moderately employed at any given time. This should not prevent them from seeking out or sharing in the strategic management process. If nurse managers do not partake in direction-setting processes, then nursing input may be missing. It is often the case, however, that nurse managers are distracted by clinical duties and administrative responsibilities that prevent them from participating in direction-setting processes of health care organizations.

Elements of the Strategic Management Process

A diagram of the strategic management process is shown in Figure 2-1.[16,17] As this figure indicates, strategy formulation (i.e., defining a plan of action) is a key element in the process. The process shown in Figure 2-1 has may similarities to managerial planning, but it focuses on strategy instead of operations. Strategy formulation precedes managerial or tactical planning. Once strategic objectives have been defined and a strategy chosen, then operations planning becomes crucial in the implementation phase. Short-range and medium-range planning are distinct efforts to achieve the strategic objectives. As such, they address operations rather than strategy.

Figure 2-1 depicts the specific elements of strategic management as a continuous or flowing process. This implies that organizations should begin by defining mission and purpose before proceeding to the next steps. Realistically, a step-wise, iterative model seldom is adopted by managers. It is rare for an organization to follow each step through the model before cycling back from control to mission and purpose. For this reason, there are a number of feedback loops depicted in Figure 2-1. There may be any number of false starts, returns to previous steps, or skipping of steps in practice as information is digested. A better appreciation of this phenomenon is possible by examining each of the elements or steps in the strategic management model.

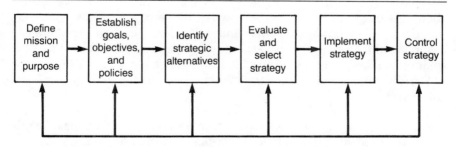

Figure 2-1 The Strategic Management Process

Defining Mission and Purpose

Organizations must establish a mission, philosophy, and purpose that guide operations. These concepts are differentiated as follows:

- Mission: a basic concern, or a definition of the primary interests of the organization. Included in this definition are the organization's specific areas of interest and inherent values and what it intends to accomplish. The mission clarifies what the organizations does and who it tries to serve.
- Philosophy: a system of values and beliefs that guides the operations of an organization. This system defines standards of conduct and establishes boundaries for objectives.
- Purpose: a reason for being. The mission is a broad statement about what an organization intends to do. The statement of purpose is more specific. It more narrowly addresses the end results that an organization is attempting to achieve.

Statements of mission, philosophy, and purpose may seem rather impractical because they seldom appear to affect operations directly. As many health care organizations and nursing departments are discovering, however, such statements are crucial in setting direction.[18]

Too many organizations or programs have a tendency to drift along without paying attention to the direction in which they are going or the direction from which they came. They lack a vision of why they exist. Even if they know where they want to go, they do not know how to get there. The result is an incremental approach to managing. Decisions lack integrity because they may not be related to an overall plan. A mission statement may alleviate these problems, but the mission must be considered as decisions are made. Mission statements also help confirm an organization's identity. Truly outstanding health care organizations have a strong sense of purpose, mission, and philosophy. Outstanding organizations know what they are all about. Distinctive organizations know where they are going. Effort is concentrated on accomplishing objectives that fulfill mission. Staff members are cognizant of the organization's aspirations. Staff are better able to make a commitment because they know what the organization stands for.

The following statements illustrate the mission, purpose, and philosophy of one HMO:

- Mission: our mission is to provide competitively priced, prepaid health care of the highest quality to subscribers. We offer a full range of acute and outpatient services to citizens in the southwestern United States. To serve our customers better, we have established a system of metropolitan clinics that serve as locally accessible options for those seeking alternative health care delivery.

- Philosophy: our philosophy is to provide the highest quality of care that is ethically compatible with prepayment. All professional staff must meet the highest standards of preparation before they are allowed to deliver care. Furthermore, the staff will operate under the prevailing standards set in the health professions for quality of care, ethical conduct, and attention to patient needs.
- Purpose: our purpose is to provide health care services that represent the state of the art. By delivering high quality and low-cost care we intend to set a standard for other health care providers. We intend to continue raising the standard for health care by implementing innovations in service delivery, technological capability, and payment policies.

The preceding statements establish a set of criteria for decision making and for operations. Personnel know the standards to which they must aspire.

Establishing Goals, Objectives, and Policies

Once a mission statement has been formulated, policies must be set that define standards for the creation and achievement of objectives. Policies are normally viewed as guidelines for action. Policies provide a framework around which goals are identified and actions for achieving the goals are guided. In this respect, policies also function as a framework for decisions. Policies define desirable and undesirable behavior. They define the standards and operating rules that will be followed. Policies guide decision making and organizational activities.

The extent to which policies guide organizational decisions can be seen in the following examples for a durable medical equipment vendor:

- It is the policy of this firm that deliveries will be paid in cash or check on receipt.
- It is the policy of this firm that only the finest equipment will be rented, leased, or sold to customers.
- It is the policy of this firm to provide employees a $500 bonus each year if operations permit.

The preceding policies establish standards for decisions. As durable medical equipment firms usually come to discover, a large number of customers, clients, or patients are unable to pay their bills. If the firms discover that they are encountering a large volume of bad debts, they may demand cash on delivery as a precautionary policy. The first policy noted above explains the organization's philosophy and prevents delivery personnel from using discretion that may be unintentionally faulty.

The second policy provides guidelines for the acquisition of medical equipment. The firm states the guidelines used in selecting equipment to be sold or rented to customers. The firm will only select the best equipment available. This is a product criterion that some customers desire. If the firm violates the policy, then customers may question the quality of equipment purchased. Furthermore, because a high price is likely to accompany quality equipment, customers want to be certain that they are getting what they have paid for.

The third policy illustrated above defines a commitment to personnel. This policy may be created to underscore the firm's interest in employee welfare. It may serve as a motivating factor in encouraging attention to costs and customers. It also represents a mechanism to encourage long-run employment. Whatever the intention, the third policy guides behavior. If profits are attained, then employees can anticipate a bonus. Because the policy is a guideline to action, a bonus is not a given as far as personnel are concerned. Only if operations permit will a bonus be allocated. This policy provides flexibility for managers, who ultimately determine the appropriateness of a bonus. Nonetheless, a visible guideline has been established that may have significant ramifications if profits are derived and bonuses are not awarded.

Goals and objectives, like policies, are guidelines for action. Goals and objectives go beyond guiding decisions, however. They define measurable end results that individuals, work units, or organizations attempt to achieve by expending effort or other resources. Long-range goals represent end results that an organization wishes to achieve in the period beyond 3 years. Medium-range goals are results that should be achieved in the next 1 to 3 years. Short-range objectives represent end results that will be accomplished in the next fiscal period. For example, a manufacturer of lithotripters decides that its long-range goal is to sell 5,000 machines over the next 3 years. Its short-range objective for the first year is to sell 1,000 units.

The standard for guiding operations has always been clear specification of measurable end results: goals and objectives. Until the long-run goals of an organization are defined, it is difficult if not impossible to set representative short-run objectives. There are numerous objectives to be defined, including service quality, malpractice avoidance, fiscal stability, profitability, staff productivity, maintenance of physical plant and equipment, fiscal integrity, commitment to research and development, market penetration, and human resource development, to name a few. The specific end results representing the objectives, however, are contingent on defining long-run goals to guide current operations.

There are many temptations to overlook a rigorous and methodical goal-setting and objective-setting process. For example, nurse managers may not define objectives consistently, assess the extent to which they are achieved, and redefine objectives as they are accomplished or new targets or interests develop. The reason that goals and objectives go undefined, are unused in guiding the evaluation of performance, or are seen merely as a process to undergo before getting back to (perceived) real issues is the lack of incentives for correctly using goals or objectives. In many health care organizations, there are traditions of operating without reference to goals.[19] Rewards are usually not directly linked to goal achievement. Under these conditions, it is irrelevant whether goals are met. No one checks to see whether goals have been defined, updated, or adhered to in terms of performance.

Despite the incentives to overlook goals and objectives in decisions and actions, most organizations cannot afford to overlook these strategic guidelines. Almost all health care organizations sense that they inhabit an increasingly competitive environment. This austere environment presents several incentives to follow more rigorously the objective-setting process.

- There are few or no slack resources in budgets, hence going beyond budget thresholds is more visible and risky.
- Fewer revenues have forced voluntary and public organizations to reduce budgets proportionately, although the same or a higher level of productivity is still demanded.
- Declining revenues have encouraged investor-owned health care corporations to set more rigorous revenue targets.
- There are few degrees of freedom for offering new services or products, yet existing product and service lines must be upgraded to attract more patients, clients, or customers.
- Reduced staffing is necessary to control costs. Under these conditions it is imperative that each staff member fully recognize and achieve job responsibilities.
- Work units, programs, departments, divisions, and entire organizations (e.g., multi-institutional systems) are increasingly dependent on each other for accomplishing specific objectives.
- To build the best competitive advantage in price and quality, organizational units must be monitored and either supported for attaining goals or reprimanded for failing to contribute to specified goals.

The preferred mechanism for responding to these incentives is to set clear, measurable end results. By setting measurable objectives, expectations are defined, a short-run plan of action is communicated, and a basis for performance review is established. By periodically assessing progress toward the objectives, it is possible to define organizational strengths and weaknesses.

Identifying Strategic Alternatives

Strategic alternatives represent the options available to health care organizations to pursue goals and objectives. Theoretically, the set of alternatives that can be pursued is broad for most organizations; that is, only resources and imagination constrain the identification of options. Practically speaking, the range of feasible options is much narrower. Nevertheless, health care organizations that refuse to be bound by traditional thinking and that introduce imaginative innovations in products or services are likely to reap extensive rewards. They also face high risk.

The range of strategic alternatives for a hospital with urgent care centers illustrates the difference between feasible and infeasible options. Assume that the hospital is located in a city with a population of 500,000 people. The organization operates five urgent care centers. The alternatives to be considered include:

1. expansion of five more outlets in the next 2 years
2. diversification into ambulatory surgery centers
3. merger with another hospital operating three urgent care centers that are not in the same vicinity as the existing five locations
4. expansion into three smaller (less than 100,000 people) metropolitan areas in the state
5. acquisition of a local hospital not currently offering satellite urgent care
6. expanded marketing to underscore public awareness
7. service and price competition to attract customers
8. reduced staffing and service hours to control overhead
9. service innovations at existing outlets
10. corporate contacts to secure managed care

Of the 10 preceding strategic alternatives, which are most feasible? From a strategic management viewpoint only options 3, 8, and 9 may be feasible. The hospital is tight on capital because it expanded by two outlets last year that were financed through debt. Thus it cannot finance further expansion, which eliminates options 1, 2, 4, and 5. Operating margins have been insufficient in view of the recent construction to allow options 6, 7, or 10. The budget is barely adequate to float current operations as they currently stand. Therefore, the only feasible strategic alternatives are to forego expansion, to merge with another hospital (by relinquishing ownership), to reduce staffing to control costs, and to introduce service innovations that have low cost.

What are the strategic options available to health care organizations today? The options are seemingly as limitless as the imaginations and innovation of staff members. This is a refreshing situation because it implies that health care organizations can determine their own destiny. The sky is the limit as far as experimentation is concerned. The downside of this freedom is the range of actual options, that is, the feasible strategic alternatives. Organizations will go through substantial trial and error before they select a promising and realistic portfolio of strategic options. During this search for a promising strategy, inevitably some organizations will make fundamentally incorrect choices and consequently suffer failure.

Evaluating and Selecting Strategy

After the range of feasible alternatives has been specified, the next step in the strategic management process is to evaluate the alternatives and to select a strategy for implementation. A choice must be made among the options. Such evaluation requires analyzing industry trends, competitive attributes of the pertinent market, consumer demographics, opportunities available to an organization, strategic capabilities (e.g., assets and endowments), strategic weaknesses (e.g., marginal financial capability, turnover in the clinical ranks, or conservatism among board members), and foreseeable threats. After analysis, the range of alternatives must be narrowed and a choice made.

Most health care managers, including nurse managers, have far to go in effectively evaluating and selecting strategy. The problem lies not so much with decision-making discretion as it does with the underlying analysis of feasible alternatives. Nurse managers are trained to be clinical decision makers. Nurse managers normally focus on specific operating problems, not on general health care industry trends. To contribute effectively in strategy choice, nurse managers must learn to broaden their horizons. Until they are able to look at the long-range goals, to envision the big picture, and to balance organizational aspirations with organizational strengths and weaknesses, strategic choices may not produce the needed or intended results.[20]

For example, a West Coast manufacturer of pharmaceuticals must decide which of two options to pursue: (1) diversification of product line to include related health products or (2) construction of an East Coast plant to serve better the eastern market. The manufacturer uses several criteria in assessing these options:

- level of capital investment
- availability of qualified personnel to implement the option

- compatibility with existing mission and objectives
- quality of product and service
- cost of product and service
- impact on existing operations
- market demand
- competitor strengths and weaknesses

As far as most evaluation criteria are concerned, this set provides substantial information for decision making. But will the best decision be made?

Notice that most of the criteria center on internal strengths and weaknesses. These are precisely the areas in which the most reliable information can be obtained. Few of the criteria emphasize external opportunities or threats. The availability of personnel, market demand, and competitor characteristics are the only criteria involving external issues. The externally centered criteria should be much broader. These data may be difficult to acquire, but they are needed to guide the analysis.

This example illustrates the tendency of health-related organizations to falter in strategic choice by focusing on what they know best: internal variables (operations). Health care managers are more comfortable limiting analysis to their own tangible experiences than considering all relevant factors impinging on the implementation of an option. In short, they do not remember the overall vision of where their organization is going and how it will get there. Health care managers at operating levels (e.g., nurse managers) tend to emphasize the past or the present. As a result, decision making may be biased toward strategic options that are not really advances but mere extrapolations of current endeavor. There is nothing wrong with this self-limiting tendency; it controls risk. It seldom permits the substantial gain that characterizes an industry leader, however.

Implementing Strategy

Organizations seek to adopt structures and processes by which their services and products are effectively delivered to customers. This involves the implementation phase, which is a deliberate attempt to operationalize the chosen strategy. Analysis or evaluation ascertains whether a new structure is appropriate for the chosen strategy or whether additional resources will be invested in specific organizational units. Implementation addresses alterations in the work force and management ranks as well as changes in the finance, accounting, marketing, and production operations management functions.

The operational nature of strategy implementation can be easily seen in these relevant activities:

- articulating and selecting an organization design from among all organizing alternatives (e.g., matrix, geographic, ad hoc, departmentalization around function, or other structural models)
- allocating resources toward strategic objectives through budgeting
- developing substrategies and tactics
- integrating strategy into the existing or altered organizational structure
- developing the organization's human resources to ensure that strategy is accepted and supported
- providing appropriate incentives to reward or discipline variations in staff support of strategic alternatives

Although there are other ingredients that are essential in implementing a chosen strategy, the illustrations above indicate that implementation involves day-to-day management responsibilities.

Controlling Strategy

Strategy must be periodically evaluated. A number of questions are relevant in controlling strategy.

- Is the strategy consistent with the health care organization's strengths and weaknesses?
- Does the strategy address recent changes in the organization's environment without merely responding to those changes (i.e., is there a broader purpose to strategy than just response)?
- Is the strategy forward-looking beyond the immediate pressures of the environment?
- Is the risk associated with the existing strategy commensurate with rewards or return on investment?
- Does an alternative strategy promise a higher return on resources invested at a lower risk?
- Can the strategy be feasibly implemented before another major alteration in strategy is needed?
- Will clinical, ancillary, and management staff continue to support the existing or proposed strategy?

These questions capture the essence of control. Deviations from intended directions must be detected and a new strategy substituted for guidance.

Focusing on Strategic Issues

The preceding discussion about the strategic management process implicitly recognizes two significant ideas. First, strategic management is predicated on a solid grounding and working expertise in all the functional areas of management: marketing, financing, information processing, accounting, operations management, human resource management, and policy formulation. Although nurse managers may not be experts in each of these functions, they must understand the main concepts and analytical techniques. This requires a working knowledge of what the concepts include, how the techniques are useful, what limitations the concepts and techniques have, and how they interface with concepts and analytical techniques in other functional areas.

Ideally, those involved in strategic management should have:

- a knowledge of accounting systems structures and how they provide organizational control
- an understanding of capital structures and how current operations and long-term financing contribute to that structure
- insight into the product or service life cycle and how that life cycle is useful for predicting impact on utilization
- the ability to motivate line workers and staff by managing rewards, punishment, and performance evaluation
- the ability to create management information systems that facilitate decision making
- knowledge of how optimally to schedule supply purchases to guarantee adequate inventory yet minimize inventory and ordering costs
- insight into when strategic plans should be revised because environmental factors keep shifting

Nurse managers should be able to see the challenge before them. In advancing nursing's contribution to patient care delivery, nurse managers must become adept in skills underlying the strategic management process. This is especially true if nurse managers aspire to top management positions.

Admittedly, many nurse managers may not be able to calculate financial investment evaluations with payback, internal rate of return, present worth, or average rate of return techniques. Health care organizations do not expect them to spend time conducting such analysis. Nevertheless, it is important that nurse managers understand the differences among the techniques, why the techniques are used, and how to interpret the results broadly for the organization as a whole. Without sufficient grounding in functional skills, it is difficult for nurse managers to move effectively to the strategic management level. How can nurse managers contribute to the direction of a hospital, nursing home, group practice, or managed care plan if they cannot read an income statement, understand depreciation, know when operations research methods should be used, adjust prices on the basis of demand elasticity, operate a computer terminal to gain access to a strategic piece of data, or design a personnel evaluation system that allows for equitable rewards?

Second, the strategic management level involves concepts. Nurse managers and other health care administrators should not be involved in specific technical analysis at the strategic management level. They should reserve their energies for strategy issues. This does not eliminate their participation in the technical aspects (e.g., providing advice and expertise during the formulation of an incentive-based compensation plan for staff nurses); it suggests that staff are responsible for the technical analyses.

Nurse managers will probably spend considerable effort upgrading their conceptual and technical skill levels in the management functions before they move to the strategy level. There are many options for making this improvement, including continuing education, degree programs, professional training, and other management development alternatives.[21] Throughout this preparation it is important that nurse managers not lose sight of the primary objective: a strategic focus.

Nurse managers will develop a strategic perspective if they expect to function effectively in high-level nursing management roles. What is a strategic perspective? Basically, it involves participation in setting the overall direction and performance of a program, department, or organization.[22] It is concerned with identifying where a nursing program or health care organization has been and where it is going. In this sense, the focus is strategic issues rather than the details of operational issues. Attention is devoted to conceiving direction. Factors that prevent the program or organization from attaining that direction are identified and resolutions developed (Figure 2-2).

An operational focus is analogous to tactical thinking. Although nurse managers seldom concentrate exclusively on strategic matters (except at the highest executive levels), operational issues demand time and threaten to distract attention from strategic issues. As suggested in Figure 2-2, nurse managers will be challenged to devote direct attention to strategic concerns and performance. It is too easy to become overwhelmed by the press of daily issues. Nonetheless, nurse managers at the executive levels should primarily monitor day-to-day operations and become involved as appropriate. In succumbing to the urgency of daily operations, the ultimate effect is to leave the strategic portion unattended.

As Figure 2-2 suggests, nurse managers should increase direct attention to strategic concerns and end results (i.e., performance) as they move up in the

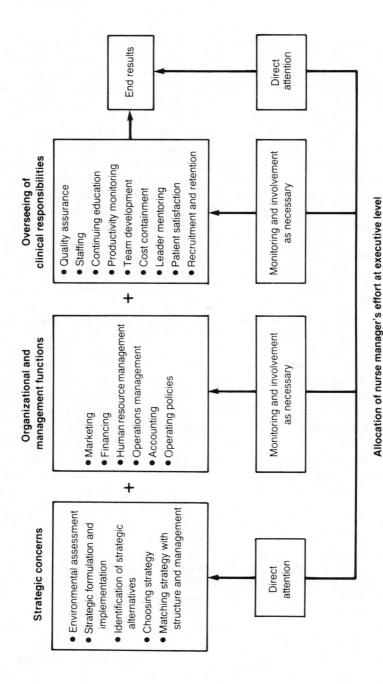

Figure 2-2 A Strategic Perspective for Nurse Managers

organizational hierarchy. This means that environmental pressures (e.g., favorability of the competitive environment, regulation, industry trends, and other external issues) must be monitored; strategy must be formulated, implemented, assessed, and revised; and concern must be given to matching structure with strategy. Additionally, nurse managers at the executive level should monitor and become involved as necessary in basic operating issues. The point to underscore is that they should only intervene as necessary, routinely checking on operations but refraining from taking a direct role in managing operations. These tasks are delegated to other managers—let them manage.

Developing a Strategic Vision

One of the most important contributions that health care managers make to an organization is a vision of where it should be headed. For example, a new chief executive officer of a rural hospital envisions that the hospital will become the central health facility in the region, providing the highest quality of care and patient service. A strategic plan is formulated and implemented with favorable results. Three years later, the chief executive officer envisions a statewide system of rural hospitals that is based on the original model. Again, the strategic planning process is undertaken and implemented. Within 2 years, the chief executive officer is envisioning a multistate system of rural hospitals in a functional multi-institutional system. The point of this illustration is that the executive did not become overly satisfied at any stage. Instead, the vision of where the rural hospitals (organization) should be going was constantly redefined. Consistent with this vision was the articulation of a strategy and a plan for implementation.

Not every nurse manager expects to provide visionary insight into a health care organization's planning. A liberal amount of creativity and imagination is needed to formulate a vision. In health care it is not unusual to discover top managers who have attained their positions because of exceptional ability to manage operational detail, but it is also possible to discover top managers who are exceptional visionaries yet miserable at handling the details of operations. Organizations must cultivate both sets of skills.

Figure 2-3 indicates some crucial factors in developing a strategic vision. Underlying this model is the assumption that strategic vision does not always imply desirable directions for an organization. In other words, a visionary is not someone who always has good news or positive prophetic visions for the organization. Instead, the message may be to terminate a particular service. Retrenchment must be seen as a legitimate option if the vision-setting process is to have sufficient freedom for providing direction for the long run.

Factors that produce strategic vision

MAXIMIZE

- Willingness to reverse algorithm of thinking
- Ability to see ephemeral nature of current events
- Willingness to look for opportunity in disaster
- Tolerance for risk
- Openess to new ideas
- Ability to anticipate pressures

= **Ability to ponder future direction of organization**

Factors that prevent strategic vision

MINIMIZE

- Tendency to follow industry or leader trends
- Tendency to focus on current events
- Failure to look for long-run implications in major environmental or policy changes
- Tendency to react to pressures
- Tendency to pursue certainty
- Pessimistic attitude toward change

= **Inability to see beyond current operations**

Figure 2-3 Developing a Strategic Vision

Those factors that produce a strategic vision must be maximized. This implies a willingness to reverse the algorithm of thinking. Nurse managers will need to listen to and consider the unusual point of view. In a sense, this suggests an openness to new ideas. Visionary nurse managers are able to see beyond current events. They do not get caught up in the ephemeral nature of operating issues. In sum, the visionary nurse manager tries to maximize free thinking. There is a tolerance to risk and a propensity to search out opportunity in disaster. By pursuing these qualities in thinking, they are able to ponder the future direction of an organization or nursing program.

Figure 2-3 also suggests that a number of factors prevent the attainment of a strategic vision. Nurse managers will seek to minimize the tendency to follow other leaders or organizations. There is little creativity in following standard formulas. The rewards are seldom substantial, even though the level of risk is low. The nurse manager who only reacts, focuses on present issues, or is pessimistic about change will be unable to see beyond current operations. By definition, this manager will not be able to form a vision that promotes organizational excellence.

CONCEPTS IN STRATEGIC ANALYSIS

The process of establishing mission and goal statements is normally guided by analysis of a health care organization's internal state and the environment in which it operates. Basically, this analysis profiles the situation that is before the organization. It helps ascertain whether objective setting is too optimistic or not challenging enough. The acronym that has been created for this type of strategic analysis, known as SWOT,[23] refers to internal strengths and weaknesses combined with external opportunities and threats. SWOT provides a convenient framework, logic, and organization for the analysis. By examining SWOT, realistic strategic objectives can be defined that address constraints and opportunities.

Figure 2-4 illustrates a matrix that is useful when assessing internal strengths and weaknesses. The goal is to evaluate thoroughly functional areas such as patient care, marketing, accounting, finance, supplies, staffing, and quality assurance relative to their inherent strengths or weaknesses. A functional breakdown does not always have to be employed. It may be more valuable to organize the analysis by departments, divisions, or subsidiaries. Additionally, the SWOT analysis should consider organization-wide factors beyond spe-

Area of analysis	Functional areas						
	Marketing	Patient care	Accounting	Finance	Supplies	Staffing	Quality assurance
Internal strengths							
Internal weaknesses							

Figure 2-4 Analysis of Internal Strengths and Weaknesses in a Home Intravenous Therapy Service

cific functional areas or departments. The point is to be thorough in examining internal strengths and weaknesses by using a convenient analytical framework.

Among the internal strengths and weaknesses that SWOT should examine are:

- subunit strategies and tactics
- implementation planning
- focus on excellence in production or service quality
- contribution to operating margin or patient care goals
- organization, department, and working unit structures
- physical plant and equipment
- technological advantages
- managerial acumen and experience
- research and development
- consumer perceptions and corporate image
- staff skills, capabilities, and deficiencies
- competitive positioning

These and many other factors are the basis for assessing internal strengths and weaknesses. It is important to underscore that there is no optimal set of factors to consider in evaluating an organization's strengths or weaknesses. It is appropriate to be as thorough as possible in the analysis.

External threats and opportunities exemplify the constraints and potential advantages that a health care organization or one of its subunits may face. SWOT attempts to profile the external factors that may prevent an organization from pursuing specific strategic objectives or, conversely, that facilitate the organization's efforts. Analysis normally centers on the following factors, among others:

- competitor strengths and weaknesses
- market growth
- demographic changes
- regulatory environment
- changing provider (e.g., physician) and patient
- substitute products and services

Like the internal factors, the external variables should be exhaustively analyzed.

CORPORATE STRATEGY FORMULATION

There are different levels of strategy in any health care organization.[24] This idea is illustrated in Figure 2-5 from the perspective of a nursing home chain.

Functional Level

In Figure 2-5 three levels of strategy are shown: corporate, business, and functional. The functional level is the most essential.[25] It represents strategy formation in major departments, divisions, or strategic business units of an organization. For example, in a nursing home in Utah that is part of a nationwide chain, functional strategies need to be established for marketing. Should marketing by the nursing home emphasize service to the local community, or should a generic strategy be adopted for the chain as a whole? As Figure 2-5 suggests, functional strategies emphasize structure and process at the operating level. The purpose is to create strategies that maximize end results.

Functional level strategy does not necessarily focus on only one organization. If, as suggested in Figure 2-5, the corporation comprises many facilities (e.g., if it is a multifacility nursing home chain), then the magnitude of the

Strategy level	Focus	Conceptual level	Illustrative decisions for a nursing home chain
Corporate	Determining what business to enter	High	1. Should the chain diversify its holdings to include any other health care services (e.g., hospice or home care)?
			2. Should the chain acquire other organizations that are consistent with the industry (e.g., rehabilitation services, retirement centers)?
Business	Determining how to compete in a business		1. Should the chain concentrate on capturing market share in the nursing home industry?
			2. Should the chain focus on high levels of patient amenities and new facilities?
Functional	Determining how to arrange structure and process of specific management functions to produce highest level of end results	Low	1. Should marketing by the chain emphasize service to the local community, or should an aggressive generic strategy be followed at the national level?
			2. Should specific facilities in the chain retain management autonomy, or should centralized control be used?

Figure 2-5 Differentiating Levels of Strategy

strategic management process is heightened but the strategic issues still involve various functions in the total multifacility organization and the specific nursing homes. Therefore, a nationwide chain of fifty nursing homes must formulate strategy for patient care standards, marketing, finance, and accounting for all the facilities. The scope of this effort is immeasurably greater than formulating functional strategies in a single nursing home, but the orientation is still the same: How should the structure and process of specific functions be arranged to produce the highest level of end results?

Business Level

Business-level strategy is the next strategy level portrayed in Figure 2-5. It is more abstract than the functional level, and its purpose is to determine how to compete in a given business line.[26] For example, a nationwide nursing home chain might seek answers to the following strategy decisions.

- Should the chain concentrate on capturing market share in the nursing home industry?
- Should the chain focus on luxury service nursing homes, or should it diversify its service line?
- Should the chain merge with another nationwide chain that emphasizes moderate rates and fewer customer amenities?
- Should the nursing home target specific customers (e.g., young children needing skilled nursing care or middle-aged clients with dementia)?
- Should nursing home facilities be sold after a specified period of time (e.g., 15, 20, or 25 years) because of deterioration of the physical plant?
- Should affiliations be made with a hospital chain or a retirement center chain?

As these questions suggest, business strategy focuses on how to compete in the nursing home industry.

Corporate Level

Corporate-level strategy, as shown in Figure 2-5, focuses on the line of business.[27] An organization must determine what business it will conduct. As time progresses and the organization is successful or encounters setbacks, the organization must reassess the line of business that it will pursue. This is truly strategic-level decision making. For example, a nursing home chain may reexamine its corporate strategy. Among the questions that must be answered in this regard are (1) whether the chain should diversify its holdings to include other health care services, (2) whether the chain should acquire organizations that are consistent with the nursing home industry (e.g., retirement centers or resorts), and (3) whether the chain should liquidate its assets and reinvest in an entirely new line of business.

For the most part, determining corporate level strategy is a challenging task. The risks are extremely high that external and market conditions may change, thereby rendering planning premises inappropriate. Furthermore, in organizations that have been successful inertia inevitably develops. The attitude seems to be: If corporate strategy is functioning, why change it? Additionally, as organizations redefine their master strategy there is a possibility that they will lose their identity.[28] Acquisitions and divestitures are occurring at an astounding rate in the health care field. Many investor-owned organizations are focusing on the bottom line. There is nothing wrong with fiscal stability or profitability; the inference is that successive revisions of corporate strategy jeopardize organizational identity. Many of the factors that made acquisitions or divestitures successful may be lost as changes are introduced in corporate strategy.

FORMULATING MASTER STRATEGIES

Master strategy is the sum of the corporate, business, and functional strategies. Master strategy formulation for an organization depends to a large extent on whether the firm has a single strategic business unit (SBU) or multiple SBUs. The differences between single SBU firms and multiple SBU firms are shown in Figure 2-6. A single SBU firm normally produces a limited range of products and services in a single industry. A multiple SBU firm usually maintains business units in at least two different industries. As Figure 2-6 indicates, the functional organization that forms the SBUs in a multiple SBU firm is responsible for specific products and services in a single industry.

Master strategy formulation is more complex in the multiple SBU firm because the business strategies in each SBU must be accounted for in the final corporate strategy. In the single SBU firm there is limited influence from other industrial sector considerations. The product or products pertinent to the industry generate constraints and opportunities for strategy formulation. In the multiple SBU firm the strategy aspects of each industry must be coalesced into a single strategy statement. This statement directs the firm while simultaneously permitting latitude in corporate strategy.

Strategic analysis in multiple SBU firms is also more complex than in the single SBU situation. Organizations want to attain a good mix of SBUs that

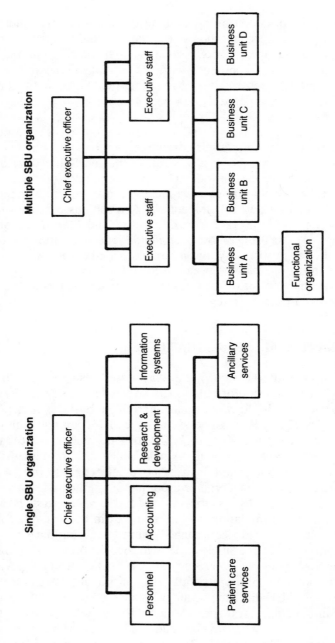

Figure 2-6 Distinguishing between Single and Multiple SBU Organizations

promotes overall growth. Although SWOT analysis can be used for any single SBU, comparisons must eventually be made among SBUs. There have been a number of models proposed for assessing the attractiveness of SBUs.[29-31] The precision of these analytical models is still rudimentary, but significant gains have recently been made in quantifying comparisons. The problem is the number and interaction of variables to be evaluated for each firm. The most sophisticated assessment models have incorporated multiple criteria, whereas initial models usually considered two factors, as portrayed in Figure 2-7.

The Boston Consulting Group (BCG) matrix assesses an SBU in two dimensions: competitive position (e.g., market share) and business growth rate. These are narrow standards. General Electric's (GE) Business Screen also employs two vectors, business strengths and industry attractiveness, but these are broader than the BCG dimensions. GE has elaborated on subdimensions for each of these vectors, which has expanded the usefulness of this assessment technique. The purpose of these techniques is to compare visually a number of SBUs simultaneously as shown in Figure 2-7 for six firms. Having used one of these techniques to compare SBUs analytically, managers are then in a better position to formulate corporate strategy.

SHAPING STRATEGIC SURPRISE

Health care organizations are concerned about minimizing the number of adverse surprises that may affect performance.[32] The uncertainties of a competitive environment tend to erode quality of patient care, to reduce the efficiency of operations, and to threaten fiscal solvency. The biggest threat is that a surprise of strategic magnitude will occur according to one of the following scenarios.

- A competitor decides to replicate another hospital's service. The competitor recognizes that the service has been helpful in attracting inpatients and diversifying the hospital's service line.
- A key nursing executive is raided by another hospital. The ability to shape a strategic business unit (i.e., nursing services) is decreased.
- A competitor suddenly withdraws a service in durable medical equipment, leaving excess demand and pressure for expansion when fiscal constraints are at their maximum.
- A competitor introduces several service amenities (e.g., a wellness program option) that cause patients to switch their health plan allegiance.

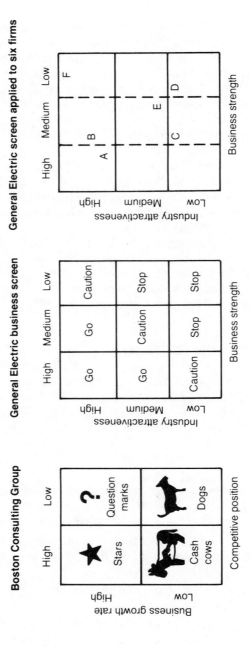

Figure 2-7 Models for Assessing Multiple SBUs

- A nationally based nursing home chain sends several consultants into a new geographic market to assess the feasibility of market penetration.

These and other similar situations represent unanticipated events that foil the strategic planning process. Careful environment surveillance and a propensity for flexibility can be built into strategic plans and resource allocations, but the element of surprise can be invoked as a strategic weapon.

Figure 2-8 presents several ideas and suggestions to prime further thinking about stimulating strategic surprise. These methods reverse the algorithm of strategy formulation. They create an element of uncertainty about an organization that keeps competitors off-guard and confused. Consequently, it is more difficult for competitors to develop strategic responses. By keeping competitors upset, strategic flexibility is improved. Hence there is more time to devise and implement strategy. The uncertainty may channel competitors in the wrong direction as far as strategy formulation and implementation. In essence, surprise helps prevent strategic retaliation. Competitors are overly cautious about responding with countervailing strategies because they are uncertain about the organization's opposing strategy.

Reversing the Algorithm of Thinking

The essential beginning for strategic surprise shown in Figure 2-8 is the willingness to reverse the normal algorithm of thinking. Algorithms are usual or patterned responses to situations or problems. For example, if a hospital discovers that its competitors use extensive advertising campaigns, it too will seriously consider what advertising program it should be undertaking. To

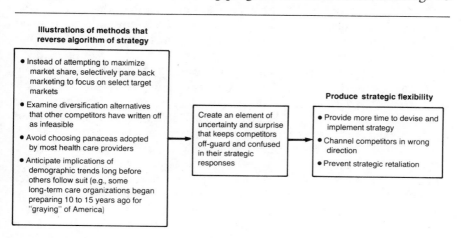

Figure 2-8 Shaping Stratetic Surprise

prepare an equivalent or more ambitious campaign is the normal response. Alternatively, consider what happens in an HMO when there is a sudden drop in enrollment. The tendency is to reduce staffing, particularly for primary care services. This is the needed algorithm to reduce costs. By cutting the staffing levels, labor costs drop and may compensate for the reduction in enrollments.

In both these examples the normal response (or algorithm of thinking) is expedient; but only over the short run. In the first example, by the retaliating hospital's advertising it may be possible to confuse the exact message that consumers receive regarding the competitors' advertising, just as is the case for all the other hospitals. On the other hand, the precise benefits to the retaliating hospital may be marginal as a result of a sudden profusion of advertising messages. The hospital needs to avoid the algorithm of thinking (i.e., to advertise) and instead reverse the algorithm. For example, it might be better to put more resources (those that would normally have gone to advertising) into developing relations with former patients. Services may be expanded. Prices may be lowered. Whatever the strategy, the hospital must be able to promote a unique advantage. It is essential to concentrate on investments that maximize return (i.e., patient relations) rather than minimize return (i.e., advertising).

In the situation of declining enrollment for the HMO, the primary questions are (1) What factors are causing the decline, and (2) How long will these factors continue to operate? If the factors are short-term in nature, it may not be advisable to pursue short-term savings (by terminating personnel) at the expense of accomplishing long-term goals (e.g., continued high service quality and low operating costs). Every time an organization treats its staff as a dispensable commodity, the ability to achieve goals is threatened. The remaining (i.e., nonterminated) personnel may be happy to have retained their jobs, but probably they will not like the implication of low esteem that the organization held for their co-workers. They may also resent the added burden resulting from the lower staffing levels. These and other possible ramifications inevitably threaten the efficiency and effectiveness of operations. Hence short-run savings may mutate into grievous long-run outcomes. It might be better to reverse the algorithm of thinking by retaining staff and absorbing the expenses to achieve better long-run performance.

How can the algorithm of thinking be reversed to create better strategy? Figure 2-8 illustrates only a few of the concepts that may lead to strategic surprise. First, a hospital may consider targeting select portions of a market for promotion. This approach is contrary to prevailing thought that the larger the market share the greater the anticipated revenues. Targeting select segments of a market may provide greater efficiency and higher returns even though market share is lower.

Another approach for reversing the algorithm of thinking is to examine the diversification alternatives that competitors have written off as being unprofitable. Admittedly, there must be an underlying rationale as to why other health care organizations avoid acquiring firms that are on the market, but it may be possible to capitalize on these strategic "rejects" (e.g., by integrating them to produce an entirely new subsidiary or to implement strategic changes that produce a good return). This suggestion for reversing the algorithm of thinking is similar to another: avoiding the panaceas adopted by most organizations in an industry. Just because every organization seems to be deriving good results from a popular strategy does not mean that the strategy has universal value. In fact, panaceas may be better avoided than pursued.

Another illustration of the reversed algorithm is to anticipate (i.e., to pay attention to and to plan according to the implications of) demographic trends. Since the early 1970s demographers have been discussing the fact that the population is aging rapidly. Have health care organizations done anything meaningful about this trend? Usually, the answer is no. What could have been done? For example, the following ideas suggest new ways in which long-term care organizations could respond to the aging American population:

- develop new services to serve the senior market
- make capital investments in facilities needed to serve the senior market
- plan for reorganization, if necessary (e.g., undertake geographical considerations), to capture large portions of senior markets
- undertake market research on senior preferences, and compare these preferences to other customer preferences as a basis for product and service changes

These ideas are only a few of the strategies that are possible for meeting the needs of the aging.

In sum, shaping strategic surprise requires innovation. Nevertheless, it is difficult to be creative or innovative when an organization is continually following algorithms of thinking. Managers need to be alert to this phenomenon of the reversed algorithm. In their strategic management role, it is vital that they move forward with fresh thinking that does not overly replicate that of competitors.

Willingness To Revise Strategy

Consistent with the need to reverse the algorithm of thinking is the willingness to revise strategy. Both ideas imply an openness to new ways of thinking. The problem facing many health care organizations is the inertia generated from past success. Good performance eventually breeds mediocrity. Unable to change dramatically the status quo, the organization proceeds down a path of little enlightened effort or innovation. Unable to conceive a better way to produce the same or better results, the organization slowly loses its competitive edge.

Figure 2-9 illustrates the problem of willingness to revise strategy. Organizations must prevent stagnation in thinking. Complacency with good performance has an insidious organizational effect, particularly on strategy. When a strategy appears to be working perfectly, there is a temptation not to alter it. The attitude seems to be: Why fix it if it is not broken? This thinking overlooks the fact that vibrant health care organizations continually ask themselves how they can attain excellence.

There are two basic options available to organizations for strategy revision, as shown in Figure 2-9. The stagnation option is pursued by most organizations. It is predicated on maintaining the status quo. Organizations that retain their initial strategy do many things to protect this strategy and to avoid change at all costs. Assume that a clinic establishes a strategy at time 1. As months and years go by there are some observable problems with the strategy, which are noted at time 2. These are not serious problems, but they are resolved in the most expedient manner. For example, the clinic may discover that it has poor leadership, discourteous nursing staff, and a poor geographic location. These problems are treated in a first-aid approach; that is, the problems are bandaged. The chief operating officer is sent to a Dale

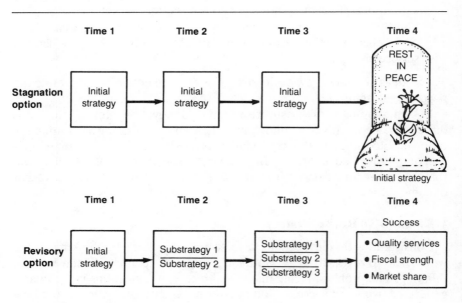

Figure 2-9 Options for Revising Strategy

Carnegie course, and the nursing staff is given in-house training on courtesy. Basically, the organization has responded in a minimal fashion to the problems.

At time 3 the problems worsen, but bandages are still applied so that the initial strategy can be retained. Some of the problems are causing the clinic to bleed profusely and thereby threaten its survival. At time 3, the executive has forgotten the material from the Dale Carnegie course and is back to his or her old habits of mismanagement. The nursing staff has acquired even more surly personnel. Meanwhile, the socioeconomic status of the market served by the clinic has deteriorated even further.

By retaining a single strategy, the clinic has established preconditions for failure. Continued adherence to the strategy with quick-fix and ephemeral treatment has not improved the diagnosis. First-aid is not the solution when a strategy needs surgery. The anticipated outcome is the eventual death of the clinic with its initial strategy still intact. May it rest in peace.

The stagnation option for organizational strategy should be avoided, but organizations do have an attractive option available to them. The revisory option shown in Figure 2-9 can be an alternative to strategic failure. Under the revisory option the clinic begins with an initial strategy at time 1. As months and years go by the clinic revises the strategy by creating two substrategies, which are acknowledged at time 2. This process of strategy revision does not stop there, however. Further variations are introduced in the strategy at time 3. By time 4 it becomes apparent that continuing the revision of strategy has produced success: high-quality service, fiscal strength, and high market share. The clinic is a vibrant organization reflecting vitality under the revisory option. Unlike the ultimate result of the stagnation option, obsolescence has been avoided.

Health care organizations and their managers need to pursue openness and vitality in strategy formulation. They must avoid becoming locked in to a given strategy. They should be willing to revise strategy as an indication of their commitment to progressive organizational growth.

FUTURE CHALLENGES IN STRATEGIC MANAGEMENT

Primarily as a result of an unsettling environment, health care organizations are facing an uncertain future. The past tendencies to define methodically a mission, strategic objectives, and strategy are slowly being undermined. Strategy is no longer safe and secure over an extended period; health care organizations are challenged to rethink how they will achieve their goals. In part this is due to expanding visions among organizations.[33] Additionally there is the proximity of competition, which has an unrelenting influence on strategy. In the final analysis health care organizations are being pressured to devote more attention to strategic management issues. Complacency and hesitance to evolve in the contemporary context will only jeopardize survival and the well-being of service delivery efforts.

Fundamental to effective strategic management is the need for innovation and creativity. Stepwise adherence to the strategic management process is only the beginning in ensuring a vibrant and growing health care organization or nursing program. At each step a generous infusion of insight, willingness to take risks, vision, experimentation, and originality can occur. This represents a singular challenge because in many respects organizational strategy has been limited to reactionary or problem-solving approaches.[34] A new dawn has arrived in health care that demands a total rethinking by all managers, however. Strategy and corporate direction are no longer givens. The fight for survival and success continually arises.

Health care organizations and nurse managers will respond to the future challenges in strategic management in various ways. For some it may mean adopting an entirely new view of time-honored relationships.[35] For others the response will consist of an expanded time allocation for contemplating health care organization environments. Whatever the precise configuration of response, the attention of health care organizations and nurse managers will be consumed by strategic challenges.

NOTES

1. G.A. Steiner, *Strategic Planning* (New York: The Free Press, 1979).

2. L.A. Files, "Strategy Formulation and Strategic Planning in Hospitals: Application of an Industrial Model," *Hospital and Health Services Administration Quarterly* 28 (November/December 1983): 9-20.

3. D.R. Gourley, "Marketing and Planning in Multihospital Systems," *Hospital and Health Services Administration Quarterly* 33 (Fall 1988): 331-344.

4. G.D. Harrell and M.F. Fors, "Planning Evolution in Hospital Management," *Health Care Management Review* 12 (Winter 1987): 9-22.

5. T.T. Craig, "Integrating Institutional Long Range Strategic Planning," *Hospital and Health Services Administration Quarterly* 28 (May/June 1983): 16-26.

6. D.H. Fox and R.T. Fox, "Strategic Planning for Nursing," *Journal of Nursing Administration* 15 (May 1983): 11-17.

7. J.L. Lukacs, "Strategic Planning in Hospitals: Applications for Nurse Executives," *Journal of Nursing Administration* 16 (September 1984): 11-17.

8. M.G. Nash and B.C. Opperwall, "Strategic Planning: The Practical Vision," *Journal of Nursing Administration* 18 (April 1988): 12-18.

9. J.A. Pearce and R.B. Robinson, *Strategic Management: Strategy Formulation and Implementation* (Homewood, IL: Irwin, 1985).

10. G.A. Steiner, *Top Management Planning* (New York: Macmillan, 1969).

11. R.C. Shirley, "Limiting the Scope of Strategy: A Decision Based Approach," *Academy of Management Review* 7 (1982): 262-268.

12. K.W. Tourangeau, *Strategy Management: How To Plan, Execute and Control Strategic Plans for Your Business* (New York: McGraw-Hill, 1981).

13. D.K. Clifford, *Managing the Threshold Company* (New York: McKinsey, 1973).

14. A.A. Thompson and A.J. Strickland, *Strategy Formulation and Implementation* (Dallas, TX: Business Publications, 1980), vi.

15. D.R. Brodwin and L.J. Bourgeois, "Five Steps to Strategic Action," *California Management Review* 26 (1984): 176-190.

16. L.L. Byars, "The Strategic Management Process: A Model and Terminology," *Managerial Planning* 32 (1984): 38-44.

17. J.M. Higgins and J.W. Vincze, *Strategic Management and Organizational Policy* (New York: Dryden, 1986).

18. B.J. Trexler, "Nursing Department Purpose, Philosophy, and Objectives: Their Use and Effectiveness," *Journal of Nursing Administration* 17 (March 1987): 8-12.

19. S.J. Carroll and H.L. Tosi, *Management by Objectives* (New York: Macmillan, 1973).

20. D.A. Aaker, "How To Select a Business Strategy," in *Strategy and Organization*, ed. G. Carroll and D. Vogel (Marshfield, MA: Pitman, 1984), 158.

21. J.N. Giger and R. Davidhizar, "Strategic Planning: Implications for Nursing Practice and Education," *Hospital Topics* 65 (August 1987): 11-14.

22. H.L. Smith and M.D. Fottler, *Prospective Payment: Managing for Operational Effectiveness* (Rockville, MD: Aspen, 1985).

23. H.H. Stevenson, "Defining Corporate Strengths and Weaknesses," *California Management Review* 19 (Spring 1976): 51-66.

24. S.K. Marrus, *Building the Strategic Plan* (New York: Wiley, 1984).

25. Steiner, *Strategic Planning.*

26. C.W. Hofer, "Toward a Contingency Theory of Business Strategy," *Academy of Management Journal* 18 (1975): 784-810.

27. S. Tilles, "How To Evaluate Corporate Strategy," *Harvard Business Review* 41 (1963): 111-121.

28. W.D. Guth, "Corporate Growth Strategies," in *Business Policy and Strategy*, ed. D.J. McCarthy, R.J. Minichiello, and J.R. Curran (Homewood, IL: Irwin, 1987).

29. Y. Wind and V. Mahanjan, "Designing Product and Business Portfolios," *Harvard Business Review* 59 (1981): 155-165.

30. C.W. Hofer and D. Schendel, *Strategy Formulation: Analytical Concepts* (St. Paul, MN: West, 1978).

31. B. Hedley, "Strategy and the 'Business Portfolio,' " *Long Range Planning* 10 (February 1977): 9-15.

32. I.H. Ansoff, "The Changing Shape of the Strategic Problem," in *Strategic Management: A New View of Business Policy and Planning*, ed. D.E. Schendel and C.W. Hofer (Boston: Little, Brown, 1979).

33. G. Donaldson and J.W. Lorsch, *Decision Making at the Top* (New York: Basic Books, 1983).

34. R.M. Burton, "Variety in Strategic Planning: An Alternative to the Problem Solving Approach," *Columbia Journal of World Business*, Winter 1984, 92-98.

35. T.J. Peters. "Strategy Follows Structure: Developing Distinctive Skills," in *Strategy and Organization*, ed. G. Carroll and D. Vogel (Marshfield, MA: Pitman, 1984), 102.

Chapter 3

Planning for Strategic Visions

There are many parallels between health care organizations and business organizations in their attitudes toward planning. Both tend to view the present circumstances that they confront as being unique. The novelty of the new environment often leads managers to the conclusion that planning is inappropriate or ultimately a waste of time. Experientially, they have discovered that competitors, reimbursement, suppliers, prices, staffing, regulations, patient demand, and related factors seldom remain constant. The same variability characterizes managerial planning environments. Consequently, health care corporations face a complex and changing set of circumstances. It must be pointed out, however, that today there are more resources, data, and technologies for addressing the changing health care or corporate environment.

Under the placid environment accompanying cost-based reimbursement, health care organizations could afford not to plan. There were many degrees of freedom to support errors and haphazard ways. This approach is entirely inappropriate today. The current health care environment ultimately distills to a planning challenge at all organizational levels. Not only do health care organizations need a vibrant and results-oriented planning process, but planning is crucial at all organizational levels. A concerted effort is needed from operating levels up to the top administrative positions.

Now more than ever, nursing is a central focus of planning not only in daily activities but in long-run strategy as well. To succeed requires a realistic and innovative strategic vision defined and endorsed by all staff. Nursing services' contribution to this process can be supported by nurse managers.[1]

61

PRESSURES FOR PLANNING

The pressures for planning that affect corporations and health care organizations are similar, as is shown in Figure 3-1. This fact should emphasize to nurse managers that active involvement in planning is an expectation that accompanies managerial roles. As suggested in Figure 3-1, service diversification has increased, competition is more intense, patient preferences are driving service delivery strategies, technological developments have accelerated, and staff demand a promising work environment. These examples are only a few of the pressures motivating managers in health care organizations and corporations to focus attention on planning activities.

Not surprising, these same pressures are acknowledged reasons for not planning. Many health care managers have seen their plans become obsolete after a sudden change in corporate structure (e.g., acquisition by an investor-owned organization), medical technology, market, or nursing service delivery variables on which plans were based. Much of the effort invested in planning is unrecoverable under these circumstances. After having to discard plans several times, it is understandable why managers begin to shift from planned action to reaction. Paradoxically, this is precisely the time when

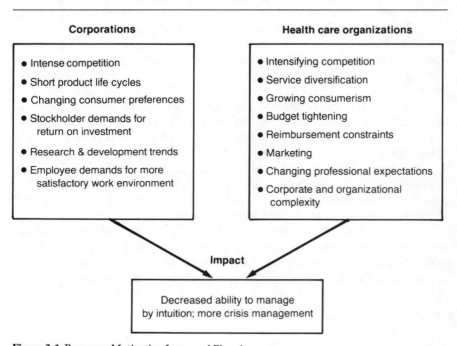

Corporations

- Intense competition
- Short product life cycles
- Changing consumer preferences
- Stockholder demands for return on investment
- Research & development trends
- Employee demands for more satisfactory work environment

Health care organizations

- Intensifying competition
- Service diversification
- Growing consumerism
- Budget tightening
- Reimbursement constraints
- Marketing
- Changing professional expectations
- Corporate and organizational complexity

Impact

Decreased ability to manage by intuition; more crisis management

Figure 3-1 Pressures Motivating Increased Planning

greater adherence to planning is appropriate even if motivation is beginning to wane.

Health care organizations and nurse managers need to prevent the drift that accompanies reacting to present circumstances. Planning is the best way to define a specific intended direction and to remain headed in that direction. Nonetheless, planning should be flexible enough to allow revisions in direction. Flexibility is needed to address sudden changes and to prevent incremental decisions that could prevent the pursuit of a specific direction. Planning provides a formal framework in which a preferred direction is identified and the means for attaining the end are specified. Planning also improves the quality of decisions because nurse managers can exercise both intuition and reasoned judgment in directing staff.

BALANCING PLANNING'S BENEFITS AND LIMITATIONS

Is planning worthwhile? This is a question that every nurse manager will consider at some point. Immersed in managing a nursing department, a director of nursing may come to a moment of introspectively questioning whether planning is necessary. Staffing levels have been steadily increasing as a result of expanded program services. Patient care has been improving. Staff nurses have expressed satisfaction with their benefits, work environment, and organizational climate. All signals point to a period of success resulting from quality care, which has been attained simultaneously with higher productivity and lower nursing costs. Why should a nurse manager plan under these circumstances? It would seem that any investment in planning at this point would be a waste of time.

Whenever health care managers become too complacent about performance and self-assured that planning has little payoff, they need to reexamine the rationale for planning. There are both qualitative and quantitative reasons behind this rationale, as shown in Figure 3-2. Qualitatively, there are arguments both for and against corporate planning. The balance of the argument seems to favor planning over not planning. Furthermore, there have been a number of empirical studies that point to the value of planning.[2-11] Admittedly, the results from empirical research do not unequivocally indicate that planning leads to better performance. Nonetheless, most of evidence to this point favors planning.

Benefits

The primary overall benefit from planning is the ability to establish guidelines for decision making. The role of nurse managers is to make

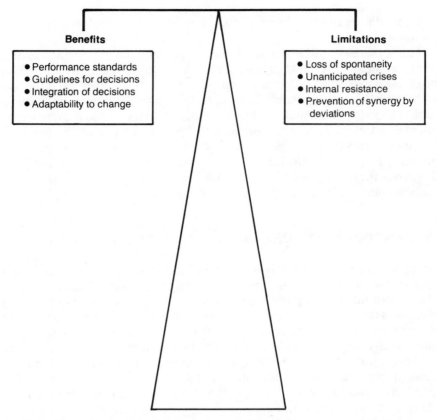

Figure 3-2 Balancing the Limitations and Benefits of Planning

decisions leading to efficient and effective delivery of patient care services. Unfortunately, not every nurse manager recognizes that planning can improve the quality of decisions. However, such an appreciation can be developed by considering several of the benefits attributed to planning.

Standards for Measuring Performance

Plans establish standards by which nurse managers can assess performance. At the core of the planning process is the definition of mission, objectives, and goals. Goals or objectives are definitions of desired performance. They are defined at specific levels in the organizational hierarchy, such as at organizational, divisional, departmental, and individual levels. The complexity of a health delivery organization in terms of service specialties, equipment, assets, number of employees, structure, patient population, and provider diversity influences the range of objectives.

A mission statement defines what an organization seeks to accomplish through its activities (e.g., our mission is to serve the health care needs of the northeastern corridor). Strategic objectives define specific performance targets for organizations (e.g., our goal is to earn a 15 percent return on investment while minimizing malpractice costs). Departmental level objectives further define the organizational goals (e.g., nursing services costs will decrease by 10 percent this year). Individual level objectives establish standards for personnel (e.g., all staff nurses will improve their productivity by 8 percent during the first 6 months of the forthcoming fiscal year). Exhibit 3-1 illustrates standards for evaluating objectives in nursing services.

Once goals are established in measurable form (i.e., there should be a specific definition of what performance levels will occur over a given period

---

Exhibit 3-1 Standards for Evaluating Objectives in Nursing Services

- The objectives for the nursing department or service or unit are written.
- The objectives were written in collaboration with nursing personnel who will assist in achieving them.
- Nursing personnel share in an annual review (or more often), and revision as needed, of the written statements of objectives.
- The written statements of objectives meet these qualitative and quantitative criteria:

  1. They operationalize the statements of mission or purpose and philosophy; they can be translated into actions.
  2. They can be measured or verified.
  3. They exist in a hierarchy or sequence that is determined by priority.
  4. They are clearly stated.
  5. They are realistic in terms of human and physical resources and capabilities.
  6. They direct the use of resources.
  7. They are achievable (practical).
  8. They are specific.
  9. They indicate results expected of nursing efforts and activities; the ends of management programs.

- They show a network of desired events and results.
- They are flexible and allow for adjustment.
- They are known to nursing personnel who will use them.
- They are quantified wherever possible.

Source: Reprinted from R.C. Swansberg, "Planning—A Function of Nursing Administration, Part II," in *Supervisory Nurse*, with permission of S-N Publications, Inc., © May 1978.

of time), then nurse managers may use them as standards for assessing performance. This is a valuable practical benefit of planning. Planning defines standards before performance occurs. In this manner it is possible to determine how well a nurse, department, or organization has performed. Without defining goals and objectives beforehand during the planning process, it is difficult to ascertain whether subsequent performance has improved or deteriorated. Planning is much more than simply setting goals, however. It includes defining tactics to achieve these goals (i.e., plans for implementation) as well as defining specific operating decisions for how resources will be deployed (e.g., budgets). Additionally, planning involves comparing defined performance standards (i.e., objectives) with actual performance. In sum, planning sets standards for measuring performance.

Guidelines for Decision Making

A physician group is faced with the following situation. Eight months after opening a small clinic in a storefront on a local commercial strip, the group is approached by a preferred provider organization (PPO) that expresses interest in the group's joining the PPO. The first 8 months in the life of the new clinic have been somewhat successful, but targeted revenues are not at projected levels. The new clinic location would expand revenues and add additional physicians.

What should the clinic manager do? Answering this question would be considerably easier if the group had bothered to plan. Without a plan there is no framework for decision making. The clinic manager must decide in a vacuum with limited time for analysis or consideration of intended direction. Even in this relatively simple situation, the value of planning is highly apparent.

Planning establishes guidelines for decision making. A plan provides a framework around which prudent decisions can be made. Without such guidelines decisions can be made according to virtually any criterion. A plan generally helps define the most feasible options, and simultaneously it directs attention to relevant, rather than superfluous, issues. In effect, plans assist nurse managers in becoming more efficient in their activities. Plans can focus nurse managers' attention on the most promising options. Nurse managers can then identify opportunities that do not relate to or support the mission or goals of a nursing program or health care organization.

If the clinic manager in the example above had formulated a business plan, guidelines would then be available for assessing the option of joining the PPO. Without a plan the clinic manager is caught in a dilemma. On the one hand, attention needs to be devoted to the original business effort. Revenues are not up to expectations. What are the causal factors underlying this situation? Until this question is answered it will be difficult to allocate time to the PPO opportunity. The clinic manager seeks to clarify the factors threatening survival of the group practice before considering expansion into another distinct service. The same factors threatening survival for the group practice may well continue after joining the PPO. In that case, the group practice is in at least twice as much trouble. A business plan would set standards for decisions regarding managed care services (e.g., a PPO, a health maintenance organization, an independent physicians association, and the like). A plan would also serve as a guideline for determining whether joining the PPO would really be a propitious opportunity or merely a regrettable distraction.

Integrated Decision Making

Planning provides an opportunity to integrate decisions. The result is fewer piecemeal decisions producing suboptimal performance or decisions that conflict with one another. Planning motivates nurse managers to adopt a broader perspective on the operations of their department, unit, team, or program. This can facilitate an improved understanding of intended direction and a propensity to include this perspective in decision making.

For example, when the nurse manager is faced with a choice of investing in two ultrasound machines, one of which costs $10,000 and will meet capacity for the next 2 years and the other of which costs $15,000 and is capable of meeting service quotas for the next 5 years, future plans can be used to make a choice. Assuming that all other crucial premises have been met to that point, it appears to be more prudent to acquire the $15,000 machine now rather than delay its acquisition. The additional expense can be depreciated over more years, price inflation will be avoided, and extra capacity is available if patient demand exceeds projections. Naturally premises can be wrong, but the intent of planning is to establish a best scenario that fits existing and forecasted constraints.

Adaptability to Change

Planning can generally help health care organizations and nursing programs adapt to change. This perspective is not universally held, however. Planning can also be viewed as the antithesis of flexibility. Plans may formalize intentions and thereby establish barriers to change. As a result, planning can equally be interpreted as preventing change. Nurse managers who view planning as a barrier to change are often those who do not revise plans or who are reluctant to change strategic direction. These nurse managers have no other choice but to remain committed to their present strategy because they have not allocated sufficient time to improving plans.

Planning should not be a static process, nor should it be assumed that once a plan is formulated it will remain viable forever. Plans should evolve as health care organizations and nursing programs evolve. Plans represent aspirations of intended directions. They articulate the next milestone that will be achieved. As a result, plans are organic rather than inorganic.

If plans are continually revised to reflect new premises, standards, aims, and constraints, they can prepare an organization or program for unexpected contingencies. Few forecasts are perfect, but by including contingency plans in the overall planning framework options can be defined in the event that primary planning premises are not achieved. Furthermore, contingency plans establish an attitude of flexibility. When change becomes necessary, an organization is conveniently positioned to adapt. In sum, planning not only generates stability and direction but also creates preconditions for change and evolution.

Limitations

Planning also has its downside. Nurse managers can become cognizant of these limitations to understand better the true value of planning. By recognizing these limitations, nurse managers are more likely to avoid relying on plans simply because they exist. Additionally, they are more likely to ask tough questions, to test premises when plans are formulated, and to convince nursing staff about the efficacy of planning. Finally, grounding in the basic limitations of the planning process can help nurse managers create more perceptive plans that acknowledge the inherent questions about future nursing trends, political events, economic conditions, health sector trends, societal values, staff values, and organizational goals.

Loss of Spontaneity

Planning has a tendency to terminate options, to restrict latitude in operations, and to limit the spontaneity of personnel. By its very nature, planning is designed to define a prescribed course of action. The danger in planning is that these prescriptions will be taken too seriously. By adhering too zealously to plans, nurse managers not only threaten the health care organization's ability to take advantage of unforeseen opportunities but also create a climate that is excessively formal. Failure to take advantage of opportunities is common in the contemporary health care environment. Failure to take action at the proper moment spells the difference between success and mediocrity. Neither health care organizations nor nursing departments can afford to bypass unique opportunities or to delay in acting on new ventures when the timing is advantageous. Planning may prevent nurse managers from acting on propitious opportunities because they are resolutely adhering to a predetermined course of action.

Planning also limits spontaneity by creating a climate of formalization. Planning can be honed to the point that discretion and spontaneity are lost. Nursing personnel may become reluctant to deviate from standardized policies, rules, regulations, or operating procedures. Staff operate under a sense of restraint. This climate makes nurse managers particularly vulnerable to overlooking opportunities and to suboptimizing key strengths. In essence, action is excessively planned and does not permit spontaneity. For example, a director of nursing may maintain such a structured, planned approach to service delivery that nurses do not look for ways to improve the process. Refinements that would result in more satisfied patients and nursing staff are not introduced because they are inconsistent with the previous plan for service delivery.

Unanticipated Crises

Virtually no one is able to forecast a crisis. If nurse managers could accurately forecast crises, then they would prevent their occurrence. It is nearly impossible to incorporate crisis forecasts in the planning process. The need to plan for contingencies has long been recognized, but contingency planning is based on anticipating events that may occur. If taken to the extreme, contingency planning evolves into an obsession with protecting every possible course of action. This could result in wasted resources (i.e., time needlessly spent on planning). Quite simply, it is impossible to prepare for every contingency. There is a certain level of risk associated with providing health care services.

The keys to managing crises effectively are to maintain flexibility and to review periodically actual direction relative to planned direction. Flexibility represents the willingness to revise strategy and tactics in the face of new constraints. For example, the small local drug store that insists on price competing with large national chains because it has planned to offer the lowest prices to consumers may be susceptible to a rude awakening. Invasion of the drug store's market by large, nationally based competitors is a crisis that may be unanticipated. Failure to reassess the planned direction (i.e., in price competition) in view of this event only worsens the crisis. The small drug store needs to remain flexible in its planned strategy. Instead of price competition, it could alter plans by incorporating a customer service orientation that cannot be matched by large chain stores even though the latter's prices are lower.

Willingness to review plans is also effective in managing crises that confuse plans. The half-life of planning is growing shorter. Long-range plans were once thought to cover 5 years in the future. As this time horizon has shortened, the need to review plans has become more important because the factors reducing the planning horizon also threaten existing plans in the sense of unforeseen crises. By periodically reviewing planning premises, nurse managers are able to reexamine these premises. They may have fresh insight into premises that were formulated years earlier. If these premises are no longer valid, then the plans that have been constructed on the premises are also fallible. Nurse managers can anticipate crises by reviewing plans and planning premises.

Internal Resistance

Planning effectiveness can be threatened by internal resistance. Staff may resist plans for a number of reasons.

- Staff may resent the implication of excessive organizational authority. Plans and the operational aspects of plans (e.g., budgets, production schedules, policies, standardized procedures, impersonal rules, and so on) are symbolic of authority. Staff may deliberately resist organizational efforts to attain high productivity, low costs, or high-quality care because they are not comfortable with the attempts to control everything. Some staff may attempt to sabotage plans in retaliation against formal authority represented in the planning process.
- Staff may resent their immediate leader or supervisor. If a nurse resents a supervisor, then such resentment may carry over into the implementation of plans. Performance targets or goals are a convenient mechanism by which staff nurses can sabotage their leaders. Through informal efforts at disrupting group cohesiveness, conniving with other disgruntled nurses, purposeful attempts at blocking co-worker productivity, negligence in duty, and similar tactics, nurses can make their supervisors appear to be managerially incompetent. Nurses can block attainment of planned objectives.
- Staff may resent personal responsibility. Plans articulate expectations. When applied at operating levels, plans define expectations for nurses' performance. Some nurses want to avoid personal responsibility. They do not want to be held accountable for specific performance levels or predetermined thresholds. Instead, they may want to be in control of expectations. Unless the planning process incorporates a participative approach, it is unlikely that staff nurses who hold this view will go out of their way to support efforts for reaching plans.
- Staff may have experienced inequitable treatment. Plans are based on predefined objectives. When staff work hard to achieve those objectives

and are not rewarded, a natural skepticism may develop. This is particularly the case when rewards are maldistributed. In these situations, it is not surprising that staff may not support the planning process.

Other factors may also generate resistance to plans. Resistance does not occur solely at operating levels. Top level personnel may resist efforts at planning for many of the reasons noted above. Staff may resent the authority held by other managers. Staff may resent their superiors. Staff may wish to avoid personal responsibility, especially for plans that are viewed as being susceptible to failure. Finally, staff may not have received an important promotion, or their work may have otherwise gone unrewarded. Whatever the causal factors, there are many opportunities for internal resistance to plans to develop.

Loss of Synergy through Deviations

Crises tend to foul planning systems. A related but distinct problem is the tendency for deviations (from plans) to snowball. A plan is a defined course of action that contains numerous ingredients. Objectives, strategy, tactics, and implementation are fundamental to plans. When strategy changes, there is a trickle-down effect. Nursing departments or programs with a simple plan have few problems adjusting to conditions demanding a new strategy, but in large organizations there is a "critical mass" underlying all plans. Reverberations may ripple through subsidiaries, divisions, departments, work units, and teams. As a result, there is inertia to revising plans.

Considering the barriers that exist to the revision of plans (even under the best of circumstances), it is predictable that deviations from plans can generate turmoil. In fact, the disruptions are serious enough to threaten the integrity of the planning efforts. Deviations prevent synergy in plans because of the ripple effect. Adjustments may vary at each level. With each adjustment there is opportunity for encroachment on the general concept underlying the plan. The result may be a less than perfect articulation of a plan throughout a health care organization.

Balancing the Benefits and Limitations

Every nurse manager must reach a decision about planning's value. The preceding discussion has attempted to weigh objectively the arguments surrounding the value of planning. The wisdom of planning has long been recognized, however. Retrospective studies on planning in large corporations confirm the inherent worth of planning. Benefits such as establishing standards for performance, guidelines for decision making, and a mechanism for adapting to change have been reaped by many health care managers and corporations.

Admittedly, the planning process does not always guarantee success. It can be implemented incorrectly, or unanticipated constraints may emerge that make it difficult to plan. Furthermore, as society increasingly embraces individualism and autonomy, planning has a tendency to conflict with the fundamental premises and objectives surrounding work in contemporary society. This is especially true when planning is taken to extremes. A climate can be created that is counterproductive to human effort. The implication for nurse managers is to avoid an excessively formal approach to planning.

Evidence from Planning Studies

On balance the previous discussion suggests that planning is a worthwhile activity for most organizations. The question remains, however, as to whether there is a more objective method for persuading nurse managers to support the planning function. In the last 15 years a growing body of research has attempted to answer this question. Although mixed results have been obtained, and although these studies have all concentrated on business corporations rather than health care organizations, the overall conclusion that can be drawn from these studies is that planning is worthwhile. In most of these studies the level of formal corporate planning has been compared with performance indicators. Corporations that formally plan appear to outperform other corporations that do not plan. They tend to have higher sales, higher return on investment, higher stock prices, and other similar attainments on financial indicators.

An overview of these studies is shown in Table 3-1. Most of the studies were completed in the 1970s. At this time, there was an explosion in empirical research. Strategic management and strategic planning were often focal points for this research. Although extensive knowledge about planning had previously been distilled in the management literature, few empirically derived results verified the experiences, anecdotes, and rules of thumb. Planning was accepted at face value as a worthwhile activity that produces better performance, but this was only a theorized relationship. Science had not caught up with practice. Consequently, the question of whether strategic planning actually does lead to better performance was a natural concern. If planning does not establish conditions for better performance, then presumably less time should be allocated to the planning function.

When planning does not achieve improved performance, it may be argued that organizations are at the mercy of their situation or context. This question

Table 3-1 Studies Investigating the Relationship between Planning and Corporate Performance

Authors	Sample	Description of Study	Results
Ansoff et al. (1970)	93 manufacturing firms	Investigated relationships between performance (principally sales, earnings, earnings per share, total assets, and earnings and equity) and type of acquisition planning. Planning was defined as the degree to which a firm determined whether and when an acquisition should be made (i.e., explicit statements were made about objectives and strategies). Planning also was defined as establishing criteria for selecting acquisition candidates.	Planners perform better and more consistently than nonplanners. Acquisition planning is particularly conducive to return on investment.
Thune and House (1970)	36 firms in six industries (i.e., drug, food, chemical, steel, oil, and machinery industries)	Examined sales, stock prices, earnings per share, return on common equity, and return on total capital employed in relation to formal planning and informal planning. Planners had established strategy and goals for at least 3 future years as well as plans for achieving the goals.	Formal planners outperformed informal planners in the drug, chemical, and machinery industries.
Herold (1972)	36 firms in six industries sampled by Thune and House (1970)	Extended Thune and House's (1970) study by creating a new measure of profit and cross-validating the planning questionnaire.	Five formal planners in the drug and chemical industries outperformed five informal planners.
Rue and Fulmer (1973)	386 firms in the nondurable, durable, and science industries	Examined economic performance indicators in relation to long-range planning.	Mixed results. Planning was most successful in the durable industries.
Karger and Malik (1975)	90 firms in chemical, drug, electronics, apparel, machinery, and food industries	Compared planners and nonplanners on thirteen economic indicators. Planners exceeded nonplanners on ten of these measures.	Planners outperformed informal planners.

continues

Table 3-1 continued

Authors	Sample	Description of Study	Results
Grinyer and Norburn (1979)	21 firms in England	Utilized structured interviews to establish characteristics of the planning process. Financial performance was measured through financial ratios, including size, profitability, performance, and growth ratios.	No association between formal planning and financial performance.
Wood and LaForge (1979)	41 banks	Financial performance including growth in net income and return on owners' investments was compared to that of four groups: comprehensive formal planners, partial planners, no formal planning, and a control group.	Formal planners tend to outperform informal planners. Planning may be indicative of more sophistication in other management practices.
Kudla (1980)	328 firms of Fortune 500	Classified planners into three categories: nonplanners, incomplete planners, and complete planners. The study related the degree of planning to risk and rate of return. Complete planners used comprehensive, systematic, future-oriented, long-range planning processes. Incomplete planners had a written long-range plan covering at least 3 years but lacked systematic planning.	No association between planning and rate of return.
Ramanujam, Venkatraman, and Camillus (1986)	207 executives in Fortune 500 firms	Investigated the extent to which dimensions of planning are associated with multiple measures of effectiveness. Planning dimensions included system capability, use of techniques, attention to internal facets, attention to external facets, functional coverage, resources provided for planning, and resistance to planning. Effectiveness of planning systems was increased by ability to predict future trends; growth in sales, earnings, and market share; return on investment; and related indices.	Effective planning must combine creativity with control. Planning is most effective when there is system capability, sufficient resources, and functional coverage.

Table 3-1 continued

Authors	Sample	Description of Study	Results
Gable and Topol (1987)	179 small-scale retailers in the Northeastern United States	Compared planners and nonplanners on percentage change in sales and profits over a 3-year period. Planners were those setting goals, conducting analyses of strengths, weaknesses, opportunities, and threats (SWOT), and preparing contingency plans, among other attributes of planning.	Planners did not outperform nonplanners on sales and profit changes.

of environmental determinism implies that organizations may not really be able to control their destinies. If organizations cannot control their direction, it may be possible for them to succeed with only a few managers. This would reduce overhead expenses. As these points imply, the question of whether planning leads to higher corporate performance is important.

A problem in associating planning with corporate performance involves the validity of research design. Although planning may be associated with higher corporate performance, as is suggested by statistical analysis, this does not mean that other management functions and even other variables are not somehow also responsible for higher performance. Planning may merely be indicative of other managerial actions or situational variables (e.g., human resource management, superlative system control, market share, asset base, number of employees, type of industry, and the like) that actually determine levels of corporate performance. In short, it is difficult to control for all the thousands of variables that might explain why one organization performs better compared with others. Few of the studies listed in Table 3-1 controlled for these other determinants of performance in the underlying study design. Most of the studies attempted to minimize the influence of moderating variables through sample selection, construct measurement, or other research methodologies. From a practical viewpoint, however, it is almost impossible to control for all the variables that might influence corporate performance.

Ramanujam, Venkatraman, and Camillus[12] expressly caution us against overinterpreting the results of the studies shown in Table 3-1. They acknowledge that planning is difficult to measure and that existing measurement efforts are rather rudimentary. This is a significant problem in drawing conclusions about the association between planning and performance. How does one measure planning? Is it best distilled from interviews with managers? Is it captured in the degree of formally written plans? Alternatively, is planning really measurable because it is a daily function? These questions are relevant in interpreting the results in Table 3-1. Most of the studies used different measures of planning, so that results may not be entirely comparable. At best only certain aspects of planning may have been measured.

Recognizing the cautions discussed above, what conclusions have been drawn about the relationship between planning and corporate performance? The following points represent a conservative interpretation of the studies.

- Planners normally outperform nonplanners on recognized measures of financial performance (e.g., sales, earnings, profitability, and related financial ratios).
- At least three categories of planning effort are observed in corporations: comprehensive formal planning, partial planning, and no planning.

- Formal planning appears to be undertaken in industries associated with routine manufacturing technologies (e.g., pharmaceuticals, chemicals, and machinery).
- Formal planning has many dimensions. It may consist of written planning statements, periodic assessment of decisions relative to planning documents, meetings among managers to coordinate and plan efforts, or simply the impression that decisions and activities are well organized.
- Planning does not always guarantee that higher corporate performance will be attained. Other factors may vitiate the positive contributions of planning.

There is sufficient evidence (despite countervailing results by the Grinyer and Noburn study, the Kudla study, and the Gable and Topol study) to suggest that planning is associated in some manner with better corporate performance. The most conservative stance would be that the results are mixed and that it is impossible to reach a conclusion about the precise relationship between planning and performance.

Having inspected the available evidence on corporate planning and performance, it is essential to raise one further point about this line of research. The premise of Table 3-1 is that, if corporate planning produces high performance for some organizations, then it will also produce high performance for other organizations. This may or may not be true. There is no guarantee that findings in corporations will necessarily transfer to health care organizations. Furthermore, there is no evidence that the planning-performance relationship has implications for individual performance. In other words, just because corporate performance is related to general planning does not mean that nurse managers' performance will be better when they are completing the planning function. The evidence in Table 3-1 is for corporations, not managers. Nonetheless, there is compelling evidence to support the assumption that what holds true for corporations should also hold true for the individuals whom organizations comprise.

PLANNING MODELS

How should planning be accomplished? What actions actually represent planning? How does the planning process vary from one organizational level to another? When should planning be detailed and technical, and when should it be conceptual? How do the various components of planning integrate in an overall model of planning? To answer these questions, a conceptual model or framework is required that defines the specific ingredients making up planning systems.

Steiner has presented a comprehensive planning model that captures the essence of planning[13] (Figure 3-3). This is an admirable model in several respects. First, it incorporates both strategic and tactical planning. Strategic planning involves determining the direction in which an organization should be headed. Tactical planning involves allocating resources that enable an organization to reach strategic objectives. Second, Steiner's model conveys the organization-wide nature of planning. Effective planning does not occur just at the top echelons. It should be implemented throughout an organization. Third, planning centers on defining mission, goals, and objectives. Steiner's model diagrams the flow of objective setting from mission to operational objectives. Fourth, the values and expectations of crucial constituents often determine what missions and strategies are adopted. Steiner's model suggests that there are many factors that support strategy formulation. Finally, Steiner underscores the importance of reviewing and evaluating plans. This is control. Planning does not occur in a vacuum. Accomplishments or failures are ultimately analyzed, and the information gained thereby is used to revise plans where necessary. In sum, the Steiner model shown in Figure 3-3 has a number of useful features that recommend its adoption.

Strategic Planning

Strategic planning normally occurs in the upper echelons. Depending on the size of an organization, a separate department may be assigned the responsibility of planning. Alternatively, a staff assistant may perform the task. In small organizations (e.g., a clinic, nursing home, or home health agency) the chief executive officer (CEO) may undertake the planning function. The key to strategic planning is not who performs the function, however, but what steps combine to represent the function. Strategic planning is an exercise that defines a vision. It involves setting specific objectives and strategies for their achievement.

According to Steiner there are four major sources of information that contribute to the formulation of master strategies by an organization.

1. External stakeholders such as patients, customers, health care providers, stockholders, suppliers, and subcontractors hold certain expectations about an organization and its strategic direction. Although the pluralism of these stakeholders prevents them from excessively influencing internal affairs, they can have a major impact on organizational governance. Their values and interests may affect how the organization defines its mission, strategic objectives, strategy, and policies.

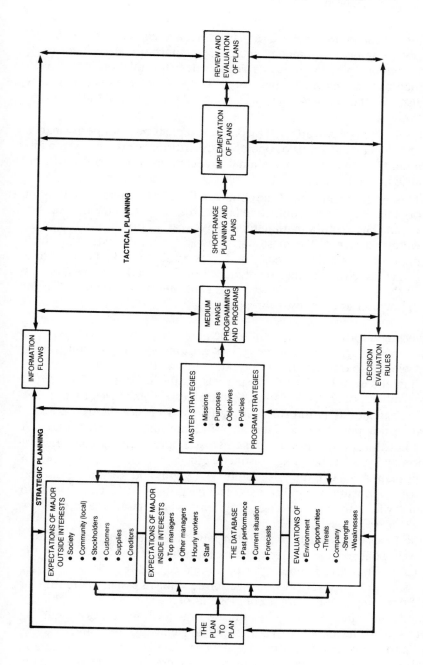

Figure 3-3 Steiner's Planning Model. *Source:* Reprinted with permission of The Free Press, a division of Macmillan, Inc, from *Strategic Planning: What Every Manager Must Know* by George A. Steiner. Copyright © 1979 by The Free Press

2. Internal stakeholders such as managerial and clinical staff members, governing board members, and other organizational affiliates (e.g., volunteers) play a significant role in strategy formulation. Not only do they possess relevant expectations, but these internal stakeholders also are the primary means by which the strategy setting process evolves.

3. Strategic plans are affected by periodic reports on prior performance and the current status of operations. Performance defines the minimum threshold of organizational expectations. Poor prior performance may limit the strategic vision.

4. The environment defines the opportunities and threats confronting an organization. These contextual factors further determine the feasible vision. They set the parameters of risk that an organization may be willing to accept. The master strategy addresses the extent to which opportunities will be pursued and interventions invoked to minimize threats. Such plans hinge on organizational strengths and weaknesses or the resources, experiences, and skills necessary to capitalize on opportunities or to avert threats.

By analyzing information pertinent to the preceding factors, managers can formulate a strategic plan that recognizes existing options and constraints. The problem is to translate this information into a strategic plan.

As Steiner's model in Figure 3-3 suggests, strategic plans are formulated around five components: (1) mission, (2) purposes, (3) objectives, (4) policies, and (5) strategies. The information inputs from outside interests, inside interests, prior performance data, and situation analyses are considered throughout the specification of these five strategic planning components. Situation analysis has become a distinctly crucial exercise in establishing a strategic plan. A SWOT analysis examines strengths and weaknesses as well as external opportunities and threats. The purpose of SWOT analysis is to determine where an organization or program is, where it wants to go, and how it will get there.

In the final analysis, a strategic plan must integrate mission, purposes, objectives, policies, and strategies. This must be achieved in light of the information from constituents, prior performance, and the SWOT analysis. The mission and purpose of an organization describe its essence or reason for being. For example, consider the components of the nursing service philosophy shown in Figure 3-4. Any health care organization delivering nursing services should elucidate such a philosophy to guide objectives and strategy.

It is also important to distinguish between the strategic planning and tactical (or operating) planning elements in Figure 3-4. Strategic planning primarily involves determining mission and strategic objectives. The chosen

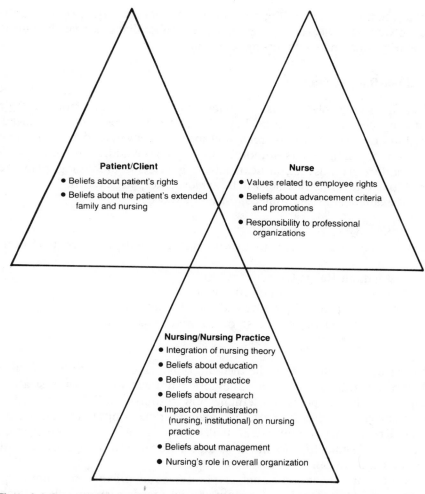

Patient/Client
- Beliefs about patient's rights
- Beliefs about the patient's extended family and nursing

Nurse
- Values related to employee rights
- Beliefs about advancement criteria and promotions
- Responsibility to professional organizations

Nursing/Nursing Practice
- Integration of nursing theory
- Beliefs about education
- Beliefs about practice
- Beliefs about research
- Impact on administration (nursing, institutional) on nursing practice
- Beliefs about management
- Nursing's role in overall organization

Figure 3-4 Components of a Nursing Service Philosophy. *Source:* Reprinted from "Identifying the Components of a Nursing Service Philosophy" by G.W. Poteet and A.S. Hill, *Journal of Nursing Administration*, Vol. 18, No. 10, pp. 29–33, with permission of J.B. Lippincott Company, © October 1988.

field of business, the overarching aims of an organization, and the socioeconomic purpose of the organization are the essential ingredients in strategic planning. Strategic plans seldom address the detailed methods by which these lofty aims and mission will be attained. That is reserved for tactical or implementation planning. As is apparent in Figure 3-4, there is no clear definition of where strategic planning ends and where tactical planning begins. In many cases, strategic and tactical elements overlap. To differentiate between the two, the manager must remember that strategic planning is primarily concerned with setting direction.

Medium-Range Planning

Medium-range planning is a step down in conceptual level from strategic planning because it addresses how strategic objectives will be achieved. Medium-range plans are still relatively abstract. They may cover a long time horizon (e.g., 2 to 7 years or more), but they do not address the immediate expenditure of funds (i.e., the next budgeting cycle). Medium-range plans are used to define how strategies will be achieved in specific terms.

For example, the following contrasts could occur:

Strategic Objective:
To increase productivity in nursing services by 25 percent in 5 years

Medium-Range Objectives:
1. To expand staff by 10 percent
2. To provide geriatric and pediatric nursing
3. To decrease the use of licensed practical nurses by 15 percent

As this example illustrates, the medium-range objectives clarify or further define the strategic objective. They are more specific than the strategic objective without precisely defining how resources will be allocated to accomplish them. Furthermore, the medium-range objectives indicate the general nature of how the strategies will be implemented. The medium-range plans provide guidelines for nurse managers, who must develop specific plans for allocating resources to reach the objectives.

A common convention among corporations is to organize medium-range plans around functional areas: manufacturing plans, marketing plans, financial plans, human resource management plans, and supporting plans from other functional areas or staff areas (e.g., public affairs, accounting, and legal affairs). Nonetheless, health care organizations normally organize plans around services.

Short-Range Planning

Short-range plans typically consist of 1-year operations plans and occasionally 2-year plans. Short-range plans seldom extend longer than these time parameters; otherwise they would begin to resemble medium-range plans.

There is one primary technique that is used in short-range planning: the master budget or the budgeting process. A budget is simply an end product of a rather lengthy forecasting and negotiation process. Service delivery forecasts precede budget formulation. A health care organization develops its best estimate of services to be delivered in the next period (normally a fiscal year). This forecast is compared to forecasts on which the medium-range and long-range plans have been formulated. If necessary, adjustments are made in long-range plans to recognize significant variations in the estimates initially proposed. This may alter fundamental planning premises. Once a forecast is established, the remaining steps in the budgeting process can begin.

At the functional or departmental level, budgets primarily consist of expense or cost projections. The budget becomes a negotiating tool between the financial or accounting staff and department managers such as nurse managers. Objectives are the central ingredient in planning. It is in the budgeting process that objectives are linked to fiscal expectations. Department or division managers must argue for a resource allocation (i.e., department budget) on the basis of past and forecasted performance. In some organizations this negotiation process becomes aggressive. Managers must be able to defend continued allocations at past levels.

Most fiscally responsible health care organizations have progressed beyond the assumption that last year's budget is a base on which additional allocations will be made. Lower budgets are just as feasible as raised budget levels. The "acid test" is the ability to progressively produce results with resource allocations. When this capacity is documented, there is a promising outlook for budget increases.

In functional areas or department units, operations planning also occurs. Aspirations by functional areas or departmental units are inevitably tied to budget constraints. For example, in nursing a recruitment-retention model as shown in Figure 3-5 may be followed. The budget is tied to three components: recruitment, retention, and evaluation. Alternatively, planning may focus on nursing care standards.[14] The point is that the budget is the essential short-range plan.

Implementation and Control

The strategic, medium-range, and short-range plans are primarily mechanisms for guiding organizational efforts. The real test of planning is its ability to direct efforts on a daily basis, that is, to move from the abstract to the implemented. Steiner's planning model in Figure 3-3 illustrates a comprehensive planning model. It is not enough just to create plans. They must be

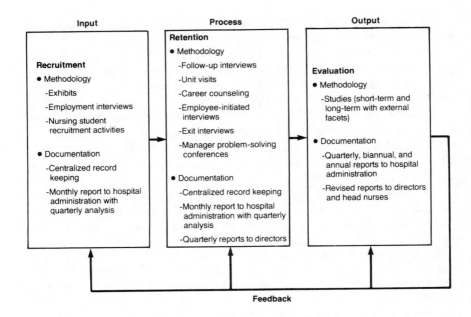

Figure 3-5 Standards for Evaluating Objectives in Nursing Services. *Source:* Reprinted from "Plan Development for a Nurse Recruitment-Retention Program" by L.L. Wall, *Journal of Nursing Administration*, Vol. 18, No. 2, pp. 20–26, with permission of J.B. Lippincott Company, © February 1988.

articulated and then put into action. Once the action occurs, control should be implemented to ascertain whether performance targets have actually been achieved. For a comprehensive planning model to work effectively each step must receive equal attention, and the cycle must be completed (i.e., from planning to implementation and then to control) before returning to planning.

PREREQUISITES FOR EFFECTIVE PLANNING

In the course of their careers, nurse managers will adopt some logical framework for organizing their planning efforts. The Steiner model has its strengths and weaknesses. Although this model sets forth the concept of planning, it does not directly address some of the specific ingredients or steps that contribute to effective planning. At this point it is appropriate to move from the conceptual to the applied. There are a number of building blocks (Figure 3-6) that determine the efficacy of managerial planning.

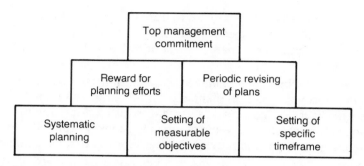

Figure 3-6 The Building Blocks Underlying Effective Planning

Top Management Commitment

There will be no effective planning unless the top echelons of an organization are committed to planning. The board of directors, chief operating officer, and related top management staff must demonstrate their commitment to planning; otherwise there will be no meaningful planning in a health care organization. No matter how vehement the argument is for planning, unless actions are used to reinforce the rhetoric it is unlikely that others will also adopt an active planning posture. Planning is definitely a function in which actions speak louder than words. Others are quick to assess the extent of commitment to planning. If planning is supported merely because it is viewed as good practice, then it is unlikely that a planning mentality will be adopted. Instead, staff will merely go through the actions necessary to convince others that they are planning. The facade masks the fact that the plans are seldom used to guide decision making.

Commitment implies more than just vocalizing how important planning is in the scheme of management values. Commitment implies all the following actions:

- *developing a reward system that identifies and compensates those who plan.* These systems are not excessively difficult to formulate. They can often be centered on a management-by-objectives program. Flexibility should be available for rewarding unusual efforts that produce substantial gains.

- *allocating resources to the planning process.* Nurse managers are often so overburdened with daily clinical problems and issues that they do not have time to plan. An expectation that planning is a fundamental responsibility implies that nurse managers will also be given sufficient resources (e.g., time or staff assistants) to allow them to plan or to delegate some operations issues to free time for planning. Not surprising, as planning becomes a routine activity the daily crises begin to evaporate, and nurse managers naturally are able to free time for planning.

- *creating a planning unit in the nursing department or organization.* The high priority assigned to planning can be reinforced by designating a specific office or individual as being responsible for planning. A planning unit reinforces the value of planning, conveys commitment to the planning function, and provides a means for standardizing planning.

- *actively participating in the formulation, review, and revision of plans.* Admittedly, a CEO of a major hospital may only have time to participate in top level planning meetings. If an executive is unable to participate, however, the absences will be highly conspicuous. The result is that others recognize the low priority given to planning by the CEO. Others will carry this realization to their own meetings with low-level managers. The process continues throughout the organization. Everyone is going through the motions, but there is little interest in actually using plans.

In sum, nurse managers only get out of planning what they put into it. They should not be surprised when others do not follow through on plans if there is little commitment coming from the top level. There is no middle ground. Planning either is or is not a vital organizational activity.

Rewarding Planning

People respond to incentives. Incentives do not always have to be based on pay; they may take the form of promotions, nonmonetary benefits, and, often, simple recognition. If there are no incentives for planning, however, then it is unlikely that nurse managers will target planning as a priority concern. The problem is how best to reward planning when most health care organizations tend to emphasize short-run performance criteria. Planning implies a long-run perspective on performance. An effective reward system for planning will acknowledge short-run accomplishments as it supports long-run performance criteria. Planners should not be penalized for accommodating a long-run perspective. A long-run view may be healthier for an organization than obsession with short-run results. Nevertheless, the importance of current performance should not be jeopardized.

When nurse managers are developing a prudent reward system, some consideration should also be given to disincentives. Nurse managers who do not perform their planning responsibilities should be penalized. If organizations do not implement these disincentives, the implication is that only exceptional planning performance deserves a reward. Anything less is acceptable but not subject to reaction by top management. For many health care organizations the introduction of penalties or disincentives (e.g., demotions, no raises, added responsibilities) is a fairly radical notion. Organizations are far better prepared to administer rewards than punishments.

Nonetheless, nurse managers should recognize that rewards and disincentives are crucial elements of any motivational system. When a function such as planning is purportedly a high priority but is not tied to the prevailing reward or punishment system, people will react accordingly. They should not be expected to make a sincere commitment to planning unless the reward system is adjusted.

Periodic Revisions

Effective planning is predicated on continuing revisions. There is a tendency to formalize plans in writing. Once they are written it takes a concerted effort to revise them. Partially this is caused by the amount of time required to generate plans in the first place. Planning is not an easy assignment. It requires a substantial time investment in meetings, analysis, and documentation. Discussions, debates, arguments, and negotiations must be condensed in an articulate format. Staff may be reluctant to experience the process again after completing a plan. Revising plans seldom requires as much effort as making the initial plan, however. The organization is already accustomed to the process, which should add efficiency to future planning efforts.

Organizations are not static. They are constantly changing. They grow, deteriorate, fluctuate, explode in a flurry of new activity, undergo irreversible losses, and in general follow individual patterns of evolution. In the same fashion, organizational plans are not static. They should be constantly evolving to address the strengths, weaknesses, opportunities, and threats of an open system. This means that nurse managers and others throughout the organization will periodically revise plans by adjusting them to new conditions and constraints. Planning should be continuous, not static.

Systematic Planning

A fundamental argument surrounding planning is the extent to which it should be systematically developed or allowed to evolve incrementally. The systematic approach correlates in many ways with other management principles and theories. Under the systems approach, organizations attempt to control their own destinies. They identify internal and external pressures threatening survival. They seek opportunities that can be exploited before organizing resources for the ensuing strategic effort. Organizations attempt to analyze rationally their environment and internal operations as a precondition for specific action. In sum, organizations can systematically analyze prevailing conditions before methodically formulating rational plans of action. The higher the degree of systematic analysis and rational thought, the better the prospects for performance.

Measurable Objectives

Planning effectiveness is enhanced when objectives are stated in measurable terms. By defining objectives, nurse managers effectively establish intended standards of performance. Objectives represent a means for evaluating actions. Objectives provide a standard for determining whether action was consistent with the standard. This process provides direction to organizational efforts. Decisions then fall in a decipherable framework. What represents subjectively good or bad decisions is predetermined. Furthermore, there is a high degree of objectivity instilled in an otherwise subjective process.

There is a tendency to define objectives in nonmeasurable terms. For example, an objective may be stated as follows: "Our objective is to increase outpatient services to the young patient population." There are too many generalities in this definition. How much of an increase in services is intended? What type of services will be pursued? Over what period of time? Which services will be the focal point? Which young patients are targeted? Are "young patients" 5 to 10 years old? 75-80 years old? These are all legitimate questions arising from a nonspecific objective.

A measurable objective would be stated as follows: "Our objective is to increase orthopedic services to men and women 30 to 40 years old by 15 percent over the previous year's utilization volume." Notice how much more specific this objective is. It sets standards by which performance 1 year from now can be assessed. This detail is fundamental in effective planning.

Specific Timeframe

Effective planning is specified over a reasonable period of time to guide short-range, intermediate, and long-range decisions. Both managerial and clinical staff tend to be obsessed with the immediate problems that they confront. They tend to delay decisions and actions because they are more interested in attending to the present. These behaviors are unnecessary. Plans should spell out guidelines for decisions to prevent procrastination. The result is a conventional wisdom of allowing 5 years for long-range planning, 2 to 5 years for medium-range planning, and 1 to 2 years for short-range planning. Opinions vary as to the precise parameters that are appropriate for the specific types of planning functions.

Recently, the timeframe for planning has shortened. It is now difficult to plan in the 5- to 10-year range because of uncertainties associated with contemporary organizational environments. The result is a shortening of the periods specified above and a tendency to react rather than to plan nursing services.[15] In many health care organizations the short run is the immediate fiscal period. Intermediate plans cover 1 to 2 years. Long-run plans fall in the 3- to 5-year range. Variances in health care markets, the general economy, public regulation, patient preferences, industry structure, social climate, societal values, competition, and related factors tend to shorten the timeframe of planning. Nonetheless, it is useful for health care organizations to extrapolate their efforts to 5 to 10 years in the future. This also elucidates current planning premises.

OBJECTIVES: THE COMMON DENOMINATOR

There is no more important ingredient in planning than objective setting. This is the process of establishing standards. Without an objective, the rest of the planning process has little meaning. Hence objectives are the foundations on which the rest of the planning process is based. If nurse managers develop skills in setting objectives, then they are that much better prepared to complete other planning steps.

The Hierarchy of Organizational Objectives

Objectives should be linked in the overall planning process as suggested in Figure 3-7. They occur in hierarchies and have a rational connection from the strategic level down to the operating level. This descending hierarchy can produce problems in terminology, however. There have always been arguments about the terminology used to differentiate among levels of objective setting. Some believe that the goals are more conceptual than the objectives. Others believe the reverse. For all practical purposes, however, this arguing over terminology overlooks the primary issue. It does not matter what objectives are called as long as they are established in a logical hierarchy.

For those who believe that terminology is important, a distinction can be made between goals and objectives. Goals represent broad statements of intended performance. Goal statements usually do not contain sufficient specifics to clarify precisely when they are to be achieved. Goals suggest organizational or individual action, but they do not specify who will be responsible for the action, when the action will occur, or how progress will be measured. In this sense, goals are broad statements of intentions. Objectives tend to be narrower in scope and to contain a higher degree of specificity than

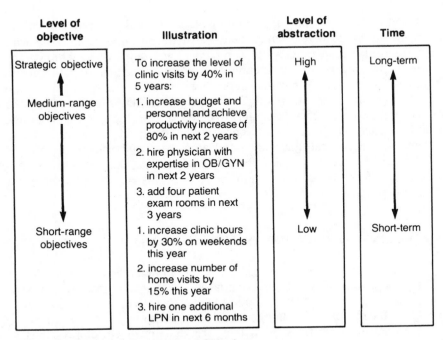

Figure 3-7 Differences in Organizational Objectives

goals. Objectives communicate intent in greater detail and thereby exclude other possible alternatives.

Some people believe that these definitions of objectives and goals should be reversed; that is, objectives should refer to organization-wide issues, and goals should refer to individual issues. Objectives would therefore be broad in scope and goals much more specific. This argument over terminology is fruitful only insofar as it distinguishes one level of target setting or end-result setting from another. Nurse managers must clarify terms and then proceed to the task at hand: creating a meaningful plan.

Guides for Defining Measurable Objectives

There are at least five steps that nurse managers should use to set better objectives in planning.

1. *Define a single intention.* Virtually every organization, department, and staff member is responsible for a multitude of objectives. Therefore, it is essential that an objective state only one intention to minimize the confusion associated with multiple objectives. For ex-

ample, the objective "to package and ship mechanical body parts" contains two intentions: "to package" and "to ship." A person may be successful in shipping parts but may do a miserable job packaging them, so that they arrive broken. By separating the intent into two objectives, performance can be better evaluated.

2. *Describe the intention with verbs.* Performance implies action. Objectives are statements of intended performance. Therefore, they should be phrased in terms of action. For example, "to produce" and "to increase" are better statements of action than "to provide" and "to improve." The former are action oriented. The latter are unspecific.

3. *Define a single end result.* An objective should specify the intention and the end result that will be attained if action is taken. For example, the objective "to increase patient services by 30 percent" indicates the intention ("to increase") and the end result ("services"). It also specifies the level ("30 percent"). In contrast, the objective "to communicate better with my nurse subordinates" does not indicate an end result, although it does specify an intention ("to communicate better").

4. *Specify the level of the end result.* The objective statement "to increase patient services by 30 percent" explains the level of the end result. This statement could be improved by adding "to increase patient services by 30 percent over the preceding period." This establishes a basis for measurement. In contrast, the objective "to increase patient services" does not specify the level of end results. It is only conveyed that services will be increased by some unknown amount.

5. *Define a timeframe.* An objective statement should define when an objective is expected to be achieved. For example, the statement "to provide 1,000 home visits by the end of the first quarter" specifies exactly when the home visits will be delivered. There is no uncertainty as to when the objective will be accomplished.

The preceding guidelines should be help nurse managers set better objectives. There is no reason for objectives to be nebulous. With enough practice, objective setting can be honed to a fine art.

The Role of Management by Objectives

Insight into management by objectives as provided by Odiorne and Raia suggests that objectives through out an organization could be linked in a planning process.[16,17] By setting goals or objectives for their respective units, nurse managers would fulfill their responsibility for planning. These objectives could then be interrelated to foster consistency and relevance to the encompassing organizational objectives.

Management by objectives began as an extension of the planning process in many nursing services settings. Gradually, it began to assume characteristics of a philosophy, thereby becoming more than an organizational planning process.[18] Management by objectives is also a guide to individual action and motivation.[19] For example, nursing staff require objectives to guide their behavior. It follows that rewards can be tied directly to specified objectives to avoid subjectivity in the appraisal process.

Management by objectives contributes to improved management in at least four respects. First, it interrelates individual, work unit, departmental, division, and organizational objectives. The hierarchy of organizational goals and objectives thereby acquires an improved synergy. Second, it encourages managers to follow through on the planning process. As a philosophy of managing, management by objectives prevents managers from adopting objectives only to neglect them in the flurry of daily crises and problems that they confront. Objectives are an integral foundation of day-to-day activities. Third, management by objectives provides a rational basis for performance appraisal. If objectives are defined beforehand, then standards are set by which performance can be assessed. Fourth, management by objectives encourages participation. By joining in defining personal work objectives, staff simultaneously share in determining the direction of an organization.

Figure 3-8 clarifies the relation between the planning process and management by objectives. It also defines the specific steps involved in management by objectives. There are many similarities between the planning models discussed earlier and management by objectives. In fact, management by

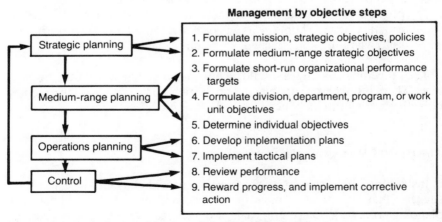

Figure 3-8 Linkages between Management by Objectives and Planning

objectives provides a detailed breakdown of the strategic planning process. In Figure 3-8, note the cascading set of objectives from strategic objectives to short-run performance targets (e.g., 1-year plans) and finally to individual objectives. The common denominator is objective setting. Like strategic planning, management by objectives establishes guidelines for action and decisions through objective setting.

Management by objectives is more than just a managerial tool; it is a valuable mechanism for involving personnel in the planning process. By partaking in objective setting, staff begin to recognize that certain performance targets are desired. When their behavior supports achievement of these targets and when rewards are allocated, the resulting reinforcement perpetuates not only the objective-setting process but also personal commitment to the objectives. In this fashion, management by objectives has contributed meaningfully to organizational commitment. Without a specific agenda of aspirations, staff have limited reason to invest in an organization other than to fulfill a trade or profession. Management by objectives provides the means to integrate individual and personal goals.

Over time, management by objectives has come to be recognized for what it is: simply sound management practice. There are still many supporters of management by objectives as an outstanding management philosophy. This view has many compelling arguments. Setting objectives to guide organizational, personal, and staff efforts provides a rationale for action. Once behavior and action are focused on a particular target, the probability increases that the target will be attained. This fundamental idea has been practiced by every successful organization and person.

NOTES

1. R.C. Swansburg, "Planning—A Function of Nursing Administration, Part I," *Supervisor Nurse*, 9 May 1978, 25-28.

2. H.I. Ansoff et al., "Does Planning Pay? The Effect of Planning on Success of Acquisitions in American Firms," *Long Range Planning* 3 (1970): 2-7.

3. S.S. Thune and R.J. House, "Where Long-Range Planning Pays Off," *Business Horizons* 13 (1970): 81-87.

4. D.M. Herold, "Long Range Planning and Organizational Performance: A Cross Validation Study," *Academy of Management Journal* 15 (1972): 91-104.

5. L.W. Rue and R. Fulmer, "Is Long Range Planning Profitable?" *Proceedings of the Academy of Management*, 1973, 66-73.

6. D.W. Karger and Z.A. Malik, "Long Range Planning and Organizational Performance," *Long Range Planning* 8 (1975): 60-64.

7. P.M. Grinyer and D. Norburn, "Strategic Planning in 21 U.K. Companies," *Long Range Planning* 7 (1974): 80-88.

8. D.R. Wood and R.L. LaForge, "The Impact of Comprehensive Planning on Financial Performance," *Academy of Management Journal* 22 (1979): 516-626.

9. R.J. Kudla, "The Effects of Strategic Planning on Common Stock Returns," *Academy of Management Journal* 23 (1980): 5-20.

10. V. Ramanujam, N. Venkatraman, and J.C. Camillus, "Multiobjective Assessment of Effectiveness of Strategic Planning: A Discriminant Analysis Approach," *Academy of Management Journal* 29 (1986): 347-372.

11. M. Gable and M.T. Topol, "Planning Practices of Small-Scale Retailers," *American Journal of Small Business* 12 (1987): 19-32.

12. Ramanujam, Venkatraman, and Camillus, "Multiobjective Assessment of Effectiveness of Strategic Planning," 347.

13. G.A. Steiner, *Strategic Planning: What Every Manager Must Know* (New York: The Free Press, 1979).

14. T. Porter-O'Grady, "Strategic Planning: Nursing Practice in the PPS," *Nursing Management* 16 (October 1985): 53-56.

15. E.M. Toohey, F.L. Shillinger, and S.L. Baranouski, "Planning Alternative Delivery Systems: An Organizational Assessment," *Journal of Nursing Administration* 15 (December 1985): 9-15.

16. G.S. Odiorne, *Management by Objectives* (New York: Pitman, 1965).

17. A.P. Raia, *Managing by Objectives* (Glenview, IL: Scott, Foresman, 1974).

18. J.A. Fain and H.H. Sheathelm, "Management by Objectives (MBO) as Applied to Nursing Service," *Nursing Forum* 21 (1984): 68-71.

19. C. Cain and V. Luchsinger, "Management by Objectives: Applications to Nursing," *Journal of Nursing Administration* 8 (January 1978): 35-38.

REFERENCES

Ansoff, H.I. et al. 1970. Does planning pay? The effect of planning on success of acquisitions in American firms. *Long Range Planning* 3: 2–7.

Gable, M., and M.T. Topol. 1987. Planning practices of small-scale retailers. *American Journal of Small Business* 12: 19–32.

Grinyer, P.M., and D. Norburn. 1979. Strategic planning in 21 U.K. companies. *Long Range Planning* 7: 80–88.

Herold, D.M. 1972. Long range planning and organizational performance: A cross validation study. *Academy of Management Journal* 15: 91–104.

Karger, D.W., and Z.A. Malik. 1975. Long range planning and organizational performance. *Long Range Planning* 8: 60–64.

Kudla, R.J. 1980. The effects of strategic planning on common stock returns. *Academy of Management Journal* 23: 5–20.

Ramanujam, V., N. Venkatraman, and J.C. Camillus. 1986. Multiobjective assessment of effectiveness of strategic planning: A discriminant analysis approach. *Academy of Management Journal* 29: 347–372.

Rue, L.W., and R. Fulmer. 1973. Is long range planning profitable? *Proceedings of the Academy of Management*, 66–73.

Thune, S.S., and R.J. House. 1979. Where long-range planning pays off. *Business Horizons* 13: 81–87.

Wood, D.R., and R.L. LaForge. 1979. The impact of comprehensive planning on financial performance. *Academy of Management Journal* 22: 516–626.

Chapter 4

Financial Management

Nurse managers and nurses have an important responsibility in responding to the financial pressures facing health care organizations. The nursing profession plays a pivotal role in the new economic environment. Nurses are a primary factor underlying health costs (because of the labor-intensive nature of care delivery), yet they are also the means by which health costs can be controlled.[1] Nurse managers strive to balance these two countervailing pressures. Nursing labor costs can be minimized by creative and efficient scheduling. Staff can participate in cost control programs that identify and resolve waste problems. Nurse managers can further identify potential business opportunities that enhance health care organization revenues. In short, there are many opportunities for nurse managers and nurses to contribute to the financial well-being of their institutions and programs. Familiarity with and ability to apply financial management concepts are prerequisites to building the power base of nursing, however.[2]

Excellence in management assumes that nurse managers are conversant in the functional aspects of health care delivery, including marketing, planning, accounting, human resource management, clinical operations management, and financial management. Breadth of preparation implies that nurse managers can adopt an encompassing view of where nursing programs and health care organizations have been and where they are going in terms of delivering patient care. A functional approach can be used to ascertain whether weaknesses exist, whether strengths have developed, and how clinical operations are predicted to affect an organization's direction. This approach identifies weaknesses that threaten organizational or program growth as well as the inherent strengths that produce distinctive capabilities.

Nurse managers can improve their ability to collaborate with nonnursing administrators by demonstrating a working knowledge of all management functions. Nonetheless, one function deserves special attention from nurse managers and others aspiring to become effective leaders in the health care field: financial management. Changes in third-party reimbursement, the economics of the nursing and medical professions, organizational diversification, and rising competition make it imperative that managers be well versed in and allocate sufficient time to financial management. Unless nurse managers develop a functional competency in financial management, they may be unable to contribute to financial issues involving their nursing program or organization.

Emphasizing financial management skills does not imply that accounting (i.e., control), operations management, human resource management, marketing, or planning are any less important than finance. Each management function is inherently valuable, just as clinical knowledge and skills are prerequisites for fulfilling the nurse manager role. Any sound financial plan depends on joint clinical and functional accomplishments: Costs must be carefully controlled (i.e., through accounting); efficiencies must be introduced in how nursing services are organized and implemented (i.e., through clinical operations management); qualified nursing personnel must be attracted and retained by the organization (i.e., human resource management); a viable marketing program for nursing services must be designed; and an encompassing plan detailing specific patient care objectives, broad nursing program and organizational goals, and organizational mission must be formulated (i.e., through planning).

As many nurse managers recognize, however, inattention to financial management issues can seriously constrain other functional areas. For example, at the organizational level failure to pay careful attention to capital acquisition and mechanisms for funding debt may prevent an organization from renewing its asset base. In this situation, the possibility exists that the organization will not remain competitive. The repercussions are felt throughout the organization, from nursing services to support services. Alternatively, failure to assess financial performance periodically in nursing departments generates a high probability that operations are exceeding budget targets. The nursing program encounters a position from which it (and the nurse management staff) may not recover. As these examples suggest, nurse managers need to hone their financial skills. This is a compelling recommendation not only from the perspective of sound management practice but also from the perspective of improving nursing services.

FINANCIAL RESPONSIBILITIES OF NURSE MANAGERS

If nurse managers expect to adopt a financial perspective commensurate with their managerial and clinical skills, it follows that they must first learn basic financial concepts and techniques. Such knowledge is a prerequisite to nurse leadership.[3] An in-depth discussion of these tools is provided in texts devoted to the subject of finance in nursing services.[4] There are, however, some especially crucial financial management responsibilities that can be underscored here. These represent prime considerations for improving the strategic management of nursing programs. A solid grounding in financial basics allows nurse managers to acquire power and to participate jointly (with other nonnursing managers) in key decision processes.[5] Without this knowledge or skill, nurse managers abdicate power and require intermediaries.

The crucial importance of upgrading financial skills among nurse managers is suggested in Figure 4-1. Decisions about budgets and financial plans are constrained by many factors outside nursing services. First, the philosophy of the chief executive officer (CEO) and the governing board relative to expenditure increases, capital outlays, equipment acquisition, or cost control affects financial decisions for the nursing program. Second and third, nursing's profile as a revenue generator (or revenue consumer) influences the extent to which funds are allocated for program growth. Nursing is often viewed as a consumer of resources rather than a revenue generator. Nurse managers are responsible for demonstrating how nursing expenditures enhance other service units (e.g., laboratory, radiology, and surgical services) that are revenue earners. In this manner, nursing establishes rights to its fair allocation of resources.

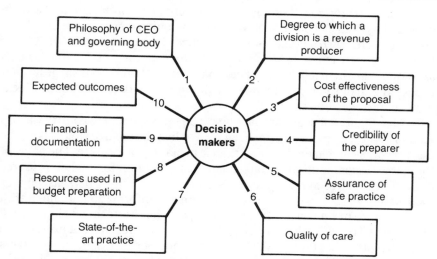

Figure 4-1 Factors Influencing Key Decision Makers in Health Care Organizations. *Source:* Reprinted with permission from *AORN Journal*, Vol. 42, p. 712, November 1985. Copyright © AORN Inc., 10170 East Mississippi Avenue, Denver CO 80231.

Figure 4-1 indicates that not just any financial plan or proposal by nursing is acceptable. A fourth factor constraining financial plans is the extent to which the proposed plans are cost effective. This cost effectiveness is related to nursing's reputation as a credible financial manager. The credibility of proposed budgets is linked to the credibility of nurse managers as financial planners. It is also supported by past efforts at attaining budgets.

Fifth, decisions about nursing expenditures and annual budgets by key decision makers are affected by the perceived thresholds of safe clinical practice. Nursing programs have too often resorted to pleas of malpractice and clinical risk in negotiating for additional financial resources. The sixth and seventh factors affecting financial plans—quality of care and state-of-the-art practice—are related to safe clinical practice. Nursing programs are expected to produce high-quality care and to maintain safe clinical practices. Hence financial planning hinges on documentation (of quality or low risk) to justify resource expenditures.

Figure 4-1 suggests that resources used in the budgeting process, an eighth factor, influence financial planning by nurse managers. For example, nurse managers use a wide variety of data in establishing personnel budgets. They rely on assistance from the chief financial officer in preparing budgets. Consequently, financial decisions involving nursing services are directly influenced by the validity and reliability of data in the planning process. Reports, information, data files, historical schedules, and similar resources ultimately determine the accuracy of proposals. Consequently, they represent a ninth factor constraining financial plans. This information is usually provided by financial personnel who may not understand the considerations and trade-offs surrounding clinical practice. Nurse managers work with financial officers in guiding their understanding of how nursing functions as an individual financial entity. The final step in Figure 4-1 suggests that expected outcomes from nursing activities influence decisions about allocations to nursing services.

In sum, Figure 4-1 suggests that nurse managers attempt to control various factors in presenting a solid financial plan to health care decision makers. In essence, nurse managers adopt a strategic management posture. The name of the game is competition among organizational units for higher resource allocations. Unless nurse managers are prepared to argue persuasively for their units by using rigorous documentation and information obtained with the assistance of financial officers, nursing may be shortchanged in the final allocation.[6] Today, health care organizations expect results, not excuses. To compete with other units in the budget bargaining process, nurse managers must have not only financial management skills but also an understanding of how decisions are made, by whom, and in view of what factors.

Financial management is predicated on basics. Without basic knowledge of financial skill areas, it will be difficult if not impossible for nurse managers to contribute an enlightened perspective on nursing services to the rest of the organization. In the case of financial management, when nurse managers lack an understanding of capital budgeting, working capital management, financial statements, ratio analysis, budgeting, pricing, capital acquisition, investment assessment, leasing, or other financial techniques it becomes difficult for them to argue persuasively for nursing programs and services.

It is assumed that nurse managers will make a sincere effort to acquire the training needed in specific financial management skills. Nursing must have a financial contribution if it intends to gain control of the professional environment and factors affecting nursing care.[7] Nursing is a business. Appropriately, nurse managers should personally cultivate the fiscal concepts and terminology associated with their business. The power of the nursing profession is contingent on nurse managers' developing these financial skills and on their effort to integrate them with other clinical and functional skills.

SENSITIVITY TO FINANCING ISSUES

Nurse managers can become more sensitive to the fact that capital is the basis on which health care organizations procure medical equipment and facilities; that is, they must become more sensitive to the infrastructure through which nursing services are provided. The nursing profession can begin to understand the issues surrounding financing of the capital asset base. Without a solid financial foundation, the ability to deliver nursing services is directly threatened (because services require supporting plant and equipment). Although the issue of capital financing was once relatively noncontroversial, health care organizations have discovered that the ground rules have changed. Not only have the sources of capital changed, but the means for paying off capital expenses have also altered significantly. For many health care organizations this is not an immediate problem because they own relatively new plant and equipment. Others have not thought carefully about replacement or renovation of plant and equipment over the coming years. This could be a strategic error of the highest magnitude.

The implications of a capital crisis in health care organizations for nursing services are numerous. Unless hospitals and other health institutions are able to maintain plant and equipment, their longevity is threatened. Inability to pay interest on leveraged assets means that health care organizations face financial disaster. At a minimum, they cannot procure new equipment (or facilities) to replace obsolete equipment (or facilities). This has a distinct effect on nursing care. Until prospective payment was introduced, nursing programs could insulate themselves from these concerns. It has become increasingly apparent, however, that health care organizations need a concerted effort from all personnel in battling the budget crunch. Nurses and other personnel should understand that inability to maintain or replace capital assets ultimately influences patient care delivery.

There are several possible negative consequences of failing to address capital financing. First, current operations must be cost driven to derive funding for long-term debt. Money spent on capital expenditures and debt service, however, is money not allocated to nursing care. Second, without new or renovated facilities it may be difficult to capture a large share of the patient market. Clientele is lost because of the poor image conveyed by deteriorating plant and equipment. Declining patient demand may imply lower nurse staffing or onerous cost-control policies. Third, without the financial means to procure the latest medical technology the organization may lose not only patients, image, and goodwill but also the commitment of nursing and medical staff members. Clinicians are attracted to health care organizations that have the most advanced technology.

A Challenge for Nurse Managers

Nurse managers have seldom been asked to play a significant role in managing capital assets, whether in terms of their acquisition or their funding. This tendency will change as the economic revolution in health care reaches its full extent. Nurse managers can serve as conduits for capital asset requests from the nursing staff (e.g., for new equipment or service delivery facilities). As such, they must be able to provide convincing arguments for acquiring capital assets that are consistent with the business plans of the nursing staff.[8] More nurse managers are projected to be involved in writing business plans in the future.[9] An important element of many such plans is the outline for financing and asset procurement.[10]

Nurse managers can provide valuable input on major purchases such as diagnostic and treatment equipment. They can offer substantial advice about facility design. Additionally, they can identify a realistic cash flow plan that recognizes workable caseload projections for nursing staff. Such fiscal plans are essential in servicing debt related to either plant or equipment. Nurse managers will also be increasingly involved in key capital asset decisions such as facility construction, creation of clinic or office complexes, and acquisition of major medical equipment (e.g., a magnetic resonance imager or a lithotriptor).

Nurse managers may serve in a consulting capacity for decisions regarding specific financing packages in a major asset project. They probably will not be involved in detailed financial planning except to contribute an understanding of how such projects will affect and be affected by nursing programs. This role is often consistent with that of the top management team. For example, CEOs typically are not involved with the specific tasks of arranging financing for capital assets. The chief financial officer and outside financial consultants design a financing procurement plan. External consultants have vastly greater experience in formulating a financing package. They know the current interest rates, expectations, limitations, and advantages among funding sources. They have greater access to capital markets because they have been operating in these markets on a continuing basis. As a result, they are best equipped to prepare a specific financing plan incorporating many considerations that would otherwise be overlooked by a health care organization's management team.

Although it may be convenient to have consultants prepare the specifics behind a financing package, this does not release other managers (including nurse managers) from their overseeing responsibilities. In the case of nurse managers, this implies a willingness to provide input in the planning and decision-making process. Like other members of the management team, nursing leaders who are involved in major facility or equipment planning have fiduciary responsibilities in the process of arranging financing. Because a consultant has been hired to procure the financing does not mean that health care managers (such as nurse managers) may overlook how a financing package affects specific clinical or support areas. Nursing, like any other major division or department, is partially responsible for determining that the financing package's logic is consistent with nursing program goals and organizational goals.

An Illustration of the Nurse Manager's Role

Consider how a nurse manager in a hospital-based group practice might contribute to financial planning. The nurse manager could provide input on:

- diagnostic and treatment equipment to be replaced and procured in expanding services in clinical specialties
- how equipment acquisition will alter the nursing staff's productivity or that of a clinical program or department
- how increased productivity will result in lower nursing costs and improved ability to service debt associated with equipment acquisition (projections may also be offered on feasible revenue streams generated by new nursing services that can be anticipated once the equipment is acquired)
- the specific clinical advantages and disadvantages attributable to certain assets such as medical equipment

- the ability of assets to attract new nurses who might serve the existing or forecasted patient base
- recommendations for long-run financial planning involving capital asset needs of specific nursing specialties and the nursing program as a whole
- trade-offs that must be made between financial risk and nursing malpractice risk by retaining certain assets or acquiring new technology
- how new equipment will alter facility design and financing requirements

These examples represent the potential input from nurse managers into financial planning exercises involving capital assets. It should be underscored that nurse managers will seldom become overly immersed in the details of financial management, but they can make a contribution to the benefit of their organization and nursing program.

TRADITIONAL SOURCES OF FINANCING

To appreciate better the effect of capital financing on health care organization operations and on service delivery efforts by nursing programs, nurse managers should be familiar with recent shifts in financing sources available to the health care field. A knowledge of trends among primary sources of financing prepares them to make better decisions about the impact on their own clinical operations and enables them to provide better advice to financial planners. Nevertheless, keeping abreast of the latest changes in health care financing is difficult as a result of recurrent changes in third-party payment policies. The prognosis is that this evolution will continue as private insurers and government payers attempt to gain greater control over health care expenditures.

An overview of the financing mechanisms available to health care organizations is depicted in Figure 4-2. There are at least six main financing sources shown, half of which have been used extensively in the past. The other half have received limited use, but the prospects are good that they will be used more in the near future. Figure 4-2 suggests that there is a major reversal in where health care organizations derive their capital asset funds. This shift should have rather powerful repercussions for nursing programs and health care organizations. Understanding this shift and its implications should prepare nurse managers to plan more effectively for their own operations. It should also enable them to contribute to the overall organizational planning process.

It is essential that nurse managers recognize the magnitude of this shift so that they may be prepared to discuss financing strategies with other managers. Trends toward higher long-term debt, use of public stock offerings, and

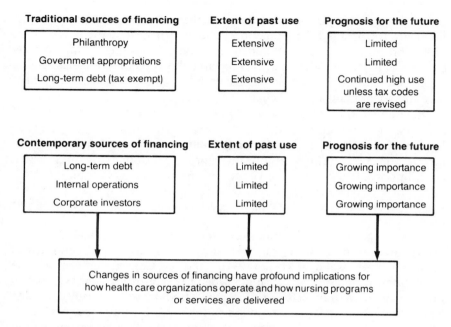

Traditional sources of financing	Extent of past use	Prognosis for the future
Philanthropy	Extensive	Limited
Government appropriations	Extensive	Limited
Long-term debt (tax exempt)	Extensive	Continued high use unless tax codes are revised

Contemporary sources of financing	Extent of past use	Prognosis for the future
Long-term debt	Limited	Growing importance
Internal operations	Limited	Growing importance
Corporate investors	Limited	Growing importance

Changes in sources of financing have profound implications for how health care organizations operate and how nursing programs or services are delivered

Figure 4-2 Overview of Health Care Financing Sources

reliance on internal operations to fund assets have powerful implications for nursing, medical, and support services. These financing sources reflect a fundamental change in philosophy away from inherently subsidized financing (e.g., philanthropy and government grants) to basically free enterprise options (e.g., long-term debt, internal operations, and corporate investments).

Health care organizations are confronting an aggressive environment in which attention is continually focused on decisions for financing capital assets. Decisions will be made on which the organization must live for 15, 20, or 30 years, which is the life span of many assets. Failure to exercise proper caution at this point can seriously jeopardize the long-run survival of any organization in addition to the well-being of specific organizational units such as nursing services.

Philanthropy and Government Appropriations

Health care organizations have traditionally relied on several sources of financing. Philanthropy and government grants (or appropriations) are the traditional funding sources for health care plant and equipment. Philanthropy has gradually declined to the point that only about 3.9 percent of all financing for hospital construction is obtained from donations and gifts. Philanthropy never was a dominant method for funding major projects because of the uncertainty in attracting large donations. Nonetheless, it was a convenient beginning for funding assets or operations (often in the form of seed money or matching and challenge grants).

Donations represent only a small portion of financing for major capital projects. This may surprise many nurse managers. The small percentage of funds raised from donations does not diminish the importance of philanthropy, however. The implication is that more must be done to increase actual contributions. In short, it would be unwise to formulate plans under which philanthropy is the key ingredient for success. Overall, it appears to be best to treat philanthropy as a convenient benefit that can be invoked at the proper time.

Nurse managers must also place philanthropic giving in the context of health care environment changes. Specifically, the health field is being driven toward a businesslike or corporate orientation. Consequently, it will be increasingly difficult to attract funds when the industry is seen as basically profit oriented. Although for-profit organizations may never truly dominate health care, they can affect the image of the field. Despite these problems, philanthropists are able to distinguish among health care organizations and their goals. Furthermore, there is a tangible sentiment on the part of the public to donate monies for health services programs.

Most philanthropy has centered on nonprofit organizations, for which donors obtain lucrative tax benefits. These tax benefits could disappear in the future, however. Furthermore, ingenious reorganization of health facilities involving linkages between for-profit and nonprofit entities has erased many of the distinctions in ownership status. Holding companies provide an option for maintaining philanthropy programs (e.g., by establishing foundations) while affiliating themselves with for-profit entities.[11] Despite these new multi-institutional arrangements, a prudent organizational strategy for financing capital assets does not rely on philanthropy.

Government grants have offered another convenient funding option for health facility construction. As with philanthropy, the promise of government grants relates mainly to the past. Today, government grants represent less than 12 percent of all funds for hospital construction; these monies are often stipulated for communities that are underserved. Government health facilities are included in this percentage as recipients of the funding. The actual allocation to community general hospitals is small. The Hill-Burton program was formerly a solid source of financing, but its importance diminished in the 1970s as the government shifted its focus from constructing hospitals to providing needed health services.

Government grants are not a viable funding source except in extreme circumstances. Various stipulations accompany government grants that make them impractical. For example, a pledge may be required to transfer asset ownership once a certain period of time (e.g., 20 years) has elapsed.

In view of these and other limitations, philanthropy and government grants are of decreasing relevance to health care organizations. They represent traditional sources of financing whose applicability has greatly diminished. It now appears that health care organizations must make the transition from basically dependent institutions (i.e., dependent on charitable giving and government subsidies) to autonomous, vibrant, aggressive, and competitive institutions. This transformation requires innovative strategic responses if health care organizations wish to succeed in the health care market.

Long-Term Debt (Tax Exempt)

Most hospital construction (more than 55 percent) has been funded through tax-exempt revenue bonds. Although this is the predominant source of construction funding for hospitals, it must be remembered that the health care field consists of many other facilities than just inpatient facilities. Hence tax-exempt revenue bonds are not the only means to fund health care organization assets. Furthermore, it should be recognized that nonprofit hospitals have been the predominant users of tax-exempt funding. During the transition to prospective payment, hospital construction slowed considerably. The forecast is that it may be stalled for years.

The advantage of tax-exempt bonds has been their low cost to investors. A tax-exempt bond is attractive to investors from at least two perspectives. First, tax-exempt status lowers the real cost of interest earned because there are no or low taxes on the interest received. Even though tax-exempt bonds have lower interest rates than taxable bonds, the effective earning power is raised as a result of avoiding taxes. The other attractive investment feature of tax-exempt bonds is their low risk. Traditionally, hospitals have presented a relatively risk-free environment for investors. This is primarily due to third-party payment supports. Clearly this factor is changing, and the change may alter the strategic choice of tax-exempt funding.

There are several serious shortcomings of tax-exempt bonds. First, it has been proposed that the tax-exempt status be removed from these bonds. It is not clear whether such legislation will ever be passed. Nonetheless, this information should be incorporated into nurse managers' understanding of the health care environment. Hospitals and health care organizations need to be more cautious in structuring capital financing plans. Excessive reliance on a single funding source reduces the elasticity of response, which is so needed in today's environment. As cost-containment pressures mount in the health field, it is essential that executives diversify the structure of their funding portfolio.

Figure 4-2 indicates that tax-exempt long-term debt has been used extensively in the past and may be used extensively in the future. Also implied in Figure 4-2, however, is a shift away from the lucrative and highly supportive funding patterns of the past. Continued reliance on tax-exempt funding is contrary to corporate involvement trends in the health field.

Figure 4-2 does not convey the fact that tax-exempt bonds offer a relatively low interest rate, which is a significant liability in periods of inflation. The low risk of the hospital and health care field may gradually dissipate as there is more corporate involvement and as third-party payers restrict capital reimbursement. Consequently, physician executives should encourage the development of a more diverse funding portfolio.

CONTEMPORARY SOURCES OF FUNDING

Health care organizations are increasingly turning to new funding sources. As an acute care–centered health system is left behind, entirely new strategies are unfolding for financing health facility construction and equipment acquisition. Furthermore, the ambulatory nature of health facilities is compounding the aforementioned trends. Thus free-standing surgery centers, home health agencies, diagnostic centers, clinics, and other prevalent service organizations must house their staff members and associated health and medical equipment. These organizations are turning to entirely new sources of financing, which will require a high return on investment and low costs.

Long-Term Debt

An option considered by many health care organizations is long-term debt or conventional borrowing. Although hospitals have avoided this alternative in the past, there is a strong likelihood that more will pursue long-term debt for capital asset acquisition or renovation in the future. The advantage of long-term debt is its ease of acquisition. In return, health care organizations make a commitment to servicing debt over a long period of time (e.g., 20 to 30 years). Long-term debt has fewer restrictions than tax-exempt revenue bonds. Under favorable financial market conditions, there may be an excellent supply of capital available from lenders. All these advantages suggest that long-term debt is a viable option in the health field.

Figure 4-2 indicates that long-term debt will be used with increasing frequency in the future. As the industry begins to resemble other corporate settings (most notably with a high preponderance of investor-owned and for-profit enterprises), health care organizations are beginning to alter their perspective on what constitutes appropriate funding.

Long-term debt can be costly as a result of prevailing market interest rates. Health care facilities, as a rule, have not been able to attain profitability levels that make such funding economically feasible. Despite third-party payment supports, there is also the problem that health care facilities confront high bad debt rates and a significant amount of free care. These factors drive down the ability to fund long-term debt. As a result, many health care organizations, particularly hospitals, have turned to long-term debt only as an option for renovating plant or for acquiring major pieces of equipment.

Some for-profit hospitals have implemented strict policies on admissions to prevent bad debts and to achieve a predefined level of charitable care. As more health care organizations adopt these practices, there could be a drive to expand facilities, to construct new facilities, and to acquire equipment that attracts paying clientele. With solvent clientele comes the ability to move easily into new capital projects by using long-term debt.

The main problem with long-term debt is high interest cost. Nonetheless, there are certain situations in which a financially lucrative project justifies accepting more debt. These situations are typically those in which the organization is an early market entrant or when a significant strategy revision dictates capital investment. In most other cases, health care organizations want to avoid becoming too leveraged because they have limited revenue-generating capacity (e.g., a finite number of beds or third-party restrictions). When it becomes necessary to capture certain opportunities, however, then debt may be justifiable.

Internal Operations

Nurse managers should be alert to the policy of relying on internal operations to fund capital assets. This certainly is not a new idea in the business sector. In fact, it is a common practice. The prevailing policy in many businesses is to plan for depreciation of plant and equipment by setting aside sufficient funds in retained earnings or special funds to cover most or all of the cost of new assets. The amount of money retained in these accounts may exceed the original investment because of inflation. This financial strategy requires discipline to avoid expending capital reserves on current operations. Such an approach is facilitated by depreciation, a tax deduction that generates savings from operations. These savings are actually the result of capital asset costs, which have already been incurred.

Internal operations is the most promising point from which capital financing can begin. Nurse managers can assume an active role in managing their programs, departments, divisions, or organizations to guarantee that an operating margin exists. In this manner, they can contribute to the strategy of funding capital assets internally. As part of their contribution, nurse managers will be involved in prolonged negotiating with chief financial officers, creating new agendas at departmental meetings, and encouraging staff to achieve fiscally responsible behavior.

Problems in Funding from Internal Operations

Business corporations, unlike health care organizations, do not have the benefit of third-party payments. Hence they must be self-disciplined in protecting their capital asset base. Health care organizations have an advantage in that most third-party payers reimburse for capital expenses. Admittedly, these allocations are often below the replacement cost of the assets. There is a significant question regarding how these assets should be valued (i.e., as historical cost, market value, replacement cost, and so forth). Nonetheless, health care organizations are able to have some of their capital assets covered by third-party reimbursement.

Reliance on third-party payment is philosophically a stumbling block for many health care organizations. This becomes particularly evident when examining capital reimbursement. There is a tendency to view third-party payments as a safety net. This instills less incentive to manage operations rigorously because there is a certain level of guaranteed revenues. In effect, third-party payments have not created the appropriate incentives to encourage fiscally responsible management throughout health care organizations.

Retrospective payment plans handed health care organizations a blank check to cover costs. This policy did little, if anything, to encourage cost control. Prospective or prepayment is another story altogether. Under prepaid plans health care organizations must control operating costs, and they must have enough foresight to protect their future. Health care organizations cannot simply raise rates when operating costs are high and when investments in capital assets are needed.

Incentives To Fund from Internal Operations

Changes in reimbursement policy introduce a more businesslike atmosphere to the management of health care organizations. This should directly affect the use of revenue from internal operations in providing for capital asset acquisition. Health care organizations have tended to overlook the value of internal operations as a means for funding plant and equipment. Obviously, a prerequisite for this strategy is that operations are efficiently run to achieve an operating surplus or margin. Nurse managers are pivotal in achieving this objective, particularly because nursing costs are a significant cost in the overall budget. Hence nurse managers represent the mechanism by which internal operations can be used to fund debt.

In operational terms, nurse managers will assume greater responsibility for instilling a performance-oriented attitude (toward profitability) among nursing staff. Health care organizations are being driven to the point that they must use operating margins to fund capital asset acquisition. The initial signs foretelling this change are already in place. With the adoption of prepaid plans, virtually every health care organization will eventually reach the point that capital assets are only procured if sufficient profitability exists to service debt.

The role of nurse managers in achieving this new orientation is especially important because they must help nurses understand why new constraints are being placed on the delivery of nursing care. This role is crucial because nurses have traditionally been outside the management control system. To attain sufficient efficiency in funding capital assets from internal operations, nurses must be incorporated as the cornerstone of the operations control system. Nurses should envision profitable operations as being synonymous with program and organizational survival. Without profitable operations, an organization—whether for-profit or nonprofit—will watch its capital position deteriorate. When the capital position deteriorates, then so too will supports for high-quality care.

Trends in Funding from Internal Operations

As Figure 4-2 suggests, internal operations have been used rather minimally in the past as a source of capital. This is partially supported by the fact that 15 percent of all hospital construction begun in 1981 was funded internally. This means that 15 percent of the capital raised for the projects came from internal sources. If health facility operations were effectively managed, it is possible that an organization could use the surplus for servicing debt or accumulate it as a lump-sum payment.

Using debt to acquire assets implies that a health care organization has not given sufficient thought to future physical plant and equipment needs. Executives have not prepared ahead of time by retaining surpluses from operating margins. Alternatively, they may not have managed operations effectively enough to produce operating margins.

Planning for Operating Surpluses

Whenever possible, health care organizations plan conservatively for capital replacement. Operations can be managed to provide sufficient earnings and periodically to replace assets. Although these practices have not always been followed in the health field, there is no reason to believe that health care organizations will have a difficult time obtaining support from management, nursing, or medical staffs.

The value of using internal operations to fund capital assets depends on the operating surpluses themselves. As hospitals have discovered, this is a significant stumbling block because the average operating margin in 1987 was −0.68 percent.[12] Half of all hospitals in 1987 were operating at a loss. The time to begin revising financial planning is now. At least two major steps are required.

1. Management must be willing to set forth in specific terms its capital budget for at least a 5-year period. Within that budget are plans relating to the replacement, renovation, or construction of a new physical plant. The capital budget should also specify the major pieces of equipment that will be acquired for new or existing services.
2. Management must increase the intensity of its effort to create and implement a viable control system. Internal funding is predicated on operating efficiency, so that every effort must be made to step up the attempts at controlling operations.

Realistically, there are several problems with these suggested steps. It is difficult to forecast changes in the health care field. Consequently, it may be difficult to define a 5-year plan for capital. Of course, this is a common excuse for not planning. Furthermore, there is a question as to how much efficiency can be obtained from some health care organizations and how quickly it can be achieved. Change may not be induced easily. Nonetheless, the health care field has witnessed a substantial redirection in cost control over the last 5 years. The remaining question is the magnitude of slack available to cut from the budgets of many departments.

Corporate Investors

An increasingly prevalent form of funding capital assets is through corporate means. These may include:

- a public offering of stock that provides a stipulated return or the option of awarding dividends (stock is more marketable when it offers some return on investment)
- a loan to a specific institution from corporate headquarters for an organization that has joined with a multi-institutional system
- actual capital from a buy-out when an organization joins a chain; for example, when a hospital sells its assets to a chain the proceeds from the

sale may be stipulated for the construction of a new inpatient facility (i.e, a certain number of beds) or a major piece of equipment plus renovation of existing plant

These and other mechanisms are available to organizations that join with corporations or that undertake restructuring.

There are many significant reasons for joining a corporate health care chain. The chain may purchase the assets of the health facility during a merger. As a result, the facility has received a lump sum that can be invested in various ways. The funds might go to retire existing debt or to repay holders of the equity. Alternatively, if there is no debt to repay the funds might be used to reinvest in program services. This might mean that a windfall is available for equipment purchases. However the transaction occurs, a large sum of capital is acquired. This benefit is tempered by the fact that ownership is relinquished or shared, but such strategies may be necessary if there are no other capital sources.

Multi-institutional systems often provide alternative sources of capital for assets. Professional associations facilitate access to capital for members, whether through direct loans or through contact with lenders. Some of these options may fall under the category of corporate investment. Probably they represent a commitment to long-term debt.

Figure 4-2 suggests that corporate investment may continue to grow in the future as a capital funding mechanism. This trend parallels the growing prevalence of for-profit health care corporations. Consequently, the corporate sources of funds could multiply significantly in the future.

Nurse managers will have to use their best judgment in interpreting these prognostications. There is no guarantee that corporate expansion will continue. The nursing home field is predominantly for-profit, but hospitals are usually viewed as community assets. A hospital may be the sole community care provider. In such a situation there may be a marginal market for care, so that the hospital barely thrives (often with community subsidies). In sum, there is no guarantee that for-profit or corporate investments will continue in the health care field. As a result, there are distinct limitations to relying on corporate investment in health care facilities.

A CAPITAL CRISIS?

Given the preceding overview of capital sources, there is ample reason for concern about how health care organizations fund plant and equipment. After all, procurement of capital assets is one of the indelible decisions made by an organization. As such, it is valued as one of the most important strategic decisions. These thoughts have heightened meaning when contemplating the warnings about a growing capital crisis in the health care field.

The implications of this capital crisis are as follows.

1. Health care organizations need to assess their capital structures to ascertain how they fit with respect to the capital crisis. After evaluating this position, they should formulate a plan that acknowledges funding limitations and capitalizes on opportunities (recognizing that failure to pursue those opportunities today may mean that they evaporate). Things are going to get worse before they get better.

2. Proposals for diversification into new product or service lines may provide a revenue buffer to resurrect the viability of the asset base. Diversification would have to be lucrative enough that net income from the diversified services is sufficient to contribute to principal repayment and interest on long-term debts or bonds.

3. Sincere consideration may have to be given to corporate or multi-institutional options. Corporate health care organizations can often fund capital assets through the equity markets.

As nurse managers can readily attest to, a capital crisis looms over the health care field.

NURSING INTRAPRENEURSHIP AND FISCAL SOLVENCY

Nurse managers can speculate about what the changes in the financial position of health care organizations will imply for care delivery. No matter how many different perspectives are applied to the capital crisis in health care, however, the same answer keeps surfacing. The common denominators underlying health facility financing are cost control and revenue enhancement. To pay for future capital costs and to cover expenses associated with program expansion, health care organizations need to control operations and to expand revenue sources. Cost control is a primary responsibility of nurse managers. Cost control has become an all too prevalent theme constraining the delivery of nursing services. Nevertheless, nursing programs are now being asked to do more than just control costs. They are also encountering requests to enhance health facility revenues. This new mission is generally captured by the term *intrapreneurship*.

Intrapreneurship in nursing settings is commonly characterized by the following attributes:[13,14]

- emphasis on creative efforts to control costs or to enhance profit generation

- reinforcement of innovative ideas through intrinsic and extrinsic rewards
- search for methods to generate revenues for nursing services and for the total organization
- enhanced financial viability of nursing programs, with expanded support (e.g., seed money) for new program efforts
- promotion of a supportive culture that retains nursing personnel and facilitates personal growth
- expansion of nursing business lines or products

These attributes reflect the underlying rationale of intrapreneurship; that is, the organization seeks new, creative, vibrant, and profit-oriented ideas that instill renewed vigor in service delivery.[15]

Intrapreneurship is precisely what nursing programs and health care organizations need today. Intrapreneurship is a mechanism for increasing the power of nursing services. Instead of taking a traditional stance as a support service, nursing is allowed more degrees of freedom through intrapreneurship. Nurses can redefine what it means to offer nursing care. To some in the profession, such a posture is threatening. They will immediately complain about safeguards on patient care quality or commercialization of nursing care. The point of intrapreneurship is not to make nursing into a crass commercial venture but to enliven the service delivery process, to reconstruct thinking about how services can be better delivered. Consonant with this new emphasis is the recognition that intrapreneurial efforts should produce a return on investment. This is an imperative in a resource-constrained health care field. In sum, intrapreneurship fosters a new way of looking at service delivery. It is an optimistic and constructive approach for improving nursing services and the return from the delivery process.

Intrapreneurship is consistent with a fresh financial posture on the part of nurse managers. Nurse leaders are openly acknowledging that profit centers are applicable in nursing.[16] For too long nursing care has been a cost center, not a revenue generator. Partly this results from excessive reliance on formal budgets and limited financial sophistication among nurse managers.[17] There is also the problem of not thinking in business terms. Systematic budgeting has routinely defined nursing expectations and program objectives.[18,19] The result is rather stale thinking about nursing strategies. In essence, nurses and nurse managers have been their own worst enemy. They have consistently failed to take an enlightened view of what nursing could be all about.

The best way to understand nursing intrapreneurship is to examine the intrapreneurial efforts that have already been undertaken by nursing programs. These examples are not presented as a panacea (i.e., the point is not that all nursing programs should immediately adopt similar practices) but rather as a point of stimulation for further thinking by nurse managers. Nurse managers must develop their own creative intrapreneurial ideas on this foundation.

1. *Community nursing center.* The Division of Nursing of Memorial Medical Center of Long Beach, California, launched a primary nursing care program to keep elderly clients out of the hospital and to meet the needs of the underserved while generating revenues for nursing services.[20]

2. *Cooperative care program.* Methodist Hospital of Indiana established a cooperative care program for medical and surgical patients. Nursing assumed a leading role in maintaining care standards and facilitating the project's evolution. The unit is housed in an adjacent hotel. Patients rely on themselves or care partners (e.g., family members) and have access to back-up nursing staff during the recovery process.[21]

3. *Overtime incentives.* Nurses are typically paid overtime when they have worked more than 40 hours per week. In one hospital a new policy was instituted to enhance nursing salaries, to increase retention, and to resolve staffing shortages. Nurses were paid overtime for all hours worked in excess of 8 hours per day. This policy improved staffing and morale but slightly raised costs.[22]

4. *Cost buster fair.* The Methodist Hospital of Memphis held a "cost buster fair" to increase nurse sensitivity to costs and factors influencing costs. This fair educated nurses and identified problems in documentation through ideas generated from participants.[23]

5. *Lottery incentive system.* A large hospital faced excessive costs as a result of high levels of absenteeism. To reduce these costs it introduced a lottery-based reinforcement system. At the end of each 4-week period a lottery was held for a $100 cash prize. Those nurses with sick leave, absences, tardiness, or early departures could not participate in the lottery. An additional lottery was held at the end of a 20-week period for those with perfect attendance (the prize was $500). The lottery system decreased absenteeism.[24]

Not every nursing program can adopt these ideas for controlling costs or enhancing revenues. Nonetheless, these efforts serve as idea generators. The challenge for nurse managers is to identify intrapreneurial efforts that they could be making for the financial health of their nursing program and their organization.

Another way to think of intrapreneurship in nursing is in terms of the products or services delivered in nursing care. In many respects, nurse managers need to think in terms of marketing their product or service line.[25] For example, a hospital might identify all its products as displayed in Exhibit 4-1. Once a nursing program has delineated its product or service line, it is in the position of being able to promote excellence in the services or products and to expand the services or products offered. At the heart of this issue is marketing nursing care as a profitable, cost-controlling, and valuable service.

TOWARD FINANCIAL VIABILITY

Nurses and nurse managers are confronted with a unique challenge. The organizations in which they have practiced face serious economic and financial pressures. For too long nursing has remained uninvolved in the strategic issues facing health care institutions. The profession has chosen to focus solely on nursing care delivery and to rely on institutional resolutions to problems affecting nursing services. Although this approach has been useful in maintaining a focused view of nursing care, it is blind to the events affecting the health care field. Now that prospective payment and competition are threatening the financial viability of their organizations, nurses and nurse managers must begin to define a more active role for themselves in solving problems.

In the near future health care organizations will need to replace obsolete plant and equipment. Facilities gradually deteriorate. New medical and nursing technology will become available. The nursing profession has remained aloof to these problems, but the capital asset problem is beginning to affect nursing directly. To pay for the debt incurred in securing new plant or equipment, health facilities will be asking more of nurses than ever before. Essentially, health care organizations will demand two things: that costs be controlled and that revenues be enhanced. In short, nursing must work not only harder but smarter. Nursing must become more innovative and intrapreneurial in responding to these crises. Although nurses may prefer to concentrate on nursing, the reality facing them suggests that an entirely different attitude is now appropriate.

Nurse managers offer the best response to financially constrained health care organizations. They are perfectly positioned to communicate the concerns and contributions (e.g., the intrapreneurial ideas) of nurses to top management. Before they can perform effectively in the management arena, however, they should be prepared to understand the financial implications of trends affecting health care organizations and to translate these into implications for nursing programs.

Exhibit 4-1 An Inventory of Nursing Products

Operations management

Quality assurance plan for nursing
Absenteeism reporting system (Lotus)
Budget variance reporting system (Lotus)
Human resource use reports
Nursing research proposal critique tool
Guidelines for revenue-producing activities
Patient classification and charging system
Guidelines for university collaboration and student placement
Policy, procedure, and protocol format

Consultation services

Hemodialysis skills—staff education and training
How to open an oncology unit
Preoperative teaching program for open heart patients, continuing education, and patient education services
Primary nursing in the surgical intensive care setting
Nursing administration and management

Publications

Discharge Teaching for Transplant Patients
Infant Stimulation: Baby Learning—Baby Play (videotape)
Leading a Balanced Life: Handbook for Diabetics
CenterNurse—A Nursing Newsletter

Education

Community education

- Food—facts and fallacies
- Focus on poison prevention
- Early cancer detection and preventing risks
- Drugs—not a dead issue
- Blood pressure screening

Patient education

- Medication care teaching tools
- Printed pamphlet series
  —Colonoscopy
  —Endoscopic retrograde choledocho-pancreatogram
  —Barium enema
  —Upper endoscopy
  —Upper gastrointestinal examination

Staff education

- Physical assessment
- Leadership
- Preceptorship
- IV therapy certification program
- Chemotherapy administration for registered nurses
- Self-learning modules
  —Infection control
  —Operating room paperwork
  —Kardexing
- A practical approach to 12-lead electrocardiogram interpretation
- Medical intensive care unit (ICU) course (university credit granted)
- Surgical ICU course (university credit granted)
- Neonatal ICU course (university credit granted)
- Perioperative course: basic operating room techniques (university credit granted)

Graduate nursing education

- Nursing administration course (area university)

Source: Reprinted from "Marketing Your Nursing Product Line: Reaping the Benefits" by J.E. Johnson, A.C. Arvidson, L.L. Costa, F.M. Heknuis, L.A. Lennox, S.B. Marshall, and M.J. Moran, *Journal of Nursing Administration*, Vol. 17, No. 11, pp. 29–33, with permission of J.B. Lippincott Company, © November 1987.

NOTES

1. L. Wilson, P.A. Prescott, and L. Aleksandowicz, "Nursing: A Major Hospital Cost Component," *Health Services Research* 22 (February 1988): 773-796.

2. J.M. Player, "The Economic Importance of Nurses," *Nursing Management* 13 (November 1982): 52-53.

3. D.R. Blaney and C.J. Holson, "Developing Financial Management Skills: An Educational Approach," *Journal of Nursing Administration* 18 (June 1988): 13-17.

4. B. Mark and H.L. Smith, *Essentials of Finance in Nursing* (Rockville, MD: Aspen, 1987).

5. E.K. Isaac, "Financial Planning: Influencing the Decision Makers," *Association of Operating Room Nurses* 42 (November 1985): 708-717.

6. R.C. Gabrielson and C.A. Lund, "Enhancing the Financial and Operational Performance of the Nursing Department," *Journal of Nursing Administration* 15 (November 1985): 28-32.

7. V. Sonberg and K.W. Vestal, "Nursing as a Business," *Nursing Clinics of North America* 18 (September 1983): 491-498.

8. J.E. Johnson, D.G, Sparks, and C. Humphreys, "Writing a Winning Business Plan," *Journal of Nursing Administration* 18 (October 1988): 15-19.

9. K.R. Gannon, "Nursing's Impact on a Business Venture," *Nursing Administration Quarterly* 10 (Fall 1985): 90-96.

10. R. Kirk, "Nurse Executives Can Mean Business," *Journal of Nursing Administration* 16 (October 1986): 7-10.

11. J.A. Alexander, L.L. Morlock, and B.D. Gifford, "The Effects of Corporate Restructuring on Hospital Policymaking," *Health Services Research* 23 (1988): 311-337.

12. J. Nemes, "Over Half of Hospitals Run at a Loss," *Modern Healthcare* 18 (18 November 1988): 92-97.

13. L. Strasen, "Promoting Intrapreneurship in the Acute Care Setting," *Journal of Nursing Administration* 16 (November 1986): 9-12.

14. E. Marszalek-Gaucher and V.D. Elesenhans, "Intrapreneurship: Tapping Employee Creativity," *Journal of Nursing Administration* 18 (December 1988): 20-22.

15. G. Pinchot, *Intrapreneuring* (New York: Harper & Row, 1985).

16. R. Anderson, "Alternative Revenue Sources for Nursing Departments," *Journal of Nursing Administration* 15 (November 1985): 9-13.

17. G.R. McGrail, "Budgets: An Underused Resource," *Journal of Nursing Administration* 18 (November 1988): 25-31.

18. M. Villemarie and C. Lane-McGraw, "Nursing Personnel Budgets: A Step-by-Step Guide," *Nursing Management* 17 (November 1986): 28-31.

19. C.S. Pollock, "Adapting Management by Objectives to Nursing," *Nursing Clinics of North America* 18 (September 1983): 481-490.

20. C.A. Pappas and C.V. Scoy-Mosher, "Establishing a Profitable Outpatient Community Nursing Center," *Journal of Nursing Administration* 18 (May 1988): 31-33.

21. R.M. Saywell et al., "Comparative Costs of a Cooperative Care Program Versus Hospital Inpatient Care for Gynecology Patients," *Journal of Nursing Administration* 19 (March 1989): 29-35.

22. M.K. Lehman, J. Staszko, and D.M. Nadzam, "Overtime Payment Methods: Meeting Staffing and Staff Needs," *Journal of Nursing Administration* 18 (April 1988): 19-21.

23. V.M. Norton et al., "Cost Buster Fair: Increasing Staff Awareness of Cost Effective Practice," *Journal of Nursing Administration* 18 (September 1988): 16-19.

24. M.A. Curran and K.E. Curran, "Gambling Away Absenteeism," *Journal of Nursing Administration* 17 (December 1987): 28-31.

25. J.E. Johnson et al., "Marketing Your Nursing Product Line: Reaping the Benefits," *Journal of Nursing Administration* 17 (November 1987): 29-33.

Chapter 5

Visionary and Inspirational Leadership

Nurse managers concerned about developing proficiency in strategic management skills face a very real dilemma. Even with the best education, their attempts to contribute to strategic issues in a health care organization may be blocked. Although nurse managers are entering a new era of power and responsibility, this does not mean that every administrator, physician, nurse, or support staff member will necessarily recognize and respect this power. Under these conditions, nurse managers are caught in a power-sapping bind.[1] The remedy is for them to become more politically active and to strategize in achieving organizational power. Without an organizational power base it is difficult to attain visionary and inspirational leadership, which is essential if the highest performance levels are to be achieved among staff nurses.[2]

The road to organizational power is paved with many good intentions. In reaching this power nurse managers can develop a better awareness of the organizational leadership context, understand how visionary leadership is influenced by key health care professionals, formulate strategies for collaboration with nurses, avoid barriers erected by management staff, and seek active involvement in policy-making and governance activities. As these strategies suggest, nurse managers will be concerned about developing a new profile that is consistent with expanded power and responsibility.

NURSE MANAGERS IN AN ORGANIZATIONAL CONTEXT

Nurses have traditionally played a supporting role in the health care system. As managers, they make a valuable contribution by setting and achieving objectives, minimizing conflict, ensuring quality of care, reinforcing productivity, and helping chart the primary direction of nursing programs.

Nurse managers are seldom prominent in charting the direction of the health care organizations housing their nursing programs, however.

As the health system has evolved, physicians and (nonclinical) administrators have always had the upper hand in determining the system's direction. It is unlikely that they will easily relinquish this power, responsibility, or privilege. In fact, much of the present health care system's conflict stems from changes in the nursing and medical professions.[3] Both nurses and physicians are hesitant to accommodate these changes.

A basic dilemma for many nurse managers is their lack of preparation to participate in an organizational context.[4,5] They may have an idealized belief of nursing practice and an unassuming view of management responsibilities. As a result, nurses aspiring to enter the management ranks remain in the gray area depicted in Figure 5-1.[6] Each step up the management ladder becomes progressively more difficult for nurses because of their grounding in clinical training and their beliefs about how health care organizations operate.

It is clear that nurses and nurse managers do not begin their clinical careers with a value system that supports or favors organized health care. Nurses are, first and foremost, clinicians. This focus on patient issues creates resistance to the consumption of scant clinical resources by organizational (e.g., profit) and management (e.g., cost control) goals. Nurse managers in an enlightened age offer one possible solution to this dilemma because they understand what motivates other nurses. Nurse managers are able to communicate these concerns to nonnursing managers in health care organizations. Nurse managers can provide a compromise between organizational needs and nurses' needs. These accomplishments are feasible if nurse managers themselves understand the goals, values, philosophy, procedures, and functional mechanisms of organizations. There is danger, however, that nurse managers do not have a clear perception of what health care organizations really need from clinical nursing departments.

Like their clinical colleagues, nurse managers sometimes never become really familiar with the methods and mores of organizations.[7] Nurse managers originate from a clinical background, in which autonomy is highly valued. They do not necessarily know how to communicate with others in organizations or others for whom organizations have always been a way of life (e.g., health care executives). Philosophically, nurse managers approach organizations and how organizations operate from a perspective different from that of other health care professionals. Nurse managers may not be prepared to offer guidance to either nurses or the health care system unless they achieve a fundamental understanding of how organizations operate.

For these reasons, it is appropriate to examine what it means to lead in an organizational context. At the center of this introspection is the aim of defining leadership in a revolutionary industry, one that is rapidly growing

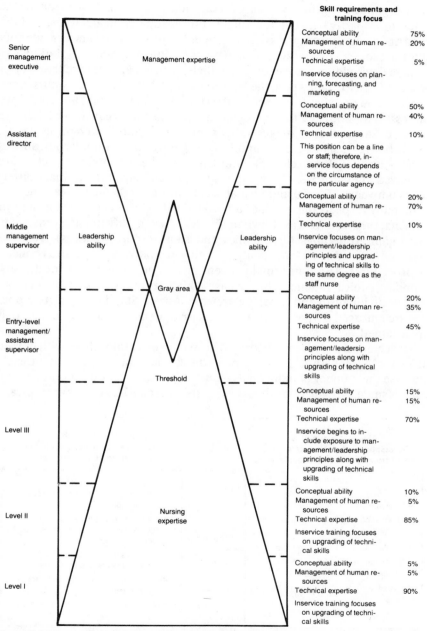

Figure 5-1 Management Progression for Nurses. *Source:* Reprinted from *Nursing Administration Quarterly*, Vol. 7, No. 2, p. 14, Aspen Publishers, Inc., © Winter 1983.

more organizational in its values, structure, and processes. By recognizing the inherent disparity between the nursing profession's clinical interest and the need to recognize organizational demands, nurse managers can identify potential sources of conflict between organizations and nurses. Solutions can then be devised that resolve these conflicts. Nurse managers are then better prepared to ascertain where the health system is headed and how nurses can play a viable and significant role in the system. Strategies that ultimately are successful for both health care organizations and nurses can also be defined.

Organization theory suggests that some significant discrepancies can be found between small groups and large organizations in numerous dimensions. A few of these relevant contrasts as applied to clinical practice are displayed in Figure 5-2. These contrasts capture many of the primary differences between informal and formal organizations in the health care field.

In many respects the qualities associated with working in small groups or informal organizations as shown in Figure 5-2 exemplify nursing practice in nonorganized settings (e.g., clinics and small group practices). Work is essentially coordinated informally, resulting in relatively unspecified policies or procedures. These informal conventions do not constrain attitudes surrounding clinical practice. Nurses have a high degree of professional autonomy. Individualism and expertise are emphasized. Standard operating policies are enforced only as necessary to ensure that patient care and clinic goals are attained.

Most clinical practice is performed in an informal atmosphere with limited need for bureaucratic policies, procedures, or controls. This is possible because the number of individuals—nurses, physicians, and support personnel—is small. Organization theory suggests that small businesses are typically

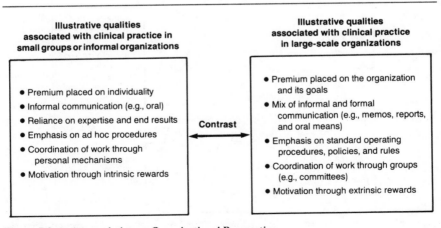

Figure 5-2 Accommodating an Organizational Perspective

those incorporating fewer than 15 people. Below that level (approximately, because a precise threshold has never been ascertained) clinical practice assumes a high degree of participation and informality.[8] Above that level health care organizations begin to institute policies and procedures to ensure standardized and quality performance by clinicians and support staff.

Figure 5-2 does not imply that either small groups or large-scale organizations represent the ideal model for nursing or the health field. Nurse managers should be open to the possibility that either an informal or a formal organization is appropriate for a given situation depending on relevant variables in that setting. Determining which organization is best suited to a certain context requires identifying relevant variables in that specific setting. The health care system itself is an excellent case in point.

For decades, medical care was delivered primarily through solo practices. Recent changes in third-party reimbursement, the supply of physicians, the competitiveness of the marketplace, consumer health behavior, and related salient factors have turned solo medical practices into high-risk financial ventures. It appears that organizations of physicians (e.g., group practices) are better suited to the competitive health care environment. There is no one best way to organize the delivery of health care. Under certain conditions solo practice is preferable, but with current economic and reimbursement policies it appears that physician groups or organizations will be more viable.

Qualities of Small Groups

Small groups, nursing teams, or relatively informal health care organizations have several significant characteristics that affect nurses' perceptions of how these organizations operate. Nurses' preferences for practicing without organizational interference is partially conditioned by the education that they receive.[9] It is also influenced by practical experience in informal settings, in which they are the primary decision makers. Consequently, nurses have a preference for small groups or informal practice situations. These informal environments reinforce nurses' values because of the autonomy that is present in them. This provides a sharp contrast to the organizational infrastructure that houses many nursing programs.

The organization chart of hospitals clearly identifies the line responsibilities of nurses. Nursing is one of several crucial functions in the organizational hierarchy. In contrast, a small group practice, nursing home, hospital, or other informal health care organization places a premium on the individual nurse. Individuality is reinforced by intimate patterns of communication in the small group. Communication is usually through direct, face-to-face contact. Oral and personal contact is immediate. Personal contact enhances the sense of individual importance and provides an immediate register on feedback. The individual nurse is able to gauge how he or she is being received and how ideas are being enacted.

A small unit, team, clinic, or informal group relies on expertise and end results. Nurses are valued for what they accomplish. In contrast, large-scale organizations emphasize authority attached to formal positions. Significant expertise and proven performance may be required to attain these organizational positions. Formal authority becomes the dominant focal point. In small groups there is less opportunity to rely on authority to legitimatize one's existence. Nurses are more likely (although not always likely) to be appreciated on the basis of what they accomplish.

Small organizational settings emphasize ad hoc procedures. There is little need for standardized procedures because nurses are educated to know when to follow algorithms and when to deviate from them. In effect, informal groups rely on relatively personal mechanisms for coordinating work. The individual seldom works entirely alone. Even in small practice settings, the nursing staff is part of a larger group. Practice is coordinated informally with physicians. There is immediate feedback. Nursing staff members do not have to wait for information to flow down a hierarchy of authority (or, if they do, the hierarchy is minimal) and for reports or memos to convey instructions. Communication is nearly instantaneous.

Another vital aspect of small clinical practices is reinforcement of internal goals. By practicing in informal settings, nurses are able to satisfy internal or personal goals. This essentially describes a system of intrinsic rewards. The value of a small group or other informal clinical setting is that individuals are basically satisfied with end results, not that someone else determines whether the setting is worthwhile. Admittedly, nurses may be motivated to accomplish many end results, such as high-quality patient care, familiarity with patients, low malpractice risk, providing care to needy people, and similar accomplishments. The point is that the individual, not the organization, determines whether the effort has been worthwhile.

Qualities of Large Organizations

There are many qualities associated with working in large-scale organizations. A sample of the most relevant concerns are portrayed in Figure 5-2. Perhaps most important is that a premium is placed on the organization and its goals. This concept is best described as an organizational imperative.[10] It has been suggested that whatever is good for people can only be achieved through organizations. Therefore, individual effort should be directed toward improving the organization.

The organizational imperative implies that individuals are highly dispensable. What health care organizations are most interested in is attaining their goals—profits, quality of care, public image, and so forth—not individual goals (i.e., those of nurses, physicians, or patients). A basic premise of organizational survival is that virtually any person can be replaced by another. Thus organizations maintain a benevolent paternalism toward their constituents. Organizations are really interested in whether and to what degree goals are accomplished.

In large-scale organizations there is a mix of both informal and formal communication. Organizations use informal communications (e.g., short conversations and lunch meetings) just as often as they use formal means (e.g., memos, reports, and written directives). Organizations tend to rely extensively on a formal system of authority and expertise, however. An individual's worth is typically determined by the position held in this system of authority and expertise.

Organizations emphasize standard operating procedures, rules, and policies. The purpose of organizations is to standardize service delivery processes and to attain efficiency and effectiveness. Because health care organizations serve thousands of clients, they need to make certain that standard protocols and procedures are implemented. Organizations cannot rely on the individual.

Work is coordinated through group and organizational methods. Committees reinforce the group effort and minimize individual contributions. Committees homogenize and democratize the process of decision making and the manner in which work is implemented. This process is normally viewed as a collaborative effort that promotes self-governance.[11] In the proper context decentralized decision making does lead to viable self-governance, but the process can serve as a mere facade of organizational control. Finally, health care organizations are effective in promoting extrinsic rewards. Hence organizations reward nurse managers with large raises, impressive titles, choice offices, support staff, the latest equipment, or other perquisites.

Implications for Nurse Managers

Figure 5-2 should sensitize nurse managers to the fact that their leadership positions are normally found in a decidedly organizational context. Nevertheless, an important group of organizational members, namely nurses, does not necessarily view itself as being chained to an organization. Nurses have been educated and socialized in clinical practice and usually have worked in small teams. Even though they may have made a conscious choice to join an organization to practice nursing, they still expect and demand the respect that is consistent with their professional role. This attitude has several repercussions.

Nurse managers face the challenge of helping nurses and other staff members become comfortable with the give-and-take of organizations. Just as organizations demand a lot from individuals, so do they provide a return. Nurse managers can assist nurses in developing an appreciation for these benefits and in overlooking the negative consequences. A first step is for nurse managers to accommodate an organizational perspective. This is the purpose of Figure 5-2. It does not imply that either small- or large-scale health care organizations are best. Each setting provides different demands and offers different rewards. Once these differences are understood and accepted, it is easier to reconcile the individual with the organization. In this respect, nurse managers need to accentuate the positive and rectify the negative.

MODERATORS OF LEADERSHIP EFFECTIVENESS

After attaining an appreciation of organizational perspective, nurse managers can become aware of factors that influence their effectiveness as leaders. Leadership effectiveness is not simply something that is willed or can be attained through hard work. Likewise, effectiveness can be prevented if the appropriate factors are not in place. Nurse managers may have little or no control over these factors, which vary from organization to organization. Nonetheless, it is still possible to define some general moderators of leadership effectiveness.

Figure 5-3 depicts several moderators of leadership effectiveness. Two sets of people are depicted as determining whether nurse managers are perceived to be effective leaders. Physicians, top management, and board members influence the strategic (and often operational) aspirations of nursing departments and nurse leaders. Managing nurses is not always an operations-level problem. As many hospitals and nursing homes have discovered, nursing staff

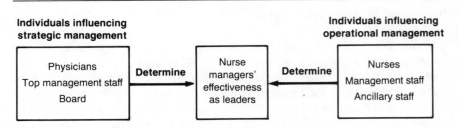

Figure 5-3 Moderators of Leadership Effectiveness

can generate significant strategic problems (e.g., strikes, drug abuse, embezzlement, and so forth) as well as strategic opportunities (e.g., cross-scheduling, staffing, career ladders, and the like). In contrast, nurses, management staff, and ancillary staff influence the operational aspirations of nursing departments and nurse leaders, specifically the ability to achieve low-cost and high-quality care. Although nurse managers may receive the proper education, experience, and support (from their health care organization), they still may not perform effectively as leaders. The moderating factors may not be controllable. By recognizing this limitation, nurse managers can allocate sufficient time to these factions and remove barriers to leadership effectiveness.

The point of Figure 5-3 is that nurse managers will focus on both strategic and operating issues. In terms of managing operating-level issues (e.g., a head nurse who is continually over budget, a purchasing employee who is absconding with nursing supplies, or a nurse who is altering patient records unintentionally), nurse managers will normally work through the chain of command.

MANAGING NURSES

Nurse managers can do more than just provide leadership for nurses. Nurse managers can also provide enlightened leadership in health care organizations, emphasize new perspectives in an organizationally oriented system, and minimize the conflict between nursing staff and health care organizations. To do so nurse managers first have to hone their managerial competency. As experience and skill are gained, they may gravitate into nonnursing management positions. Furthermore, as other organizational members become accustomed to their presence, acceptance in executive-level positions could increase.

As nurse managers progressively cultivate their leadership capabilities, they will focus primarily on nurses. Figure 5-3 suggests that nursing staff have power because of their ability to influence medical care and strategic decisions in health care organizations. Therefore, nurse managers attend to the goals, considerations, personalities, and input of the nursing staff in establishing a power base.

It may be useful to view the nursing staff as a reserve of untapped ideas. For too many health care organizations, there is an adversarial or even noncommittal relationship between nursing staff and management staff. An adversarial relationship blocks valuable input from nurses regarding how the service delivery process can be altered. This is a tremendous reservoir of knowledge to underutilize. Nurse managers can bring this knowledge to the full use of the organization.

A number of strategies can also be identified and derived by establishing a collaborative relationship with nurses. Figure 5-4 indicates that these strategies can be used to incorporate nurses more fully into organizations. By employing these strategies, nurse managers foster a collaborative effort between nurses and organizations.

A collaborative effort should promote both nurse and organization goals. This is the leadership philosophy to present to nurses who maintain a healthy skepticism of how the organization values their services. It is not unusual for nurses to believe that health care organizations have gone out of their way to prevent nurses from attaining personal and professional goals. Unless nurse managers are able to point to specific efforts on the part of health care institutions to address nursing issues, attempts to restructure nurse attitudes may be fruitless.

The idea of integrating individual and organizational goals as shown in Figure 5-4 is a crucial concept facing organizations and people. The ability to bring individuals and organizations together to meld values represents a major frontier in management. There is great interest in raising health care organization productivity to drive down costs while simultaneously raising the quality of care. Many panaceas have been proposed as resolutions. Although these concepts (e.g., job enrichment, management by objectives, Japanese-style management, quality circles, and searches for excellence) have value in the proper context, they overlook the importance of reciprocity between the individual and organization. When there is a balance in reciprocity, incredible possibilities surface for improving health care delivery.

Reciprocity and the resulting collaborative relationship between nurse and organization are contingent on the strategies outlined in Figure 5-4. Nurse managers interested in forging a better bond between staff members and their organization can consider creating a positive mindset, emphasizing mutual goals, respecting the individual worth of each nurse, and promoting personal involvement of every staff member. Admittedly, implementation of these strategies is more difficult than surface appearances suggest. Nonetheless,

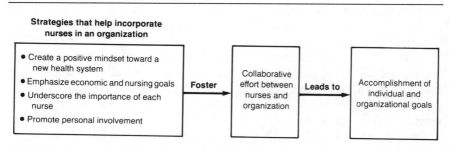

Figure 5-4 Deriving a Collaborative Effort from Nurses

nurse managers should periodically assess the extent to which their attitudes, behaviors, and decisions serve as an example for other nurses. In this fashion, collaboration may eventually evolve without artificiality and with sincerity.

Create a Positive Mindset

Nurse managers can develop a collaborative effort between the nursing staff and the health care organization by creating a positive mindset toward changes in the health system. Nurse managers could maintain an enthusiastic posture toward health system changes. Their positive attitudes could serve as a model for staff. Such attitudes are precisely what is needed by the nursing profession to cope with the impact of powerful external forces. The organizational nature of the health system, third-party policies for cost control, and the economic shortage of nurses mandate the development of a positive mindset to overcome adversarial constraints.

By focusing on possibilities instead of limitations, nurse managers can identify how this evolution will benefit nursing practice and the profession as a whole. Resistance will accomplish little besides wasting effort and fostering a perception that much was done in vain. The nursing profession and nurses need leaders who are comfortable with system changes. The nurse manager provides a role model of one who is determined to see the health system prosper while promoting nursing practice in the system. In essence, the nurse manager creates a positive mindset toward a reorganized health care system.

Emphasize Economic and Nursing Goals

Nurse managers can act as advocates for nursing practice goals. Figure 5-4 suggests that they can provide leadership to nurses by acknowledging the importance of economic and patient care goals. Admittedly, this may be difficult because the nursing profession has always placed a premium on quality of care and less emphasis on cost of care. Recently, the profession has cultivated a conscious effort on the part of nurses to institute cost controls in clinical practice. This goal has not yet been attained, however. Health care organizations continue to strive to keep costs down and to provide an infrastructure for remaining competitive by delivering a superior service to patients.

Quality nursing care will always be the interest of the health system, but it must be achieved within economic realities. Nurse managers provide the means by which nurses and organizations reach an understanding that economic performance is only one of several measures of success. Few health care organizations are able to deliver care just to attain profits. It is also true, however, that health system retrenchment is forcing both nurses and organizations to rethink how care is delivered. As nurse managers come to participate more in this process, it is vital that they remain committed to achieving both economic and patient care outcomes.

Underscore Individuality

The tendency for health care organizations to dominate individuals is a challenge to nurses, whose professional education emphasizes autonomy. Some nurses are reluctant to become just another provider on a large nursing staff. They recognize that the individuality of clinical practice can be lost in the maze of large health care organizations. When this occurs, they have become just another assembly-line worker.

These fears are well founded according to organizational philosophers. As organizations assume more importance than individuals, the result is a propensity for alienation among nurses and other providers. The best way to prevent alienation is to involve staff in key decisions. Additionally, the importance and dignity of each nurse must be continually reaffirmed. The person who has the most potential for eliciting participation and promoting personal dignity is the nurse manager. Nurse managers are perfectly positioned to work toward integrating nurses harmoniously into health care organization infrastructures. Nurse managers are pivotal in bringing organization and individual together.

Promote Personal Involvement

One of the best ways to integrate nurses into an organization is to promote their personal involvement in setting and meeting goals. When nurses are encouraged to become joint or collaborative partners, several things happen. First, nurses begin to sense that personal goals are as important as the organization's goals. Nurses attempt to maximize the time allocated to doing what best suits their interests as well as those of the organization. Second, nurses become actively involved in professional social patterns, which improves opportunities for collegiality. This is a meaningful strategy for nurses who are interested in achieving collegial networks. Third, nurses become an asset for organizations by attending appropriate meetings and participating in issues to which they might make worthwhile contributions. This facilitates sharing of knowledge and coordination of work.

Nurse managers can promote personal involvement of nurses in their organization by:

- making certain that each nurse rotates in assignment on nursing committees

- varying the leadership structure of committees and special projects
- facilitating continuing education and research (e.g., by requiring all staff to deliver a presentation at some point during the year)
- establishing quality circles around clinical specialties, subspecialties, or core teams

These strategies for personal involvement can work, but only if nurse managers act sincerely in implementing the strategies among all staff members.

MANAGING THE MANAGEMENT STAFF

Managing the nursing staff may represent one of the easier leadership challenges to nurse managers. Most nurses honor the professional education and experience of nurse managers. This leadership advantage can be more than offset by adverse relations with management staff, however. Nurse managers must somehow bridge the gap between nursing staff and management staff. Power of position alone will not ensure that this is accomplished. Although a nurse manager may hold a powerful organizational position, there still remains the problem of constructively drawing out the best from all staff members.

Figure 5-5 presents an overview of the responses that nurse managers can anticipate from management staff. It is vital to place these responses in perspective because most of them appear to be negative. The negative attitudes of health care administrators toward nurse managers stem primarily from confusion in the nursing profession. Although nurses' involvement in management positions is widely accepted in the profession, there remain numerous questions about how best to develop nurse managers.[12-15] Just as

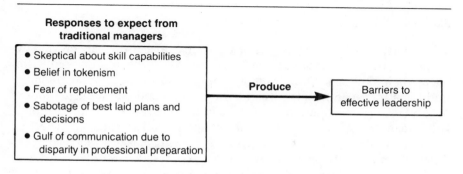

Figure 5-5 Barriers to Effective Leadership Caused by Management Staff

there is controversy over the appropriate educational degrees needed for clinical nursing,[16] so too is there uncertainty about the best education and training for nurse managers.[17,18] The literature offers numerous discussions about how to teach management concepts to prospective nurse managers[19-23] as well as recommendations for evaluating nurse manager effectiveness.[24,25] Nonetheless, agreement about what roles nurse managers fulfill and what expectations exist for their management capability has not been achieved.

The confusion surrounding what nurse managers are, what they should be, and what skills and abilities are appropriate to complete their responsibilities eventually affects other clinical and managerial staff in health care organizations. Nurse managers may be defined in a narrow sense as an administrative body for nursing services.[26] Potential management candidates are recruited from the clinical staff.[27] This narrow vision of nurses in management positions is inconsistent with the challenges facing nursing programs and health care organizations today. Traditional nurse managers (e.g., supervisors, head nurses, and assistant directors) are now much more involved in issues affecting executive-level decisions, including conflict management, budgeting, goal setting, and problem resolution.[28] Nurse managers cannot effectively complete their assignments (e.g., pricing nursing services, strategic planning, and marketing) unless the entire nurse management team supports them.

Ultimately, a narrow vision of nurses in management will influence the nonnursing managers with whom nurse managers work. If nurse managers maintain a limited vision of their role and contribution to health care organizations, then why should any other managers perceive them differently? To capitalize on the new power and responsibility available to them, nurse managers must accept the opportunities made available by increased power and responsibility by acting accordingly. Otherwise, they can anticipate the management staff's continuing to view their contribution negatively.

Skepticism about Skills

The barriers to effective leadership by nurse managers that are erected by traditional (usually nonclinical) health care managers begin with skepticism about their skill capabilities. Simply because of nurses' clinical training, traditional managers maintain a certain degree of skepticism about the ability of nurse managers actually to fulfill the requirements of managerial positions. Nurse managers are viewed first as nurses and second as managers. There is a continuing question as to how a nurse could possibly make a good manager. After all, traditional managers have probably observed plenty of token nurse managers who did not produce much in the way of positive results. Why should they expect that a nurse who has received some management education will be any different? Yet the same question could easily be asked of every manager.

Effective leaders do not have to rely solely on prior education (whether nursing or managerial) to convince others of their capability and right to fulfill a managerial role. Leaders demonstrate capability in their daily assignments and actions. In some instances this means that leaders procure additional knowledge before making key decisions or attending meetings to discuss those decisions (e.g., they may refresh their understanding of the different methods of evaluating a budget shortfall). In other cases, managers can admit a lack of expertise to acquire assistance from a management staff member. The point is that leaders can remove skepticism by demonstrating confidence in their personal capabilities, acquiring more knowledge, and sharing expertise with staff.

Tokenism

Consistent with the skepticism surrounding nurse managers and their skill capabilities is the belief that nurses are often selected for token management positions. Some managers view nurse managers as token representatives whose function is to placate or serve the interests of nursing staff. This is a significant barrier to effective leadership. It implies that management staff may be unwilling to participate in managerial assignments and direction-setting processes with nurse managers. In other cases, nonnurse managers may maintain a personal grudge because nurse managers have prevented them from reaching their own executive aspirations.

Fear of Replacement and Sabotage

Traditional managers may present a barrier to effective leadership because they fear replacement. This idea is linked to the potential for sabotage of nurse managers' best laid plans and decisions, as shown in Figure 5-5. Nonnursing managers may fear replacement if they expect that a nurse manager will begin replacing the management team with colleagues or other nurses. Nonnurse managers may resent the fact that a nurse manager occupies a position that they expected to fill one day. Mix these ingredients of resentment and fear together, and it is not surprising to find subtle sabotage. Managers could attempt to obstruct accomplishments by nurse managers.

Gulf of Communication

Finally, Figure 5-5 suggests that a gulf of communication may exist between nurse managers and other managers because of a disparity in professional preparation. Nurses are admired for their clinical preparation, which continues with them into managerial roles. In a certain sense there is no going back. Clinical nursing preparation cannot be removed. The result is difficulty in communication due to differences in terminology and conceptual frameworks. Nurse managers often do not speak the same language or think along the same lines as nonnurse managers. This difference is primarily attributable to the gap between clinical preparation, which nonnurse managers lack, and managerial education, which nurse managers lack.

Realistically, nurse managers have a limited set of options for resolving communication problems (and other barriers) with their managerial counterparts. One option is to seek commensurate management education and development. Another is to demonstrate a willingness to clarify confusion in communication. A third option is to demonstrate capability. All these solutions recognize that nurse managers confront significant barriers to effective leadership that are caused by bias on the part of managers.

MANAGING BOARDS OF DIRECTORS

Nurse managers can concentrate on collaborating with the board of directors or trustees if they wish to function effectively as leaders.[29] Not all nurse managers occupy positions that allow them to interface with the board, but many will have opportunities to work with a board member or subcommittee when involved in strategic projects. For these reasons it is valuable to consider some ways to facilitate interaction with the board.

As Figure 5-6 indicates, nurse managers inevitably have to address characteristics of governing boards that facilitate or prevent nursing input. Some nurse managers hold positions in which interaction with the governing board is feasible. Despite this advantage, nurse managers may let the opportunity pass and thereby fail to capitalize on a potential avenue for improving the condition of nursing services. It may not always be possible for nurse managers to cultivate relationships with a governing board. When these propitious opportunities do arise (e.g., when presenting formal reports or working with board subcommittees), then every effort should be made to use them to their maximum.[30]

Characteristics Facilitating Input

There are several characteristics of boards that facilitate input by nurses (Figure 5-6). Generally, board members are seldom knowledgeable about the specifics of operations. They are not involved in the day-to-day manage-

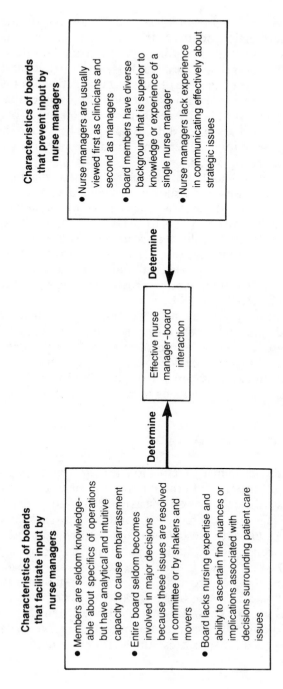

Characteristics of boards that prevent input by nurse managers

- Nurse managers are usually viewed first as clinicians and second as managers
- Board members have diverse background that is superior to knowledge or experience of a single nurse manager
- Nurse managers lack experience in communicating effectively about strategic issues

Determine

Effective nurse manager–board interaction

Determine

Characteristics of boards that facilitate input by nurse managers

- Members are seldom knowledge-able about specifics of operations but have analytical and intuitive capacity to cause embarrassment
- Entire board seldom becomes involved in major decisions because these issues are resolved in committee or by shakers and movers
- Board lacks nursing expertise and ability to ascertain fine nuances or implications associated with decisions surrounding patient care issues

Figure 5-6 Salient Factors To Consider in Interacting with Boards of Directors

ment of the organization, nor should they be. The purpose of the board is to provide strategic direction, not to run the organization. Consequently, nurse managers have a distinct advantage because they know how the organization (specifically, nursing care) operates. This is a tremendous advantage because it provides leverage (in expertise) that can be beneficial in discussions of strategic issues. Nurse managers must not forget the limits of this knowledge advantage, however. Most board members have achieved a governing position because of power, assets, or skills. Board members have the analytical and intuitive capacity to cause extreme embarrassment if their particular strengths are taken for granted.

The entire board may not become involved in certain decisions surrounding nursing care because these issues are resolved in committees or by key movers and shakers on the board. The best point for influencing a key decision issue is therefore not at a board meeting but behind the scenes. Nurse managers should carefully cultivate acceptance from relevant committee members or the significant powerful individuals. Board members are alert to hidden agendas. The best approach is to inform them of an opportunity or decision, to solicit their input, and to provide nursing's perspective before presenting the issue to the entire board.

Nurse managers may discover that governing boards of health care organizations have a significant lack of knowledge about nursing care. This lack of expertise suggests that they are unable to ascertain the fine nuances or implications associated with nursing care or decisions surrounding it. This is a distinctive advantage that nurse managers should use to influence the board's analysis of any given nursing or patient care issue.

Characteristics Preventing Input

Nurse managers have many factors to battle in their attempts to provide input to boards of trustees.[31] Perhaps none is so significant as the fact that nurse managers are usually viewed first as clinicians and second as managers. Once the nurse manager is stereotyped, it is difficult to shake the stereotype. Therefore, it is essential to present an image of both a manager and a nurse. This may be difficult in view of the time spent in preparing for the professional nursing role. The best advice is to balance nursing and managerial images.

Another characteristic of boards that prevents input by nurse managers is the governing board's diverse background. Their combined perspective is generally superior to the knowledge or experience of a single nurse manager. The cumulative knowledge base prevents nurse managers from taking advantage of their own expertise because the board has a more comprehensive knowledge base.

Finally, Figure 5-6 suggests that nurse managers may lack experience in communicating effectively about strategic issues. Nurse managers may not be able to effectively provide input to the board because they do not have a working knowledge of the strategy and tactics employed by boards. The focus of clinicians is patient care. Failure to cultivate a strategic management viewpoint wherein organizational direction is emphasized could inhibit nurse managers' ability to communicate about strategic issues.

INSPIRATIONAL LEADERSHIP THROUGH SHARED GOVERNANCE

There is a growing awareness in the nursing profession that leadership is needed to stem problems of job dissatisfaction among nurses.[32] Dissatisfaction ultimately generates high costs (as a result of turnover) and threatens patient care. Self-governance through decentralized and participative decision making has received considerable attention as a methodology for treating an otherwise unhealthy nursing culture.[33] A number of different approaches have been tried in nursing with mixed success.[34-37] Consequently, nurse managers should be alert to shared governance as a mechanism for visionary leadership. The idea of sharing power and decision-making authority may seem paradoxical because it has taken nursing leaders so long to acquire such power and authority.[38] Nonetheless, truly inspirational leaders are prepared to share and are capable of sharing power, and in the process they amplify their authority, respect, and commitment.

Participation in or decentralization of authority is the extent to which staff are consulted concerning or allowed to make decisions.[39] Participation is believed to limit the extent to which employees feel alienated by their work or the organization. By participating in decision-making processes they have greater incentive to make a commitment to an organization.

Or do they?[40]

It is often said that if a worker is permitted to participate in making decisions, he will work harder. But work harder at what? At making the decision? At implementing the decision? Or at implementing *other* decisions? Suppose, for example, workers are permitted to decide for themselves *when* coffee breaks should be taken (though management still determines how long they should be). The discussion itself may well be quite lively. But will the mere fact of participation lead to workers taking their breaks only at the times agreed upon? Will they be less likely to take excessively long breaks? And will they also produce more on the job? And, to consider a related question: When will decision making within the small group lead to greater support of the goals of the entire organization? Many managers assume that participation in regard to a relatively trivial problem will lead to higher productivity generally. Perhaps this will occur at times. But when? Why?

There are many reasons to believe that participation will lead to increased productivity, but delegation of decision-making authority is not always the answer. Findings on employee participation indicate the following relationships:[41]

1. Participation in decisions sharply increases the acceptance of decisions.
2. The process of participation affects the attitudes only of those who are actually consulted; those outside the process are not influenced.
3. Participation in inconsequential decisions does not affect general attitudes.
4. The effects of participation may be mediated by personality. People who naturally accept authority and express low need for independence react positively where little participation is used.

Thus employee participation (in decisions) leads to mixed results.

Participation is often confused with other management techniques such as democratic leadership or job enrichment.[42] Perhaps the biggest problem in current thinking about participation is confusion about the delegation of authority. Delegation of authority to make decisions is a distinctly different concept from participation in operations. When an organization supports employee decision making, the process is viewed as decentralized decision making. Conversely, when an organization does not delegate decision-making authority to employees, centralized decision making exists. The responsibility and right to make a decision represent a different concept from participation, which involves consulting, expressing views, or performing personal analysis.

The differences between delegation of authority and participation are shown in Figure 5-7. Managers can structure decision making along two dimensions: delegation of authority and participation.[43] The end result is a two-by-two matrix. Participation involves requesting and receiving employee input, not allowing employee decision making. Participation is juxtaposed with the delegation of authority, which confers the actual right and duty to make decisions.

A nursing department may promote decentralized decision-making authority in combination with participation. In this case, decisions are mainly

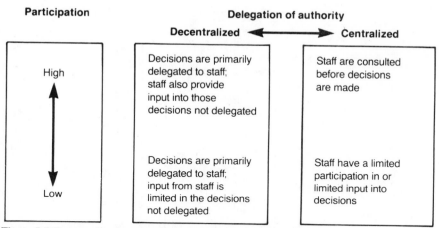

Figure 5-7 Decentralization of and Participation in Decision Making

delegated to staff. For those decision issues that are not delegated, staff retain the ability to participate in the decision-making process. In contrast, staff may encounter a condition in which authority is centralized and participation is low. There is limited decision making on the part of staff and almost no participation or consultation in the decision-making process. Between these two extremes lie most management compromises.

Centralized authority combined with high participation suggests that the decision-making power is retained by top management. Staff are only consulted when decisions are made. Staff have little decision-making power. In contrast, authority may be highly decentralized and participation low. In this case most decisions are delegated to staff members, but participation is limited in those decisions that are not delegated to them.

In achieving visionary leadership, nurse managers should recognize that participation and delegation of decision-making authority are entirely different concepts. Participation is not a panacea for health care organizational ills, especially the job dissatisfaction of nurses. Participation and delegation of authority together are appropriate elements for certain specific settings. Participation as well as the delegation of decision-making authority imply that staff are capable of handling the responsibilities delegated to them.

Shared governance suggests high participation in decision making and decentralization of authority. Figure 5-8 presents a conceptual model that clarifies how participation and delegated authority relate to shared governance in nursing. According to this model, shared governance (i.e., participation in decisions regarding nursing responsibilities) on the left-hand side of the model leads directly to satisfaction, commitment, and performance on the

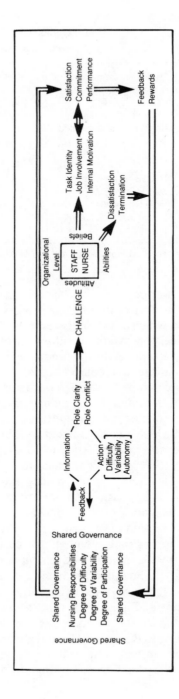

Figure 5-8 A Model of Shared Governance in Nursing. *Source:* Reprinted from "Making Shared Governance Work: A Conceptual Model" by D. Allen, J. Calkin, and M. Peterson, *Journal of Nursing Administration*, Vol. 18, No. 1, pp. 37–43, with permission of J.B. Lippincott Company, © January 1988.

right-hand side of the model. As might be anticipated, not all nurses respond equally to opportunities in shared governance.[44] The factors depicted between shared governance and job satisfaction illustrate some of the variables influencing this relationship. Nurse managers should not assume that shared governance automatically results in higher job satisfaction, commitment, or performance. The intervening variables must be examined and managed to ensure that shared governance has a fair chance of succeeding.

Staff nurses are affected by information about their work and task identity. First, shared governance increases the amount of work-related information accessible to nurses. They can then make decisions that reduce role conflict, or they can clarify their role expectations by acquiring more information. For example, if nurses are involved in collaborative practice, then by acquiring more information about decisions they should make in patient care relative to physician decisions they can reduce role conflict and increase role clarity. The model suggests that this will lead to higher job satisfaction.

Second, shared governance also clarifies task identity, job involvement, and internal motivation. Task identity involves the perceived importance of a nurse's job in delivering patient care. To the extent that nurses perceive their jobs as being important in patient care, are willing to invest themselves in their work (i.e., are highly involved), and are internally motivated, shared governance will lead to higher performance. Shared governance relies on nurses' skills and incorporates them in crucial decisions. This raises their task identity and involvement. It also reinforces their internal motivation.

Despite the benefits noted in Figure 5-8, shared governance is not a panacea. Health care organizations differ in how extensively and sincerely they implement shared governance. Similarly, nurses vary in their values and what they seek from practicing. Consequently, nurse managers should recognize that shared governance is an important, but not a fail-safe, tool in their repertoire of skills leading to innovative and inspirational leadership.

NOTES

1. D.E. Cavanaugh, "Gamesmanship: The Art of Strategizing," *Journal of Nursing Administration* 15 (April 1985): 38-41.

2. L.B. Lundborg, "What Is Leadership?" *Journal of Nursing Administration* 12 (May 1982): 32-33.

3. S.R. Eastaugh, "The Impact of the Nurse Training Act on the Supply of Nurses, 1974–1983," *Inquiry* 22 (Winter 1985): 404-417.

4. H.A. Hanson and S. Chater, "Role Selection by Nurses: Managerial Interests and Personal Attributes," *Nursing Research* 32 (January/February 1983): 48-52.

5. J.P. Smith, "Nursing Managers Need Education Too," *Journal of Advanced Nursing* 5 (1980): 243-244.

6. S. Gleeson, O.W. Nestor, and A.J. Riddell, "Helping Nurses through the Management Threshold," *Nursing Administration Quarterly* 7 (Winter 1983): 11-16.

7. R. Bergman, "Changing Perspectives in Preparing Nurse Administrators," *Nursing Administration Quarterly* 3 (1979): 73-84.

8. M. Wellington, "Decentralization: How It Affects Nurses," *Nursing Outlook* 34 (January/February 1986): 36-39.

9. A.H. Nowell and G. Nowell, "Participation Management as a Strategy for Nurse Adaptation to Hospital Unit Management Systems," *Hospital Topics* 64 (January/February 1986): 28-42.

10. W.G. Scott and D.K. Hart, *Organizational America* (Boston: Houghton Mifflin, 1979).

11. L.M. Johnson et al., "A Model of Participatory Management with Decentralized Authority," *Nursing Administration Quarterly* 7 (Fall 1983): 30-36.

12. C.H. Jordan, "Nursing Administrator—A Legitimate Career," *Nursing Administration Quarterly* 3 (1979): 53-56.

13. D.J. del Bueno and D.D. Walker, "Developing Prospective Managers. Part I. A Unique Project," *Journal of Nursing Administration* 14 (April 1984): 7-10.

14. D.R. Sheridan et al., "Developing Prospective Managers. Part 2. The Process," *Journal of Nursing Administration* 14 (May 1984): 23-28.

15. D.J. del Bueno and D.R. Sheridan, "Developing Prospective Managers. Part 3. The Results," *Journal of Nursing Administration* 14 (June 1984): 23-27.

16. L.S. Houston and G. Cadenhead, "DRGs and BSNs: The Case for the Bureaucratic Nurse," *Nursing Management* 17 (February 1986): 35-36.

17. R. Thorpe, "Supervision: Is a Masters Degree Really Necessary?" *Supervisor Nurse* 10 (January 1979): 33-35.

18. B.J. Austin, "An Alternative Management Experience for RN-BSN Students," *Journal of Nursing Education* 23 (May 1984): 204-206.

19. H.H. Plasterer and N. Mills, "Teach Management Theory—Through Fun and Games," *Journal of Nursing Education* 22 (February 1983): 80-83.

20. L.H. Oechsle and C.M. Volden, "Teaching Leadership in Nontraditional Settings," *Nursing Outlook* 32 (November/December 1984): 313-315.

21. C.B. Stetler et al., "A Modular Approach to Management Development," *Journal of Nursing Administration* 10 (December 1980): 19-24.

22. M.A. Brandt and R.M. Craig, "Follow the Leader: A Learning Exercise," *Journal of Nursing Education* 24 (April 1985): 139-142.

23. E.J. Sullivan and P.J. Decker, "Using Behavior Modeling To Teach Management Skills," *Nursing and Health Care* 6 (January 1985): 41-45.

24. J.M. Athans, "Evaluating the Effectiveness of Supervisory Development Programs in the Hospital," *Hospital Topics* 63 (March/April 1985): 20-26.

25. L.F. Nelson, "Competence of Nursing Graduates in Technical, Communicative, and Administrative Skills," *Nursing Research* 27 (March-April 1978): 121-125.

26. P.B. Cushnie, "Executive Team Development," *Nursing Clinics of North America* 18 (September 1983): 467-472.

27. C. Maese, "Management Development: Putting the Concept to Work," *Texas Hospitals* 37 (December 1981): 38-41.

28. R. Kirk, "Management Development: A Needs Analysis for Nurse Executives and Managers," *Journal of Nursing Administration* 17 (April 1987): 7-8.

29. M. Walker and K.K. Choate, "Nurses as Policymakers," *Nurse Educator* 9 (Spring 1984): 39-42.

30. R.A. Culbertson, "The Governing Body and the Nursing Administrator: An Emerging Relationship," *Journal of Nursing Administration* 9 (February 1979): 11-13.

31. E.K. Singleton and F.C. Nail, "Developing Relationships with the Board of Directors," *Journal of Nursing Administration* 16 (January 1986): 37-42.

32. D. Przestrzelski, "Decentralization: Are Nurses Satisfied?" *Journal of Nursing Administration* 17 (November 1987): 23-28.

33. L.M. Johnson, "Self-governance: Treatment for an Unhealthy Nursing Culture," *Health Progress* 68 (May 1987): 41-43.

34. M.E. Ortiz, P. Gehring, and M.D. Sovie, "Moving to Shared Governance," *American Journal of Nursing* 87 (July 1987): 923-926.

35. B. Hatfield, "How To Develop a Complete Nursing Management Program," *Hospital Topics* 65 (March/April 1981): 12-14.

36. M.E. Peterson and D.G. Allen, "Shared Governance: A Strategy for Transforming Organizations, Part I," *Journal of Nursing Administration* 16 (January 1986): 9-12.

37. M.E. Peterson and D.G. Allen, "Shared Governance: A Strategy for Transforming Organizations, Part II," *Journal of Nursing Administration* 16 (February 1986): 11-16.

38. A.G. Taylor, "The Decision-Making Processes and the Nursing Administrator," *Nursing Clinics of North America* 18 (September 1983): 439-447.

39. A. Lowin, "Participative Decision Making: A Model, Literature Critique, and Prescriptions for Research," *Organization Behavior and Human Performance* 3 (1968): 68-106.

40. G. Strauss, "Some Notes on Power-Equalization," in *The Social Science of Organizations*, ed. H.J. Leavitt (Englewood Cliffs, NJ: Prentice-Hall, 1963), 68-70.

41. A.J. Melcher, "Participation: A Critical Review of Research Findings," *Human Resource Management* 15 (Summer 1976): 12-21.

42. C.R. Forrest, L.L. Cummings, and A.C. Johnson, "Organizational Participation: A Critique and Model," *Academy of Management Review* 2 (1977): 586-601.

43. W.C. Hamner and D.W. Organ. *Organizational Behavior: An Applied Psychological Approach* (Dallas, TX: Business Publications, 1976).

44. D. Allen, J. Calkin, and M. Peterson, "Making Shared Governance Work: A Conceptual Model," *Journal of Nursing Administration* 18 (January 1988): 37-43.

Chapter 6

Organizing To Implement Nursing Strategies

For the most part, one primary model has traditionally been used by health care organizations to structure their operations. This is the bureaucracy. Both loved and hated, bureaucratic structures have dominated the world of health care organizations. When functioning at their optimum, few other structural designs allow services to be produced as efficiently as bureaucracies. Nevertheless, there are many dysfunctions that accompany even the most efficient bureaucracy. As these have become identified there has been a search for a better organizational design. Nurse managers are particularly interested in discovering organizational structures that deliver services as efficiently as bureaucracies while avoiding the impersonality, overemphasis on efficiency, and rigidity of bureaucracies. New structures that support the professional and personal needs of nurses are needed now more than ever.

Health care organizations are experimenting with a whole new spectrum of contemporary forms. There is a search for fundamentally organic structural designs that will eliminate the mechanistic qualities of bureaucracies.[1] This quest is reinforced by competitive, cost-control, and corporate influences in the contemporary health care environment. There are few restraints on structural innovation and experimentation as long as potential designs produce results. The building blocks of organization are being assembled into entirely new forms. Consequently experimentation by health care organizations has produced numerous alternative structures, including matrix, constellation, and ad hoc designs. Much of this evolution has occurred in the last two decades, and the prognosis is that the innovation will continue. This renaissance in organizing and structural experimentation could produce vibrant designs that instill vitality in health care organizations and provide a better basis for effectively implementing nursing strategies.

THE BUREAUCRACY

The term *bureaucracy* usually conjures up a vivid image in our minds. Often the term is used in a pejorative sense, and people tend to associate bureaucracy with negative experiences. Seldom is a bureaucracy linked to positive experiences. Nevertheless, a bureaucracy does have its advantages as an organizational form. In fact, the bureaucratic form is the most pervasive organizational structure in the health care sector. Therefore, it is essential to understand the characteristics, attributes, advantages, disadvantages, and future of this design. Loved or hated, the concept of bureaucracy has received much attention and comment throughout history.

Max Weber, a German sociologist, is generally identified as the father of bureaucracy.[2] In Weber's view there are three sources of legitimate authority that affect bureaucracy. First, leader-oriented or charismatic authority represents power accumulated through some unique characteristic or exceptional virtue that instills confidence, trust, or faith in the leader. John F. Kennedy exemplifies a charismatic leader. Weber's second source of authority is embodied in a patriarch: a benevolent master who acquires power because he founded an institution around certain ideals. A patriarch could be exemplified by the father or mother in a family. The third source of power, according to Weber, is bureaucracy or legal domination. Power is modeled after a machine in that authority is precisely measured and divided according to a rational plan. Power originates at the top or upper echelons of an organization. It is successively delegated or partitioned according to predetermined policies, rules, orders, and procedures. Unlike charismatic or patriarchal authority, bureaucratic authority cannot be obtained from either birth or inheritance. Authority therefore is attached to a position. It is this interplay of formal power and individual position that forms the central ingredient of the bureaucratic paradigm.

Main Features of Bureaucracy

The primary attributes of bureaucracy are best understood by examining the following definition: A bureaucracy is a large hierarchical organization of careerists that is operated by rules and regulations for purposes of efficiency. Essentially every word in this definition is important for understanding the specific elements of the bureaucratic organization. The definition incorporates Weber's six main features of bureaucracy: (1) the division of labor, (2) the hierarchy of authority, (3) rules and regulations, (4) impersonality, (5) conditions of employment, and (6) a specialized administrative staff.[3] An overview of these elements is presented in Exhibit 6-1.

Exhibit 6-1 Elements of Bureaucracies

Bureaucracy: a large hierarchical organization of careerists that is operated by rules and regulations for purposes of efficiency

Bureaucratic elements

1. *Division of labor*—Work tasks are successively partitioned or broken down into small units
2. *Hierarchy of authority*—The chain of authority is based on position, power running from the highest executive to the lowest employee
3. *Rules and regulations*—A system of predefined policies, procedures, and guidelines creates uniformity of performance
4. *Impersonality*—Each employee strives to keep personal attitudes, opinions, perceptions, and beliefs from hindering equitable treatment of all clients
5. *Conditions of employment*—Employees are hired for a lifetime
6. *Specialized administrative staff*—A special staff of administrators is hired to support bureaucratic operations

---

Division of Labor

The concept of division of labor was defined in 1776 by Adam Smith in *The Wealth of Nations*.[4] This economist observed that, when tasks are successively broken down or partitioned into small units, expertise can be cultivated. Division of labor or specialization creates efficiency because a person is able to learn a given task in great detail. Although the division of labor is normally viewed in terms of clinical responsibilities (e.g., specialties and subspecialties), it can be found throughout a health care organization. Division of labor is the basis on which many hospital bureaucracies achieve their high levels of efficiency.[5] With division of labor it is possible to take full advantage of every staff member's unique skills and training.

The division of labor in a bureaucracy is exemplified by a large urban nursing registry that processes 50,000 requests for temporary nurses each year. Although the registry may include ten people who review and make a recommendation for each request, this approach prevents attaining a high level of efficiency. Therefore, the registry divides its processing staff into rational work units. Some are assigned clerical tasks. Others are assigned the task of interviewing nurses and selecting appropriate clinical positions for them. Other staff are responsible solely for matching the nurses with temporary positions. There are many other possible partitions in the division of labor for this registry. Efficiency is attained by dividing work according to tasks.

Subdivided tasks should lead to reasonably high levels of performance because a specialist is matched to a task. There are few guidelines specifying how far to go in dividing labor, however. For example, the extreme division of labor in medical laboratories and some nursing programs has resulted in dysfunctions (e.g., staff boredom, high absenteeism, reduced quality) that counteract inherent efficiencies.

Hierarchy of Authority

In Weber's bureaucratic model all organizational positions are arranged in a hierarchical fashion. This is the chain of command. Each person is responsible for subordinates beneath him or her and is accountable to those superiors directly above. This hierarchy defines the legitimate operating sphere for both subordinates and superiors. It limits the range of activities and the decision-making discretion of every bureaucratic member. The hierarchy of authority enables personnel to know their position in the organization. It also establishes effective communication and decision making.

The hierarchy of authority ultimately loses its ability to help personnel understand their role in the organization. A nursing department or program that is positioned low in the hierarchy of a massive state health department may lose sight of the appropriate person to whom to refer a client's or patient's unique problem. This may be a bewildering experience for patients who do not know how to progress through a bureaucracy. To rectify this problem some bureaucracies have established ombudspersons to cut through bureaucratic mazes for the sake of clients or patients.

Rules and Regulations

According to Weber's ideal bureaucratic model, rules and regulations must be written and rigidly applied. Rules are designed to increase efficiency through uniformity of performance and continuity of operations. Rules help make tasks more programmable, which reduces learning time on the part of the personnel. Rules and regulations may also be viewed as guidelines. If they are followed closely, then identical treatment will be given to every case. Discretionary action is prevented. Performance is standardized, and with standardization comes improved efficiency.

Implementation of impersonal rules and regulations represents a formal approach to work coordination. Work plans, schedules, procedures, and orders are well defined in advance and are communicated to staff, and each task has its proper sequence. Nevertheless, these written and rigid rules produce a number of dysfunctions. For example, a nurse parking her car in an improper parking space at an urban medical center may receive a ticket from a bureaucracy (the medical center's security department). The ticket and fine are levied because the nurse did not adhere to a rule enforced by the bureaucracy. The ticket and fine are administered even though the nurse was called up for emergency staffing on the weekend. The parked automobile is simply in the wrong slot; considerations to the sacrifice that the nurse is making in her personal schedule or to the oversupply of available parking slots is not given by the security department. Thus police officers are removed from making excessive discretionary judgments. They are merely evaluating whether rules and regulations have or have not been followed. Security officers thereby achieve greater productivity because they administer more parking tickets over the course of a day. They are removed from the time-consuming process of judging each individual case.

Impersonality

The ideal bureaucracy should promote impersonality on the part of all organizational members. Weber suggested that bureaucrats should not allow their personal emotions to affect performance. Bureaucrats should strive to keep personal attitudes, opinions, perceptions, and beliefs from affecting the completion of their tasks. By removing personal biases, Weber believed, a bureaucracy's clientele will receive equitable treatment. Justice will be promoted. Many people cringe at the notion that impersonality should be purposefully cultivated. They recognize the banality that an impersonal attitude may foster. In some respects, however, promoting impersonality produces greater democracy. Equitable treatment is desired even though impersonality prevails.

Although an impersonal attitude provides more equitable treatment, it also may reflect a less compassionate and less enthusiastic approach to health care delivery. It is probably difficult for most people to differentiate between impersonality when it is purposefully being cultivated and lack of enthusiasm as a secondary and unintended consequence. Patients tend to focus on observable negative job behaviors, including lack of enthusiasm, lack of attention to detail, preoccupation with unusual problems, and socializing among staff members. Which bureaucratic and impersonal behaviors are most frustrating depends on the patient's perspective.

If impartiality could be implemented instead of impersonality, it might be much easier for patients to accept this treatment. They might then understand that impersonality is purposefully built into the system. Treatment without emotion is designed to help achieve greater efficiency. The impersonality represents a deliberate effort to provide clients or patients with better service. If Weber's theory were followed literally, then patients or clients would applaud rather than complain about impersonal treatment. They would affirm that the bureaucrat's good works are efficiency in the making.

Although many examples illustrate the failed good intentions of impersonal bureaucratic action, few are better illustrations than the situation in some county hospital outpatient clinics. Patients can stand in any number of lines for hours waiting to fill out appropriate forms, waiting to move toward the cashier's line, waiting to have an examination, waiting to take a diagnostic test, waiting to receive pharmaceuticals, and finally waiting to process additional information and forms. This waiting process should not necessarily be interpreted as an affront on the part of the bureaucratic county hospital. It could be interpreted as a series of procedures designed to handle the inflow and outflow of a large number of patients. Consumers, patients, and clients seldom see it this way, however.

Conditions of Employment

The fifth element of the bureaucratic paradigm recommends that each staff member be employed for an entire lifetime in a given setting. The conditions of employment assume that staff will want to stay for life, that they will create a lifelong career in the bureaucracy. This bureaucratic feature is retained in promotion and compensation systems throughout many public bureaucracies. Such policies encourage lifelong careers by rewarding seniority and by advancement according to tenure. Promotion according to the number of years employed, however, may not consider performance other than as measured by loyalty or sheer endurance.

Efficiency is gained because a person performs a task for a long period of time and thereby develops extensive knowledge of that task. Through long tenure with the organization, the person moves up the hierarchy of authority. While moving from level to level employees acquire other education and experience, which enables them to supervise the operations of the department or the bureaucracy.

These advantages overlook the fact that most employees have a shorter time perspective for employment these days. The traditional working values of security and loyalty to an organization are being replaced by loyalty to profession or career and subsumed by a desire, in many instances, for career mobility. Furthermore, the person demonstrating skill and improved productivity may not receive sufficient rewards in a system that is based on years of employment.

Specialized Administrative Staff

According to Weber, the sixth feature of bureaucracy is the creation of a specialized administrative staff. The specialized staff of administrators stabilizes operations and fine tunes the bureaucracy to a point of great efficiency. Nonetheless, many argue that bureaucracies have grown to such a point that their size alone is dysfunctional. Others analyze the size of bureaucracies and underscore that a large portion of normal bureaucracy is not directly contributing to the production of services. A high percentage of bureaucrats are probably involved in ancillary administrative tasks. As a result, administrative positions today often exist solely for the support of other administrative positions. The original intent of an administrative position facilitating the production of a good or service has been lost.

For example, many hospitals have analyzed the ratio of clinical nursing staff to administrators. Third-party payers, nurses, and health care organizations themselves are alarmed at the large amount of funds devoted to administration. The argument is not that the funding of administration should cease but that funds are being misallocated away from clinical activities. This has encouraged some hospitals to prune their administrative and managerial ranks. Consequently, the specialized administrative services on which nurses have relied in the past are often no longer available. These trends may adversely affect service delivery.

The Size of Bureaucracies

As we have seen, the definition of bureaucracy contains six elements. A bureaucracy is a large hierarchical organization of careerists that is operated by rules and regulations for purposes of efficiency. It should be noted that the only significant word in this definition that has not been discussed is size. By itself, size is not the key factor that defines a bureaucracy. There are large bureaucracies as well as small bureaucracies. Most large health care organizations have several bureaucratic elements, but it is the bureaucratic elements themselves that define whether a bureaucracy is present or not.

Size is not the sole criterion by which a bureaucracy is defined. A small medical laboratory that displays the main features of Weber's definition represents a bureaucracy just as well as a group of 10,000 employees in an investor-owned nursing home chain. Similarly, a group of 100,000 nurses in a professional organization that has little structure is not necessarily a bureaucratic organization. The criterion for determining whether an organization is a bureaucracy is the presence of Weber's bureaucratic elements.

Limitations of Bureaucracies

Not too surprising, the literature on bureaucratic structures during the last 40 years has openly criticized bureaucracy. Many of these criticisms are well deserved and have been valid in hundreds of bureaucracies, but the dysfunctions that critics have pointed out also reflect changing times and values. The formal structure that worked so well for society's organizations in one period is not necessarily the appropriate structure in another period.

A major limitation of the bureaucratic organization is its tendency to ignore the individual. A limited view of human motivation accompanies the bureaucratic model. Little thought has been given to the individual as a crucial ingredient in the bureaucratic machine. Even Weber questioned the role of humans in a machinelike organization to the point of expressing fear that people would simply become cogs in the machine. These problems are particularly evident to nurses working in large health care organizations. A bureaucratic climate is seldom conducive to professional or personal fulfillment.

The bureaucratic model provides few opportunities for individuals to realize personal significance within organizations. Individuals are less important than the organization as a whole and its efforts to achieve various ends. The bureaucracy is a machine, and the people whom that machine comprises are merely components in its structure. Motivation of the individual is achieved through standardized rewards that are received for service to the bureaucracy. Foremost in this equation, of course, is pay and security. A theory of individual motivation is therefore quite limited in bureaucratic organizations.

A second major limitation of bureaucracy results from its closed-system approach to managing. Bureaucracies typically do not address changing external environments. The bureaucracy is viewed as a machine, and like other machines it functions best when its internal parts are maintained and tightly integrated. The goal of managers in bureaucracies is to maintain a smoothly functioning internal organization. External events are disruptive because they are not integral elements of the machine. For example, when Medicare instituted prospective payment, the stability of hospital bureaucracies was severely disrupted. Before the introduction of prospective payment, hospitals experienced few survival-threatening pressures. Admittedly, not every hospital operated like a finely tuned machine. After prospective payment, however, hospitals were thrown into disarray.

A third limitation of the bureaucratic form is its "one-best-way" philosophy of managing. The bureaucracy may be appropriate for some organizational settings, but it is not necessarily appropriate for all settings. It is not the "one best way" of organizing. Nonbureaucratic nursing departments, home health agencies, ice cream stores, sporting goods stores, educational institutions, car dealerships, research and development organizations, restaurants, department stores, medical clinics, and savings institutions illustrate that there is more than one way to develop a good organizational design. The bureaucratic organization is simply one of several structural forms that might be utilized when pursuing organizational goals.

The Downfall of Bureaucracy

A growing number of authorities are expressing concern about the ability of bureaucracy to survive in the future (Figure 6-1).[6,7] They believe that

Max Weber Bureaucracy creates a confrontation between people and a machine.

Victor A. Thompson Bureaucracy generates an obsession with rules, regulations, and procedures that eventually become dysfunctional.

Warren Bennis Bureaucracies are unable to provide individual-organizational reciprocity or to adapt to external environmental pressures.

George E. Berkley Bureaucracies are crumbling pyramids; human relations philosophies are dissolving forces.

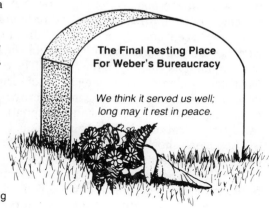

The Final Resting Place For Weber's Bureaucracy

We think it served us well; long may it rest in peace.

Figure 6-1 Predictions of the Downfall of Bureaucracy

bureaucracy as it has served humankind up to now will no longer be acceptable in future society. Many reasons are offered for the potential downfall of bureaucracy, and a number of different organizational forms are suggested to fill the vacuum created by destroying the bureaucratic form. Weber offered a most significant criticism of bureaucracy. He noted,

> It is horrible to think that the world could one day be filled with nothing but those little cogs, little men clinging to little jobs and striving towards bigger ones.[8]

Weber himself predicted that the attempt to construct a perfect machine would eventually result in a zero-sum game. Neither the organization nor the individual could possibly win in this game. In effect, Weber suggests that bureaucracies possess a deficiency that leads inevitably to their demise.

Weber's criticism is only the first of many related attacks that are indicating the potential poor health of the bureaucratic organization. Thompson's analysis of bureaucracies suggests that organizations will deteriorate because of the behavior of the bureaucrats themselves.[9] A distinct personality type arises in response to the formal authority that is characteristic of the bureaucracies. According to Thompson, "bureaupathic" behavior is exemplified by rigid adherence to rituals, rules, regulations, and procedures and, at extremes, the overextension of authority patterns. Bureaupathic behavior is a disease state whose symptoms include red tape, delay, superfluous procedures, and adherence to trivial legitimate authority. Many nurses have encountered such personalities in the course of their clinical duties. A bureaupathic manager (perhaps a nurse manager) follows policies to the letter, even though the policies are the antithesis of low cost or humane patient care.

A more recent analysis of the fate of the bureaucracy is offered by Warren Bennis.[10] Bennis suggests that two major shocks have affected bureaucracy that will limit its viability in the future. The first is that the legitimacy of the bureaucracy hinges on resolving issues of reciprocity and adaptability. Reciprocity involves the degree of conflict between individual and organizational goals (e.g., between a nurse and a hospital). A bureaucracy is designed to satisfy organizational rather than individual goals.

The second shock to bureaucracy, according to Bennis, is the problem of adapting to environmental forces (e.g., a hospital's attempt to meet competition). Bennis believes the downfall of the bureaucracy is inevitable because of the increasingly turbulent environment; changing societal characteristics (e.g., increased education of the general population); alterations in work-relevant values (e.g., the rising emphasis on career mobility); revisions in work tasks (e.g., greater technical nature, greater complications, and less programming); and changes in work goals (e.g., more differentiated and more conflicting objectives). Organizational structures will become more temporary and oriented toward solving problems. The bureaucracy, however, is far from temporary; it is permanent. It is normally oriented toward maintaining a formal structure and continuing the services that it provides.

George E. Berkley, in *The Administrative Revolution*, views the fate of bureaucracy in much the same fashion as Bennis.[11] He envisions the rapid demise of bureaucracies. Berkley believes that society is undergoing a change from crumbling pyramids (i.e., the hierarchy of authority) to a shelter without walls. In other words, Berkley foresees a shift from highly structured bureaucracies to more flexible and temporary organizations. Berkley attributes this shift to a number of factors, including improved managerial techniques (e.g., management by objectives); the development of more lenient and positive leadership philosophies (e.g., MacGregor's Theory Y and Japanese management styles); the use of staff specialists; and the improvement of human motivation techniques.

The wall-dissolving forces in the administrative revolution include employee mobility, planning, new organizational goals, and the trend toward bigness. According to Berkley, these factors dissolve the walls (i.e., the structure) of the traditional bureaucracy. This structure, which sheltered and structured a person's working life, is undergoing transformation toward more flexible organizations.

The sentiments of the preceding authorities on organizations have been echoed resoundingly in nursing. Clinical practice can be enhanced where decentralization and participation lead to teamwork, job satisfaction, and harmony among nursing staff.[12] Care delivery can be supported. In many respects, the choice is between a collegial model and the authoritarian bureaucracy. The former is viewed as more consistent with the delivery of humane and conscientious services.[13] Despite the preference for nonbureaucratic models, nurse managers will discover that they often must balance bureaucratic authority (as managers) with professional autonomy (as nurses and nurse mentors).[14]

CONTEMPORARY ORGANIZATIONAL MODELS

At this point it is appropriate to question where health care organizations will go from here in their designs. The bureaucratic model is unable to meet many individual and organizational needs. As a result, health care organizations have increasingly turned to more flexible designs. In reality there is no single best structure that is being adopted today. Consequently, it is appropriate to examine the leading models to understand how contemporary organizations vary. Two models illustrate the innovation in structuring organizations: matrix models and integrative models.

Matrix Models

Matrix designs are renowned for their use of teams or projects as the basis for organizing. Matrix structures are appropriate in health care organizations because they allow coordination across normal departmental lines (e.g., a nurse manager coordinating quality assurance functions). Central to the design of effective teams is the integrator.[15] The integrator is primarily assigned responsibility for coordinating work.[16] Integrators occupy a formal role in the organization and are delegated authority to fulfill the integrating role. The integrating role can be phased out when a project is completed, but the position usually persists as a result of a continuing stream of new projects.

What are integrating roles? Where are they found in matrix organizations? How are integrating roles different compared with traditional organizational methods? Answers to these questions are fundamental to understanding the matrix organization.

Integrating Roles and Lateral Relations

Integrating roles are responsible for the timely completion of a project. Integrators are delegated authority to work with line and staff members in completing an assigned project. The integrator facilitates project completion by planning its course, bringing various people interested in the project together to achieve a consensus on project decisions, removing barriers to the scheduled completion, and consulting with major leaders whose staff are responsible for accomplishing project tasks. A crucial question regarding integrators is how they accomplish the coordination of work. Galbraith, a leading scholar in matrix theory, believes that integrators coordinate work through personal contacts, thereby establishing trust and facilitating decision making.[17]

First, the integrator must be capable of developing contacts, know how to maintain contacts without jeopardizing other interpersonal relations, and seek to make additional contacts. The integrator knows and is capable of working together with people throughout the organization. Many project directors in their integrating roles have direct access to top management either through their immediate superior or on an individual basis. Integrators develop a clarity of perception regarding the total project. They are able to identify and resolve problems.

The integrator's influence stems from personal contacts. In this sense, integrators use lateral or diagonal relationships to obtain cooperation for a project. Diagonal relationships suggest that integrators are not bound to traditional vertical or horizontal movements when working with other people. They may freely associate with staff throughout the organization. These personal relationships or contacts can be used in a forceful manner when necessary to accomplish the task. After being invoked, however, the future power of the personal contact may be diminished. It is the threat of power, without direct use, that is probably most valuable to integrators.

The second major characteristic of the successful integrator is the ability to establish trust. When an integrator establishes a plan to reach full service capacity (e.g., a special pediatric screening program) by a specified date so that the marketing department in a health maintenance organization can begin its promotional campaign on schedule, a mutual trust has been formed. The integrator may not be directly responsible for the program's failure to meet full service capacity, but that impression could result if the plan is not attained. Integrators must use various means to ensure that deadlines are met; otherwise trust may be destroyed.

The third skill characterizing integrators is the ability to facilitate decision making. Timely decisions capture propitious opportunities and take advantage of unique organizational resources (e.g., an opportunity to procure a state health department contract for managed care). Integrators facilitate decision making. The integrator brings parties together who have a vested interest in the decision. This may be done either through formal (e.g., standardized forms or memos) or informal methods (e.g., telephone conversations, group meetings, or luncheon conferences). These communications articulate concerns and express intentions.

Integrators also determine which decision alternative is most promising for a project and obtain consensus from the concerned parties. They must bargain to achieve a consensus on decisions. Personal contacts are used to bring pressure to bear on appropriate individuals. This strategy should be used cautiously to avoid jeopardizing decisions. Finally, integrators should constantly reinforce the continuity of decision making.

Illustrations of Integrating Roles

Integrators are typically located in four basic organizational positions: a staff position with intermittent integrating responsibilities, an integrating staff position, a line position with intermittent integrating responsibilities, and an integrating line position.[18]

The staff position with intermittent integrating responsibilities can be found in many bureaucratic organizations. Projects invariably arise that require staff-level assistance. These high-priority, short-term projects are generally assigned to a staff member with a particular functional expertise. An example of an intermittent integrator is the staff director of public relations (Figure 6-2). The hospital may have a short-term planning project for new equipment acquisition. If the public relations director has shown skill in planning and feasibility analysis, this person may be assigned dual task responsibility: for planning the new acquisition and for maintaining the public relations program.

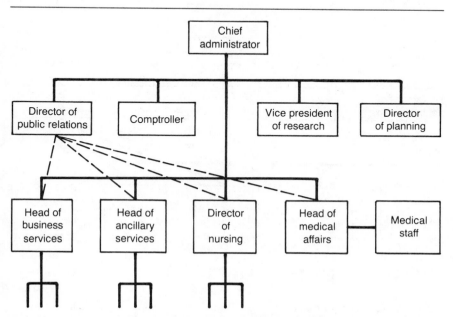

Figure 6-2 Integrator in a Staff Position with Intermittent Integrating Responsibilities. (Dashed lines indicate integrating roles.)

Integrators in staff positions usually command a high degree of respect because of their personal contacts and individual expertise. As with many staff positions, the formal power of the position may be relatively weak even though the line organization's formal authority is strong. The staff position with intermittent integrating responsibilities does have a distinct advantage, however: The integrating role vanishes when the project is completed. The vice president of public relations returns to public relations when the short-term planning project is completed.

A second form of matrix organization exemplifying an integrating role involves a staff member with permanent integrating responsibilities. Such an integrator is shown in Figure 6-3 as the director of planning. This individual is permanently responsible for ensuring that planning is integrated among divisions.

At first glance, the staff position with permanent integrating responsibilities appears to be no different from the staff position with intermittent integrating responsibilities. This is true in concept but neglects the operational aspects of the integrating role. Short-term projects are limited in duration. They represent a constraint today but are no longer a problem tomorrow. Thus staff integrators with permanent responsibilities have greater legitimacy as a result of the continuing nature of their assignment. For

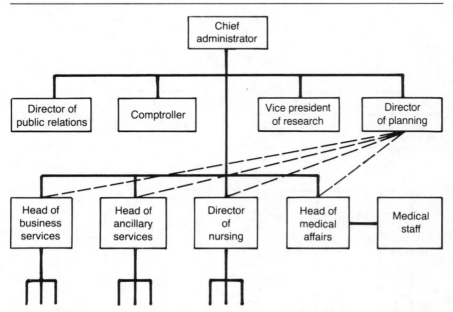

Figure 6-3 Integrator in a Staff Position with Permanent Integrating Responsibilities. (Dashed lines indicate integrating roles.)

example, assume that the hospital in Figure 6-3 decides to establish a formal program of management by objectives. The director of planning is the logical coordinator (or integrator) for this project. Because the project is conducted on an annual basis (i.e., because it is permanent), the continuing nature elicits commitment on the part of other organizational members.

Integrators may also be found in a third type of position in the matrix structure. An example of the integrator who occupies a line position with intermittent integrating responsibilities is shown in Figure 6-4. In this example, the head of business services has been assigned the role of integrator. A new service (Z) has been created as the hospital's attempt to meet several competitive services offered by other hospitals in the community. Because the hospital is heavily promoting service Z, the head of business services is delegated responsibility to manage all aspects of the service during this strategic period and to ascertain the long-run financial feasibility of maintaining the service. The head of business services is responsible for integrating billing, collection, nurse staffing, and ancillary support required by service Z.

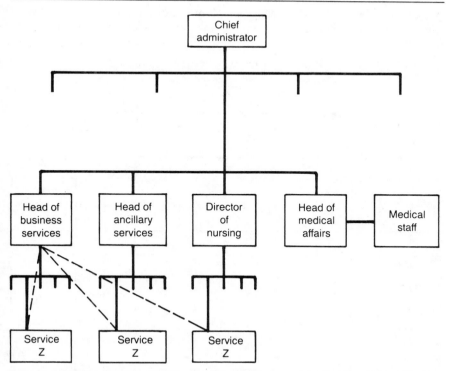

Figure 6-4 Integrator in a Line Position with Intermittent Integrating Responsibilities. (Dashed lines indicate integrating roles.)

The use of line personnel (such as the head of business services) as intermittent integrators is advantageous because of the power held by line positions. Line managers are well versed in a specific function and have an appreciation of how services relate to other line functions. On the other hand, several disadvantages are also apparent when assigning a line member to the role of intermittent integrator. Line managers usually have been delegated extensive responsibility. Increased responsibility may hinder the integrating role or cause suboptimization of line activities. This sacrifice may be necessary if the project is strategically crucial to the organization. If not, it may be prudent for a lower-level line person to assume the role of integrator.

Figure 6-5 depicts a situation in which the integrator is positioned in a permanent line position. This is the matrix structure typically utilized by health care organizations. The permanent line position is assigned responsibility for integrating the work on specific projects in the functional departments. When most people refer to a matrix organization, this structure is generally what they have in mind.

The project directors (i.e., for projects A, B, and C) who report to the project coordinator are all integrators. They do not supervise work but rather integrate work in the business services, ancillary services, nursing and medi-

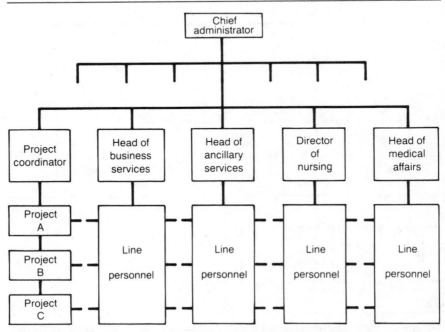

Figure 6-5 Integrator in a Permanent Line Position. (Dashed lines indicate integrating roles.)

cal affairs departments. Although they may have responsibility over various subordinates, they typically facilitate some aspect of coordination. Both the project coordinator and the subordinate project directors occupy permanent line positions. Their function is to integrate the efforts of business services, ancillary services, nursing, and medical affairs for a specific project. Integrators often operate without formal authority.[19] Nonetheless, because of their persuasive contacts (in the chain of command) they are able to coordinate work on specific projects.

Benefits of Integrating Roles

The integrating role and the matrix organization have a number of benefits and limitations. A particularly worthwhile aspect of the matrix organization is its ability to achieve resource efficiency. Efficiency is attained from pooling line personnel who may be recycled to other assignments once a project is completed. Figure 6-6 displays the organizational structure for a home health agency. The agency is relatively small, having two major staffing functions: home care assistance and personal nursing services. In this example, assume that a head manager has been assigned to each function and that 25 home health aides and 30 nurses are employed. As a result of the constant influx of new clients, the director has decided that service coordinators (integrators) will be assigned to assist in serving specific clients.

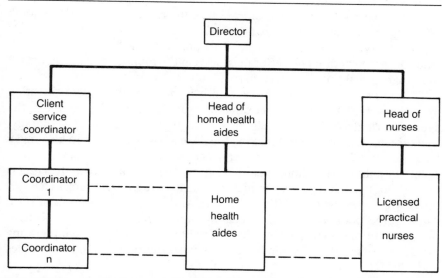

Figure 6-6 Organization Structure of a Home Health Agency. (Dashed lines indicate integrating roles.)

Note that home health aides and nurses are part of large work pools. They are assigned to specific clients by their respective department heads. The client coordinators discuss the requirements for home care and nursing services with the department heads. The coordinators may request or recommend that a certain home health aide or nurse be assigned to a client. For example, Sally, an aide, may be skilled in organizing a house in disarray. The coordinator requests that Sally be assigned to the initial home visit to prepare the house for the nurse's visit.

The efficiency of this matrix organization is evident in three respects. First, the aides and nurses are members of work pools that increase or decrease in size according to the queue of clients. This pooling circumvents the disruption that would result in traditionally structured departments. Fluctuations in labor pools are planned according to client demands; there is no inefficiency due to idle capacity. Second, the client coordinators are recycled once a client is served. If a client coordinator is assigned to a client who only needs services for two visits, there will be a subsequent assignment of the coordinator to a new client as services for the first are completed. Third, the best staff can be assigned to the most difficult clients. When a client requires special attention, enough flexibility is present to allow special assignments. It is feasible to match skills with client requirements, and in the end this enables more efficient service delivery.

Another major benefit of the integrating role is observed in flexibility. As the number of clients increases or decreases, the agency can adapt. Its temporary structure allows modification of the resource base. In the home health agency example of Figure 6-6, the crucial participants are the director, the client service coordinator, the head of nurses, and the head of home health aides. Regardless of increases or decreases in the number of clients or staff, their managerial positions remain relatively stable.

The matrix structure in the home health agency also allows diversification into other service functions. For example, assume that over the last 2 years the agency has had to reject many clients who require intravenous (IV) therapy. The director has considered making the necessary investment to hire registered nurses. Clients needing IV therapy could be integrated at a number of points with the existing home health services. The organizational structure is flexible enough to allow the expansion. A head of registered nurses (RNs) is hired who oversees the staffing of this third department, or pool, of staff. Initially, this pool of RNs will be smaller than the pools of aides or licensed nurse practitioners (LPNs), but this is a limited problem for the integrating role. Future growth in the number of RNs can be accommodated as for aides and LPNs.

Limitations of Integrating Roles

There are many benefits to using integrating roles and matrix designs, but nurse managers should be aware of the potential pitfalls or limitations that accompany matrix theory. In particular the matrix design violates both the unity of command and the hierarchy of authority, and it is an inappropriate design where work is not divided around projects. Each of these limitations deserves further comment.

Violation of the unity of command principle is perhaps the most glaring fault of matrix theory. According to traditional organizing principles, people in an organization should have one, and only one, superior to whom they report directly. This principle is violated in the matrix theory at a most crucial spot: the staff level. Consider the case of the home health agency presented in Figure 6-6. The aides will discover that they are receiving orders from two sources: the head of home health aides and a client coordinator. Although conflict does not necessarily have to develop among these parties, opportunities for it to do so are numerous.

Violation of unity of command can occur, for example, when the home health agency is operating near capacity. One aide, Karen, has just begun working with a new client. The client coordinator, Sam, is aware of Karen's careful attention to detail and is confident about having her serve this client. During the midafternoon of the second day Sam visits the client to check Karen's progress. He notes that Karen is doing light-duty housework. Almost in rage, Sam asks why Karen is not following his instructions. Karen replies that the head of home health aides, Ted, has asked her to delay personal hygiene chores for the client until the housework is done. This situation provides an uncomfortable confrontation between Ted and Sam. Ted explains that the agency director specifically requested that the housework be rushed through as a favor to the head of nurses even though Ted had not been "officially" ordered to direct the aide's work in this way. Obviously, the problem must be resolved between Sam, Ted, and the agency director. But what about the operating level employee, Karen?

When caught in the unity of command violation, there are several reactions that may be forthcoming from personnel. Most often they side with the superior whom they perceive to have the greatest control over their job and retention. Other employees simply switch to the project for which the greatest concern is expressed. Alternatively, some focus on the project of the supervisor to whom they spoke last. None of these solutions is a satisfactory one from the perspective of the organization. Thus conditions are ripe for employee dissatisfaction. The best solution to violations of unity of command is also the root of the problem: integration must be continually developed and monitored.

The second disadvantage related to matrix models of organization is the problem of hierarchy of authority. An integrator is delegated authority to integrate work, not to produce a service. Thus integrators fill neither true line nor true staff positions. Without formal line authority, the bargaining position of the integrating role is weakened.

The third crucial limitation associated with integrating roles and matrix designs is excessive reliance on projects as the basis for structure. If a health care organization has only one or two services, there may be little reason to restructure around integrating roles. The key to adopting a matrix form is the diversity of projects. Nonetheless, the number of diverse projects is an insufficient criterion for use of a matrix form. Instead, the organization, its climate, and potential improvements (as well as costs) to be accrued by adopting this flexible organizational form must all be evaluated carefully.

Functions of the Project Manager

Integrators are primarily responsible for completing three management functions: planning, organizing, and controlling.[20] First, an integrator or project manager is accountable for the planning function. This means that project goals or objectives must be formulated carefully. Unlike broad organizational goals, which tend to be abstract, project goals should be easily measured and therefore also easily verified. In conjunction with the goals, a project manager must devise tactical procedures for achieving the goals and objectives. The focus is on accomplishing the project in a predetermined time span.

Integrators are responsible for organizing work through providing key leadership. This means that they are the prime source of information about projects. Being the central source of project information establishes the integrator as the main decision maker for the project. As the central organizing point, the integrator must know what resources are needed to assist in project completion. The integrator must establish a project completion schedule and then clearly communicate it to others. An intimate knowledge of project requirements and their contribution to total project costs is essential to maintaining control. All these leadership functions are important in the management of matrix projects.

A third crucial aspect of program or project management is the ability to control the project. Each integrator is ultimately held accountable for the completion of a project. The finished project is only one measure of success, however. The integrator must periodically evaluate progress to determine strengths and weaknesses. Intervention strategies must be formulated to resolve deficiencies. Weak links in the product chain should be identified and strengthened to improve function.

In sum, the matrix structural model is a contemporary design that centers on integrating roles. The integrator is a person who is capable of facilitating project completion by bringing organizational members together. The integrator plans the direction of a project and ascertains when deviations from the plan are occurring before implementing corrective action. Whether through removing barriers to the project (both individual and organizational) or through discussing the project with other managers, supervisors, and subordinates, the integrator's focus is constantly on facilitating projects that the organization deems valuable.

Integrative Models

The search for comprehensive, practical organizational designs has occupied the thoughts of many in the health care field. Some insight has developed out of systems and contingency theories. Integrative theory is a branch of contingency theory that brings together many variables, especially organizational structure. It is a multiple-outcome approach to organizing that incorporates key variables responsible for successful organizational performance.[21] Integrative theory includes the comprehensiveness of systems theory while focusing on relevant variables in specific settings.

Structural-Comparative Theory

The evolution of organization research since the 1960s has been particularly fruitful. The work of Blau, Woodward, Starbuck, Lawrence and Lorsch, Thompson, and many others supports a macroview of organization that is essential for attaining distinctive performance.[22-27] This background has led to a model described by Neuhauser and Andersen as the structural-comparative model.[28] According to Neuhauser and Andersen, a framework for understanding the management or administration of organizations is based on four variables: environment, structure, process, and performance. These variables are interdependent, as shown in Figure 6-7.

The structural-comparative model depicts an open systems approach to managing. It essentially defines an integrative model in which nurse managers must address the interface of environment, structure, and process (i.e., individual and group behavior) to achieve specific performance levels. The structural-comparative theory suggests that both structure and process are crucial variables in the service delivery process. Both structure and process influence performance. As an integrative model, the structural-comparative

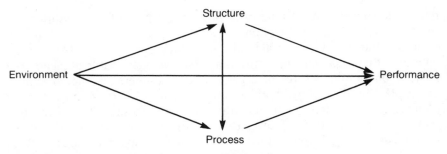

Figure 6-7 Structural-Comparative Theory of Organizations

model is a step up from the closed organization theory offered by bureaucracy. Nevertheless, the structural-comparative theory provides little more than a model of broad relationships. As a result, nurse managers may have difficulty translating the theory into practice.

Configurational Theory

The configurational theory of organizing focuses on three groups of variables: internal organizational design variables (structural variables), contextual variables, and organizational performance.[29] The main theme of integrative theory is that exceptional performance can be achieved by matching the appropriate internal organizational design variables to the external context. A primary deficiency of bureaucracy is its failure to acknowledge the external environment. In comparison, the configurational theory suggests that external factors should be considered carefully when managing organizations. The theory also goes beyond other structural-comparative theories by more extensively specifying management variables.

Efficient and effective performance cannot be achieved unless a proper configuration of internal design variables and context variables is attained, as shown in Figure 6-8. An improper configuration among either the internal design variables or context variables will result in a suboptimal level of performance. Performance is dependent on the management of internal design and the context variables (i.e., independent variables). To be specific, the performance variables (i.e., efficiency and effectiveness) depend on the internal design variables (i.e., work specification, control, reward system, decision making, and work coordination) and on the context variables (i.e., environment, organizational size, technology, and goals).

The environment is central to the philosophy of the configurational theory. In defining the dimensions or characteristics of the task environment, a core typology of environmental dimensions is developed.

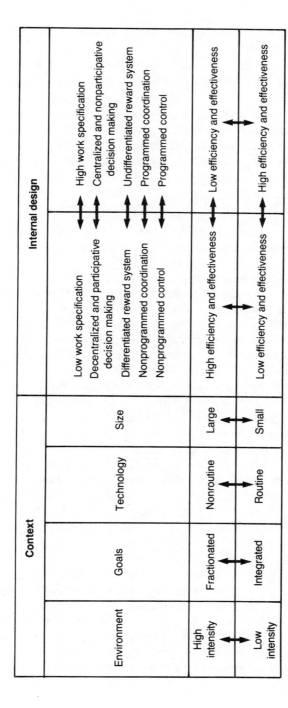

Figure 6-8 The Configuration Theory of Organizations. (The horizontal and vertical arrows indicate that these variables lie on a continuum.) *Source:* Reprinted from *Human Relations,* Vol. 30, No. 3, pp. 275–302, with permission of Plenum Publishing Corporation, © March 1977.

- *Complexity* refers to the number of external factors with which an organization has to contend.
- *Diversity* refers to the extent to which the external factors are different from each other in terms of the nature of the problems that they pose for the organization.
- *Instability* refers to the rapidity with which external factors change over time. Instability may range from a situation in which changes occur rapidly to a situation in which changes occur slowly or hardly at all.
- *Uncertainty* (unpredictability) refers to the extent to which the external factors can be predicted to occur and whether the nature of the problem or the content of the event can be predicted.

Two additional environmental dimensions, hostility (competition) and dependence (reliance on the environment for resources), can be observed in some management environments. These dimensions serve as modifying variables.

When the organization's environment is perceived to be at one end of the continuum represented by the four dimensions, it is defined as an intense task environment. It is intense because its characteristics are numerous (complex), of a diverse nature, changing over time (unstable), and unpredictable (uncertain). Examples of intense environments are rural hospitals in locations with a fluctuating local economy. An environment at the other end of the continuum is defined as a nonintense task environment. In this case, the organization experiences only a few factors (noncomplex), and these are relatively homogenous (nondiverse), do not change much (stable), and are therefore somewhat predictable (certain) in nature. An example of a nonintense environment is a nursing home that is a sole community provider in a community with a rapidly aging population.

The configurational theory of organizations suggests that internal structural variables should be matched, adjusted, or aligned to meet the demands of the context. Why are internal organizational states modified for conditions outside the organization? Today few organizations function as closed systems. Most are highly dependent on outside clients, patients, customers, suppliers (for raw materials, resources, and parts), broad economic trends, legal sanctions, competitors, technological progress, and changing societal values. These forces make it practically impossible for organizations to function independently without concern for forces around them. Hence the environment becomes a key input for the design of an organization.

A medical clinic can be used to illustrate the implementation of the configurational theory. The clinic manager wants to improve the efficiency (or profit) and effectiveness (or patient care quality) of the clinic. Better performance can be achieved by matching the internal structure with the context of the clinic. The clinic manager must first evaluate the external context. How large is the clinic (i.e., How much profit is desired over last year's performance, and how will the number of dissatisfied patients be reduced)? What is the technology (i.e., Is the clinic providing specialty care or general medical practice)? What is the nature of the external environment (i.e., Are attorneys looking for medical malpractice suits, are more clinics entering the area, and are staff nurses hard to obtain)?

Once the clinic manager has developed an appreciation, or perception, of the context, the internal organizational structure can be constructed. Assume that the context is perceived to be nonintense: The clinic is small (i.e., there are six physicians), a 10 percent profit is desired with 15 percent fewer dissatisfied patients, family practice services are delivered, and no other competitors are in a 1-mile radius of the clinic.

For a nonintense environment, the clinic manager must develop an internal structure that reflects a programmed method of work coordination, programmed controls, nondifferentiated personnel rewards, centralized decision making, and high work specification. This can be accomplished easily in the clinic. Work will be completed through well-defined procedures. Each patient receiving care will be highly controlled; that is, the clinic manager will personally discuss with the patients as they leave whether their needs were attended to by the nursing and physician staff members. Personnel will be paid through a defined salary. All major nonclinical operating decisions will be made by the clinic manager. According to the configurational theory, once the structure defined above has been implemented in the clinic, improved performance should result in better patient care and higher profits.

THE PROSPECTS FOR ORGANIZATIONAL DESIGNS IN THE FUTURE

Bureaucracies, matrix organizations, and integrative designs are all viable designs for organizing. What direction will health care organization structures take in the future? From many perspectives, the health care field is at a crucial crossroads. It has reached a point where formal bureaucracies have lost their elasticity for change. This model has served society well over the centuries, but its viability is increasingly in question. Health care organizations are beginning to realize that no amount of tinkering will minimize the inherent deficiencies of a highly structured organization that cannot serve the needs of patients or staff. Health care organizations will need to consider entirely new, innovative designs in the future.

Although the health care field is poised at this crossroads, there is some concern about new options. There is growing recognition that organizational structures are unable to respond to patients or the marketplace. This has led to an examination of alternative structural models. The result is a hybridization that seldom performs as effectively as the original model.

Clearly, formal bureaucratic structures are increasingly less viable for health care organizations and for nursing. It has been suggested that nursing would benefit more from ad hoc organizations that rely on:[30]

- group decision making
- use of experts
- shared communication and coordination
- fluid organizational structures
- decentralization

Even though nurses may prefer such structures, it should be recognized that these changes are inconsistent with the power and interests of physicians and nonclinical managers (i.e., traditional health care managers). Consequently, nurse managers must view the evolving organizational growth of their institutions from a long-term perspective.

NOTES

1. T. Burns and G.M. Stalker, *The Management of Innovation* (London: Tavistock Publications, 1961).

2. M. Weber, *Essays in Sociology*, ed. and trans. H.H. Gerth and C.W. Mills (London: Oxford University Press, 1946).

3. Ibid.

4. A. Smith, *The Wealth of Nations* (New York: Modern Library, 1937).

5. W.V. Heydebrand, *Hospital Bureaucracy* (New York: Dunellen, 1973).

6. F.A. Kramer, *Perspectives on Public Bureaucracy* (Cambridge, MA: Winthrop, 1977).

7. R.P. Hummel, *The Bureaucratic Experience* (New York: St. Martin's Press, 1977).

8. Weber, *Essays in Sociology*.

9. V.A. Thompson, *Modern Organization* (New York: Knopf, 1961).

10. W. Bennis, "Organizational Developments and the Fate of Bureaucracy," *Industrial Management Review* 7 (1966): 41-55.

11. G.E. Berkley, *The Administrative Revolution* (Englewood Cliffs, NJ: Prentice-Hall, 1971).

12. J. Hirsch, "Organizational Structure and Philosophy," *Nursing Administration Quarterly* 11 (1987): 47-62.

13. A.M. Fitzpatrick and C.C. Gaylor, "Max Weber or Jesus Christ: In Whose Image?" *Health Progress* 66 (October 1985): 35-38+.

14. J.C. Clifford, "Managerial Control Versus Professional Autonomy: A Paradox," *Journal of Nursing Administration* 11 (September 1981): 19-21.

15. J. Galbraith, *Designing Complex Organization*, (Menlo Park, CA: Addison-Wesley, 1973).

16. P.R. Lawrence and J. Lorsch, "New Management Job: The Integrator," *Harvard Business Review* 45 (November/December 1967): 142-151.

17. Galbraith, *Designing Complex Organizations*.

18. J. Galbraith, *Organization Design* (Reading, MA: Addison-Wesley, 1971).

19. J.F. Mee, "Matrix Organization," *Business Horizons* 7 (Summer 1964): 70-72.

20. J. Galbraith, "Matrix Organization Designs," *Business Horizons* 14 (February 1971): 29-40.

21. H.L. Tosi, *Theories of Organization* (Chicago: St. Clair Press, 1975).

22. P.M. Blau and W.R. Scott, *Formal Organizations* (San Francisco: Chandler Publishing Co., 1962).

23. P.M. Blau, *The Dynamics of Bureaucracy* (Chicago: University of Chicago Press, 1955).

24. J. Woodward, *Industrial Organization: Theory and Practice* (London: Oxford University Press, 1965).

25. W.H. Starbuck, "Organizational Growth and Development," in *Handbook of Organizations*, ed. J. March (Chicago: Rand McNally, 1965), 73.

26. P. Lawrence and J. Lorsch, *Organization and Environment* (Cambridge, MA: Harvard University Press, 1967).

27. J.D. Thompson, *Organizations in Action* (New York: McGraw-Hill, 1967).

28. D. Neuhauser and R. Andersen, "Structural Comparative Studies of Hospitals," in *Organization Research on Health Institutions*, ed. B.S. Georgopoulos (Ann Arbor, MI: Institute for Social Research, 1972), 128.

29. S.M. Shortell, "The Role of Environment in a Configurational Theory of Organizations," *Human Relations* 30 (March 1977): 275-302.

30. Barbara Fuszard, "Adhocracy in Health Care Institutions?" *Journal of Nursing Administration* 13 (January 1983): 14-19.

Chapter 7

Competition-Driven and Customer-Oriented Strategies

With a great amount of fanfare and visibility, health care organizations are pledging their allegiance to excellence in meeting customers' (i.e., patients') needs, delivering low-cost care, maintaining high standards of quality, and reaching fiscal solvency. This reorientation basically began when investigators identified the leading corporations in America and the management practices that allowed them to qualify for excellence.[1] This focus on excellence has encouraged health care organizations and nursing programs to examine the quality of their output along numerous dimensions, including patient care, cost, productivity, staff job satisfaction, service quality, market penetration, consumer satisfaction, and other key outcome measures. Although a laudable philosophy, managing for excellence soon began to resemble a panacea.

The problem with panaceas is that, once the ideas have been adopted by many organizations, they usually are no longer considered a master strategy option. This is illustrated by past popular management concepts such as managing by objectives, organization culture, quality circles, Japanese management styles, searches for excellence, and one-minute managing. Each of these ideas was once popular with health care managers and the general public. Each concept was ephemeral and enjoyed an explosion of interest, only to be left behind in the search for a new panacea. Consequently, the half-life of these ideas is decreasing because they are discarded rapidly after their initial popularity. Health care organizations are gradually realizing that panaceas cannot substitute for effective implementation of traditional management skills.

Nurse managers will continually be exposed to and partake in this grasping after final solutions. The problem confronting nurse managers is to analyze the integrity of concepts and to ascertain whether further investment should be made in them. Discretion is vital. For example, consider the interest shown in Japanese management styles. The Japanese economy was extremely successful in the 1980s, and forecasts suggest that this performance will continue in the future. There is a natural tendency to assume that Japanese management strategies and tactics are responsible for Japan's phenomenal industrial success (although others argue that Japan's reconstruction after World War II resulted in new industrial plant and equipment, which enabled high productivity). Many corporations and health care organizations want to know how they can adopt Japanese management practices to become equally successful. Painfully, many have discovered that a management approach in one culture has limitations in another culture.

This is not to suggest that Japanese management styles or other similar popular approaches are fruitless. On the contrary, nurse managers need to concentrate on identifying the most promising and applicable elements of a creative or innovative idea.[2] Thus the notion of quality circles is viewed as having considerable promise for nursing programs in hospitals even though Japanese management theory may not be applicable throughout the hospital.[3] Not every element of a new idea or theory is appropriate or applicable to a nursing program, health care organization, industry, or economy.

DISCRETION IN SELECTING NURSE MANAGEMENT STRATEGIES

Although the popularity of the search for excellence appears to be waning, it is crucial to question whether there are still some valuable ideas that nurse executives can adopt for their own approach to managing and for devising competitive, customer-oriented strategies in nursing services. Are there some valuable concepts that should become integral elements of a philosophy underlying nurse management? Japanese management has not achieved universal application in American health care organizations, but many nursing programs did adopt ad hoc and structural changes to facilitate quality circles. The importance of nurse managers' selectively formulating their personal management strategy (and that of their department or program) is illustrated in Figure 7-1.

Management ideas and theory progress in an evolutionary manner under the influence of ongoing research and practice. At any given point in time (t_1), there are additions, deletions, and modifications to the recognized body of knowledge. At later points (t_n), it is possible to observe a more powerful body of knowledge as a result of adding new concepts, deleting incorrect theory, and integrating all appropriate concepts. For example, management theory was improved considerably through the addition of concepts from management by objectives. Setting objectives and measuring the performance of

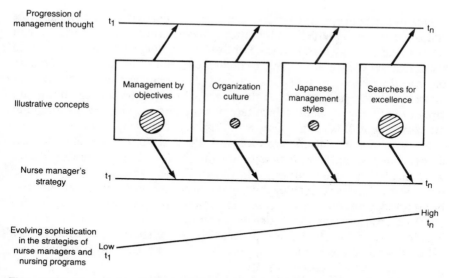

Figure 7-1 A Discretionary Approach to Developing a Nurse Management Strategy

personnel, departments, divisions, programs, or organizations against those objective standards instilled greater rationality in operations. The field did not simply terminate its evolution at that point, however. Other developments in thinking continued.

Management thought evolved through various new additions such as organization culture, Japanese management styles (and their derivatives), searches for excellence, and other contemporary ideas. Over the long run, from t_1 to t_n, management concepts have become more robust and varied. Within any theory at any given time ideas have an inherent integrity (e.g., basic principles of managing), an ephemeral and limited appeal to a specific audience (e.g., behavioral modification), and a promise for redirecting theory (e.g., the contingency view of managing).

As Figure 7-1 suggests, nurse managers formulate an ensemble of these ideas into a personal strategy. The foundation of that strategy at t_1 may be constructed on education or experience. As time progresses toward t_n, nurse managers modify that body of knowledge by adding new concepts and deleting old ideas. The most prevalent contemporary concepts, such as management by objectives, organization culture, Japanese management styles, and searches for excellence, intersect with this knowledge base and influence the strategy adopted by nurse managers (depicted by the circles with diagonal lines in Figure 7-1).

Not every concept will be embraced wholeheartedly in a management style, nor will every idea be automatically incorporated either in whole or in part during strategy formulation. For example, a nurse manager who values authoritarian control is unlikely to delegate responsibility to staff members or subordinate nursing units. Instead, this nurse manager will create mechanisms that allow him or her to retain control. Hence the concept of quality circles in nursing services to facilitate patient care may be neglected by the nurse manager. It is inconsistent with this individual's style of managing.

Nurse managers will strive to adopt only the best elements of new management strategies that have high external validity (or generalizability). Figure 7-1 indicates this selectivity with the diagonal lines. This conveys that nurse managers carefully select concepts; that is, a higher percentage of ideas may be adopted from concepts such as management by objectives and searches for excellence rather than ideas such as organization culture or Japanese management styles (hence the size differences of the shaded circles of Figure 7-1). In sum, a discretionary approach should be used in formulating a personal and nursing program strategy.

Implications for Excellence

The implications of the evolution of a strategy for excellence in nursing services as described above are not important. If nurse managers intend to help other nursing staff members improve nursing care that is oriented toward customers and sensitive to competitive pressures, then they must keep abreast of the latest management ideas. This is shown in Figure 7-1 as evolving sophistication in a personal strategy. Beginning at t_1, creative additions to strategizing are stimulated by new concepts. If nurse managers have made prudent decisions in formulating a strategic management posture, they will be well prepared to lead organizations. The promise of evolving into a first-rate nurse manager depends on exercising discretion in the selection of new and often tantalizing concepts.

PRINCIPLES OF EXCELLENCE AND NURSING SERVICES

A discretionary approach to a personal management strategy suggests that only a few or portions of the latest concepts will be wholly embraced by nurse managers. This also applies to the pursuit of excellence in nursing programs. It is difficult to argue against the pursuit of excellence in health care or, for that matter, in any other endeavor. This is especially true because the guiding objective of health care has always been attaining the highest quality care possible. Consequently, it is only logical that nurse managers contemplate the strategies that they could be formulating and implementing to make nursing services into something distinctive. Such an approach is consistent with traditional thought and philosophy in nursing services and health care delivery.

Table 7-1 illustrates how principles of excellence, one of the most recent advances in management thinking, can be selectively applied in a medical group practice. The purpose of Table 7-1 is to clarify that distinctive ideas can also lead to distinctive health care delivery if they are properly applied. Not every corporation applies or advocates all the ideas of a given concept. A single strategy for attaining excellence may be more philosophically and

Table 7-1 Principles of Excellence in a Medical Group Practice

Concept*	Illustration in a Medical Group Practice
Bias for action	The group assesses its range of clinical specialties biannually with the intention of adding additional physicians when appropriate
Staying close to the consumer	Nurse practitioners are incorporated in treatment and diagnosis to ensure that patients receive personal treatment
Autonomy and entrepreneurship	The success of an occupational and industrial health clinic at a major corporation encourages the medical group to expand its services to other corporations
Productivity through people	The group extends its service delivery productivity by using nurse practitioners in various clinical capacities
Value driven	Medical and nursing staff members meet quarterly to review the group's quality of care and cost of care performance with the intention of maintaining minimum risk and lowest price
Stick-to-the-knitting	Affiliation with a long-term care facility and home health agency are declined
Simple form, lean staff	The group maintains a chief operating officer, a director of nursing, and a medical director (rather than organizing around clinical specialties)
Control with participative management	An ad hoc committee comprising nursing and physician staff periodically assesses strategic and tactical plans involving clinical services

*Source: *In Search of Excellence* by T.J. Peters and R.H. Waterman, Harper & Row Publishers, © 1982.

practically important to some corporations than others. The same is true for nursing departments and programs as well as for health care organizations. Furthermore, it should be remembered that health care organizations (and hence management strategies) seldom remain static. They are ever changing. Consequently, ideas such as principles of excellence are only as good as the results that they consistently produce.

Bias for Action

A bias for action suggests that nurse managers are committed to helping their departments, programs, and teams pursue new levels of goal attainment. They are interested in progress that results in improved patient care or cost control beyond current standards. A bias for action suggests risk taking and implementing plans before their uncertainty is reduced to the lowest level. This implies that feasibility studies are less comprehensive because conclusions are needed immediately. Analysis is not taken to its ultimate limit in proving the potential for success. The purpose of implementing a bias for action is to facilitate a nursing program's or health care organization's effort in better serving patients and beating competition.

For most nurse managers, a bias for action has an inherent conflict with methodical analysis and the built-in safeguards that accompany clinical practice. Nursing care seldom supports risk taking when patients' welfare is involved. Deliberate, analytically driven decision making may be extremely difficult for nurses to leave behind in their managerial roles. Nonetheless, without highly responsive nursing programs and staff (e.g., a willingness to staff an outpatient program until permanent staff can be acquired) health care organizations may be less able to meet or beat competition. Flexibility in service delivery—a bias for action—could eventually characterize nursing programs and nurse managers that thrive in the resource- and reimbursement-constrained future.

A bias for action does not imply totally discarding analytical methods or analysis itself before reaching decisions or implementing plans. It simply means that after a certain point continued analysis leads to indecision. The marginal benefits of further analysis decrease as time goes by. The health care organization may lose its competitive advantage, or new factors may prevent the pursuit of an option (e.g., interest rates may go up substantially and prevent acquisition of diagnostic equipment whose purchase would have been feasible at previous lower interest rates).

A bias for action in a medical group practice may be illustrated by commitment to a biannual assessment of clinical specialties. The purpose of the analysis is to ascertain whether a new medical specialty (and clinical staff) should be added. Whether or not a specialty is added does not constitute the main issue. Rather, commitment to periodically reviewing the need for a new specialty—a bias for action—differentiates effective from ineffective management strategy. Although the ultimate decision may be that no action is taken, such a decision is better than no review whatsoever.

Staying Close to the Consumer

Corporations have observed that better results are attained when the focus is consumers. Health care organizations and nurse managers should not forget that the demand for their services is predicated on satisfying patients and clients. If patients are not pleased with how a particular service is delivered, they may take their business elsewhere. Admittedly, patients still depend on clinicians for decisions regarding inpatient care, but there is a greater propensity for consumerism, choice, and mobility in the marketplace today. Therefore, it is imperative that health care organizations orient themselves toward serving the interests of their patients.

Nurse managers recognize that health care organizations traditionally have not been as consumer oriented as most business organizations. This has minimized the understanding and application of patient-oriented services as based on the principle of staying close to consumers. There are several reasons for this occurrence:

- Decisions regarding where patients receive inpatient care have primarily been determined by providers, not by patients.
- A shortage of physicians made patients happy to receive care even though it was on the terms of the physician. These terms often implied high psychic and real costs to the consumer.
- Third-party payments were generous in benefits covered and costs paid regardless of the amenity level surrounding services delivered. Few incentives existed for cost control because patients did not feel directly the impact of high costs. Premium payments on health insurance were covered extensively by employers.
- There is an inelastic demand for medical care. Disease generates a high demand for health care services. There are relatively few medical care suppliers, and there is a prevailing high demand for service because medical care is not a discretionary good. Morbidity creates an inelastic demand.

Until the 1980s the preceding factors (and others) have allowed health care providers to remain aloof from patients. Almost all these causal agents have changed in the last decade. Change in health care organizations and by providers has been slow, however.

There are many ways to illustrate the new focus of health care providers and organizations on patients, clients, and consumers. For example, physician services are more attuned to patient needs as a result of fundamental alterations in medical technology, the supply of physicians, reimbursement, and the evolution of group practices. All these diverse pressures are forcing physicians to reconsider their relationship to patients. The same is true for health care organizations such as hospitals. Innovations in delivering care on an outpatient basis, commitment to early patient discharge, and growing emphasis on health maintenance within the specifications of prepaid plans are several causal factors that have generated alternatives to lengthy inpatient stays. Furthermore, employers are presenting their employees with managed care plans that predetermine where beneficiaries receive either primary or acute care.

Table 7-1 illustrates this concept for a medical group practice. A medical group may decide that it needs to improve productivity (i.e., number of patients served) dramatically. It decides to hire several nurse practitioners to assist in the process of delivering primary care. These nursing professionals receive their overall supervision from a nurse manager who consults with a physician. This arrangement allows the group practice to focus on the needs and satisfaction of its patients. Because many of the primary care tasks are completed or initiated by the nurse practitioner, physicians can increase their productivity (i.e., in diagnosing and treating patient conditions).

In pursuing excellent patient care, the medical group may be willing to trade off some physician productivity for patient satisfaction. Under this condition the nurse practitioners are still responsible for delivering primary care, but a physician oversees every patient through an exit examination. The primary purpose of minimizing the physician's allocated time in patient care is to stay close to the patient. This not only gives the patient the impression that care is received from a physician but also allows the nursing staff to utilize fully their care delivery skills. Although the policy of a physician's conducting an exit examination for every patient is duplicative, it may reinforce the principle of patient service. This additional effort may also be worthwhile if it helps physicians remain in touch with consumers.

Autonomy and Entrepreneurship

Excellence in business corporations is attainable when autonomy and entrepreneurship are reinforced. Entrepreneurial effort is an idea with definite implications for health care organizations and nurse managers. The more a nursing program, team, department, or division develops new ideas that result in a good rate of return or improved patient care, the greater the freedom to pursue other successful endeavors. In this sense, health care organizations should actively (and perhaps aggressively) support the efforts of nursing programs and other service units that generate creative and productive ideas. Corporations that have attained excellence observe that units demonstrating a willingness to act as service champions also need autonomy to pursue their efforts fully.

Schumacher has suggested that these entrepreneurial efforts can be reinforced in even the most bureaucratic organization.[4] Naturally, some danger exists that excessive autonomy will be abused and that the nursing unit will overly pursue its goals while hindering the attainment of organizational goals. This problem can be prevented if reward and accountability systems reinforce organizational goals, however.

As far as health care organizations are concerned, there is considerable justification for promoting entrepreneurship in nursing programs. The days of low-level competition are gone. It is imperative that health care organizations nurture services, departments, programs, or products that have distinctive competence and that serve as models to other organizational units. The key is to make excellent services highly visible and for nurse managers to market such efforts.[5,6] By maintaining a high profile for nursing services that are championed by the organization, the value ascribed to these units can be reinforced. Furthermore, these efforts alert consumers to unique or distinctive services with highly attractive features. Nurse managers are responsible for developing distinctive programs and then striving to make certain that they are marketed in and outside their organizations.[7]

An illustration of autonomy and excellence in a medical group practice is a new occupational and industrial health program. To increase patient visits, the group practice enters into coalitions with several local business corporations. The first clinic at a corporation shows promising results. The medical group is able to utilize more fully its staff of nurse practitioners in primary care. The contract with the first corporation provides added revenues for the group practice. Patients with a need for continuing care are identified and incorporated in the total patient load. The corporation discovers that it can provide highly accessible care at a reasonable cost. It conveys this result to several business associates, who contact the group about a similar program.

At this point the group practice must determine the extent to which it will specialize in occupational and industrial health. For a group practice, this is a momentous decision. By following the principle of autonomy and entrepreneurship, however, the group practice decides to expand the occupational and industrial health program. Furthermore, a specific program unit is created in the group practice to nurture this distinctive and entrepreneurial effort. In other words, the occupational and industrial health program becomes a separate department or even a subsidiary. Now it can devise ingenious plans for expanding services within the constraints of the total group practice. Autonomy is permitted for decisions about staffing, resource allocation, and specific services to be delivered during the negotiation process with corporate customers.

As nursing managers, nursing programs, and health care organizations advocate and reinforce autonomy and entrepreneurship, they will be better prepared to provide a service orientation that is consistent with the competitive environment.[8] The health system needs new methods of organizing and delivering services. Intense competition is growing among hospitals for patients at the acute and primary care levels. Autonomy and entrepreneurship could provide a feasible response to these forces and at the same time help nursing programs and health care organizations progress toward excellence.

Productivity through People

Business organizations have discovered that the best way to attain high productivity is through effectively managing people. This is especially true in service sectors because the common denominator is people. This concept also applies in many industrial sectors, where people control machines, equipment, and other production assets. Unless people are satisfied, productivity can suffer. This realization is not foreign to the health care field. Health care managers are generally highly cognizant of the need to emphasize human resource management.

Although nursing programs and health care organizations have traditionally supported their staff members, it appears that further consideration (to this relationship) is necessary in view of growing resource constraints. Many health care organizations are cutting staff to control their costs. Hospitals have been especially notable for cutting nurse staffing to conserve resources while simultaneously pushing for higher productivity from remaining nurses to compensate for staff reductions. This produced a great deal of animosity among nurses and hospitals. Not only do nurses observe that they have fewer staff members to work with, they also notice that they are being asked to provide more services. Despite demands for higher productivity, salaries are seldom raised commensurately. The result is a significant morale problem with undesirable consequences: turnover, absenteeism, medical risk for patients, dismal working climate, and similar problems.

Nurse managers need to be highly ingenious in selecting strategies to promote staff productivity. High productivity through people may lead to excellence, but it should be recognized that attaining high productivity is difficult given existing constraints. Even with team development, incentive compensation, primary nursing care, career ladders, and other recent developments, it may be difficult to raise nurse productivity to desired levels.

As Table 7-1 illustrates, a group practice might try to increase physician productivity by substituting nurse practitioners at the primary care level. If health care organizations want to improve productivity, they may have to alter traditional methods of providing care. In the case of a medical group practice, this policy could be controversial depending on physician personalities, the goals of the group, and prevailing reimbursement regulations. If the practice is basically fee-for-service, then nurse practitioners might be inappropriate. In contrast, a group practice that participates in a prepaid plan may discover that the nurse practitioners complement service delivery efforts quite admirably.

Productivity through people is an excellent idea, and one that is needed by any nursing program or health care organization. Health care is no different from other economic sectors in this regard. Although nursing departments and health care organizations already have a long history of supporting their staff members, the general environment or context has changed radically. The constraints presented by this environment reduce the flexibility of nurse managers in leading and directing staff nurses. This suggests that greater innovation will be needed in how staff are managed.

Value Driven

Corporations have found that excellence is often associated with a commitment to a defined set of values. As a result, there is interest not only in communicating these values to staff but in working to ensure that these values influence the structure, process, and results. Value-driven corporations have charismatic leaders who embody the values of the organization. These leaders provide a visible model while reinforcing the prevailing value set. Such leaders are able to drive corporations toward higher performance because there is less uncertainty about what the business stands for.

Nurse managers may be able to apply this principle in some situations if they have a charismatic nature, are able to instill the mindset of value orientation in the nursing staff, or can focus staff attention on a limited set of goals. As far as the charismatic nature is concerned, research has yet to explain why some people are more gifted with this talent than others. Consequently, it may be more fruitful for nurse managers to focus staff attention on a specific value set. The challenge is to create an almost fanatical obsession with nursing service and health care organization goals. Excessive reinforcement, however, can have a deleterious effect as well.

For example, the medical group practice in Table 7-1 decides that two goals drive the organization: minimum medical risk and low prices. In an effort to reinforce the preeminence of these goals, medical and nursing staff meet quarterly to review the medical group's quality of care and cost of care. The purpose of such meetings is twofold: to ensure commitment on the part of each staff member (i.e., colleagues have a similar vested interest in the group's goals) and to provide a periodic, comprehensive review of effort toward achieving these goals. These fundamental steps are essential in creating a mutually accepted and self-reinforcing set of values.

Values represent the fundamental thread that binds a nursing unit and staff together. A value is essentially a concept of the desirable. Hence the important aspect of value-driven nursing programs and health care organizations is a shared view of what constitutes the desirable. Unless all nursing staff share in the belief of desired behavior and performance, then suboptimization may occur. There will be a high tendency for individuals to pursue their own agendas, which may conflict with the team's, patients', and organization's interests. Congruent effort is essential in achieving excellence.

Conflict between individual nurses and their organization is inevitable, but successful health care organizations are able to match individual goals with organizational goals. Inevitably, there will be disparity between what is best for a nurse and what is best for the health care organization. There may be disagreement between what a nurse feels is a priority and what the organization intends to accomplish.

The best means of preventing value conflicts is extraordinary attention to recruitment and selection of nursing staff members. Without this attention to value congruency, there may be few opportunities to establish a good match between nursing staff and organizational goals. Even where such effort is undertaken, there is always the potential need for successively redefining the desired goals by either the individual or the organization. Maturation is a prevalent phenomenon for both people and organizations.

In summary, value-driven health care organizations maintain an almost fanatical obsession with specific values and goals. For the group practice illustrated in Table 7-1, the focus may be the quality of care, the cost of care, and the amenity level accompanying service delivery. Whatever the goals, the ability to obtain agreement among the staff about a distinctive set of values is the fundamental point from which excellence begins. By focusing attention on the values (concepts of the desirable), a context is developed that is conducive to improved decision making and performance.

Stick-to-the-Knitting

Corporations have learned that a balance must be achieved between entrepreneurial effort and stability. A stable organization is able to pursue economies of scale. It is better able to concentrate on fine tuning of operations. Excellence is also achieved when stability is improved through innovation. Identifying new markets that complement the overall organization is essential to the infusion and renewal of vitality in an organization. Over the long run, it is the balance of stability and innovation that helps promote excellence.

Many health care organizations, particularly hospitals, are faced with a threatening environment. Not only are revenues decreasing, but patient demand for some services is curtailed because of changes in benefits and the incentives accompanying managed care (e.g., copayments and deductibles). These are upsetting events because the health care field has always been viewed as an extremely stable industry. The introduction of prospective pricing, alternative delivery systems, the undersupply of nurses, hospital closures, and similar trends are factors that have shaken this stability. As a result, there is a search for panaceas for current problems. With no foreseeable solutions to declining average length of stay, admissions, and occupancy, some hospitals are diversifying their services to expand their revenue base. Diversification is viewed as an innovative solution to a critical condition.

The problem with expansion through diversification is its haphazard nature. Granted, the problem of declining revenues is a significant problem because hospitals have traditionally held fairly limited visions of their services. Nevertheless, falling revenue is not a sufficient reason to adopt immediately any attractive investment opportunity that suddenly appears. A guiding rationale should underlie diversification. Health care organizations, especially hospitals, face a difficult challenge in balancing this rationale with the need to be more innovative in defining their line of business. In other words, the health field needs an infusion of creativity, innovation, experimentation, and diversification. Discretion is a prerequisite to change, however.

Corporations are often enticed down paths of excessive diversification because some opportunities appear to be too good to pass up. Consequently, less emphasis is given to how opportunities relate to organizational mission, purpose, goals, and values compared with the expected return on investment. Diversification opportunities also confuse how operations will be structured because a logical, compatible framework among services and productive functions is seldom predefined. Without an effective infrastructure, it becomes impossible to link programs together and thus to provide excellence in either service or product.

The culmination of these ideas is the recognition that health care organizations need to stick to their knitting. They must concentrate on those services that they produce best. Deviation from these efforts is encouraged to the extent that a logical connection is maintained with the overall service delivery effort. Health care organizations and nurse managers are particularly cautioned about sticking to the knitting at a time when there may be excessive pressure to diversify services. It takes extraordinary courage and the development of rigorous assessment criteria to resist popular trends in the health field.[9] With health care organizations setting their sights on a new definition of service delivery, it is extremely important that they also avoid overdiversification. By taking on too much in the way of new services, they may inadvertently limit their options.

An example of sticking to the knitting for the medical group illustrated in Table 7-1 involves a proposition by a long-term care facility to secure continuing medical referral for its skilled nursing patients. The long-term care facility is interested in covering patients' primary medical care. This appears to be a propitious opportunity for the medical group because the long-term care facility provides a relatively captive audience. But is it in the best interests of the medical group? Perhaps not. The medical group may specialize in pediatrics or family practice and not be overly oriented toward geriatric medicine. Hence the consistent patient base may not fit well with the group's efforts. It would not allow the medical group to stick to its knitting.

For nurse managers the message of stick to the knitting is valuable because it forces them to focus on specific nursing program goals. By questioning where new opportunities will redirect a nursing program, nurse managers can maintain a specific emphasis in the effort to attain excellence. Overextending into areas that offer a good return on investment but jeopardize the ability to continue providing excellent nursing services is a problem that nurse managers can help their organizations avoid.

Simple Form, Lean Staff

Corporations have discovered that excellence is easier to attain when there are few administrative layers. Excessive managerial levels block valuable information, distort facts and perceptions, and breed rumors. As a result, decision makers may not make high-quality decisions because the intervening bureaucratic layers hinder information flows. The remedy is to cut through the bureaucratic layers, thereby providing decision makers with a crystal-clear perspective of external and internal events that affect the organization. They gain better insight into how the organization is functioning. Only with a clear view of these issues can decisions be made that drive organizations toward excellence. When excessive administrative layers or a complex structure blocks perspective, the quality of decisions ultimately will deteriorate.

The principle of simple organizational form and lean staff is readily apparent in the field of business, but the health care field has much to learn in this regard. Most health care organizations maintain at least one line of organizational authority (i.e., management) and sometimes two (i.e., the medical staff) or three (i.e., the nursing staff). Often, these lines of authority are readily depicted on the formal organizational chart, but in some cases they are merely implied. The result is possible confusion in decision making surrounding service delivery.

Health care organizations and nursing programs should be actively pursuing a simple organizational form with lean (management) staffing. This principle is congruent with the need to keep overhead costs to a minimum. The result of maintaining relatively simple structures with minimal managerial staffing is a hands-on approach to managing. The end results are more effective management and the ability to achieve organizational excellence. Many factors hinder this notion because managers become comfortable with administrative assistants and staff support. This also implies, however, that they are removed from operations and not in a position to implement control.

An example of simple form and lean staff is easily seen in the medical group practice contemplating reorganization. As Table 7-1 suggests, the group has decided to maintain only one manager of operations along with a medical director and a director of nursing. None of the clinical specialties or subspecialties uses a clinical department chairperson. All physicians report to the medical director. The manager is in charge of the business operations. This relatively simple form provides sufficient management of operations. Strategy is contributed by the medical director, the director of nursing, and the manager of operations. The group avoids the cost of physicians' investing time as clinical chairperson's. Overhead expenses are also avoided. The medical director spends less time on clinical care, but this is offset by the gains from the clinical chairperson's not devoting time to administrative issues.

As many health care organizations have discovered, the amount of administrative work to be completed somehow magically grows to exceed any number of available administrators. A point is eventually reached where administrative costs exceed the value gained from administration. Nurse managers need to be alert to this problem not only in terms of inefficiency but also in terms of the blockages that are introduced to effective decision making.

Control with Participative Management

A final determinant of excellence is the ability to combine control with participative management. This is a significant challenge that involves delicate balancing of countervailing forces. Adjustments in organizational structure and delegation of authority often have to be made over years before a harmonious balance is attained. The idea is to delegate sufficient authority in decision making that managers feel (and indeed actually are) responsible for and participate in controlling operations. Simultaneously, control must be centralized to ensure goal attainment.

The best control is almost always achieved at the lowest level in organizational hierarchies. The responsibility of top management is to analyze lower-level managers, their capabilities, the significance of their decisions, and the need to improve performance. By delegating the responsibility to make decisions and to control performance (i.e., the consequences of decisions), a healthier morale can surface in the management staff. There is a tendency for operating level managers to exercise great caution in view of their added authority and the desire to prove their capability in handling responsibilities.

The alternative to a participative management structure (with decentralized control) is highly centralized control. In complex organizations such as health care organizations, centralized control is not always a prudent strategy. Centralized control means that decisions are made at or near the top of the hierarchy of authority. The impression is that top management does not trust the capabilities of staff to make the right decisions or to complete tasks in a responsible manner.

A preferable alternative to authoritarian control systems in the health care field is a participative approach. Such systems motivate and reinforce individual responsibility. For example, in a medical group practice an ad hoc committee comprising staff physicians and nurses, clinicians who are not otherwise involved in management issues, functions as a control mechanism. The committee meets periodically (e.g., every quarter) to review strategic and tactical plans developed by top management. Alternatively, the committee might meet periodically to assess clinical accomplishments. The point is that clinicians are integrated into the control system of the group practice. The control system has the purpose of promoting high-quality care and low-cost service delivery. Hence clinicians are directly incorporated in the management control system.

PRIMARY FACTORS DRIVING EXCELLENCE

Nurse managers can easily recognize that not all the principles of excellence discovered in the corporate world are necessarily applicable in health care management. Some principles may be more relevant than others as conditions in the health care field change. Consequently, nurse managers are never totally relieved from continually questioning whether their strategies are promoting mediocrity or excellence. No one is going to do this for them. They should personally analyze the results of their endeavors to determine whether it is time to switch approaches.

Notwithstanding the responsibility to remain vigilant in assessing the effectiveness of management strategies, some of the principles of excellence are more applicable in health care organizations than others. The primary principles supporting excellence in health care and nursing services are summarized in Table 7-2. A careful reading of the health care environment indicates that some of the principles for achieving excellence are more relevant than others. With the appropriate environmental changes, other principles may rise in importance. Nurse managers can monitor the context to ascertain when such changes take place.

Table 7-2 Primary Principles Supporting Excellence

*Principle**	*Rationale for Relevance*
Bias for action	Prospective payment and competition require distinctive reactions from nursing programs and health care organizations to lower costs and meet competition. Without these strategic reactions, there is a danger of not adapting to the constraints and opportunities of the environment.
Staying close to the consumer	The delivery of health, medical, and nursing care has been influenced by reimbursement policies; specifically, cost-based reimbursement has removed the incentive to serve patients. With the evolution of prospective payment and managed care plans, opportunities are increasing for patients to switch providers. This acts as an incentive to health care providers to concentrate on serving their customers.
Autonomy and entrepreneurship	Increased competition means that nursing programs and health care organizations must promote services that have distinctive competence. Autonomy should be given to programmatic efforts that maximize innovation. Centers of excellence can be formed around these distinctive services.
Stick-to-the-knitting	There are pressures for diversification that result from competition and prospective payment. The implication for health care organizations and nursing programs is that they must not stretch themselves too thin into areas of limited or no competence.

*Source: In Search of Excellence by T.J. Peters and R.H. Waterman, Harper & Row Publishers, © 1982.

A PERSONAL MANAGEMENT STRATEGY

Nurse managers may be interested in how they can translate the concepts of excellence into a personal management strategy. In other words, what should nurse managers do to develop their own managerial strategies for promoting and for achieving excellence? Are there any implications from the corporate principles of excellence for nurse managers? These questions are basically answered in Table 7-3, which explains how each of the principles requires a specific posture or set of actions on the part of nurse managers.

Many of the specific recommendations in Table 7-3 have already been explained in the foregoing evaluation of principles of excellence. Nonetheless, a brief summary of these strategies provides a useful profile of the posture that nurse managers should strive to achieve in promoting excellence. The overall thrust is conveyed by the bias for action. A personal management strategy for nurse managers should be based on making decisions as quickly as possible once relevant information is available. Indecision results in missed opportunities. On the other hand hasty action results in excessive problems, so that nurse managers must be decisive and then implement decisions in a manner that produces immediate results and allows for long-run growth.

A bias for action and the resultant propensity to make decisions is supported by a distinct priority: continued reflection on patient needs. Therefore, decisions and the programs or services surrounding those decisions should be patient oriented. Contemplating what a specific decision implies for patients can temper ensuing analysis of other criteria surrounding decisions (e.g., return on investment, quality of care, or community service). Fanatical attention to patient service is a unique concept in the health care field, but it is a tradition that must be developed if health care organizations expect to reinforce patient loyalty.

Nurse managers can be innovative in their management styles while at the same time acting as entrepreneurs. This means that new, even unusual, ideas are thoroughly examined before they are discarded. A nursing program or health care organization can only remain vibrant if it promotes creative ideas. Innovation and the commitment to examine extreme proposals is a beginning basis for creativity. Nevertheless, there is also a need to temper these proposals with a realistic attitude toward how services will be expanded or modified. Nurse managers can avoid the tendency to overly diversify services and products. They should produce excellence over a small range of services rather than mediocrity over a large range of possibilities.

Beyond these suggestions, the effective nurse manager should be concerned with creating a management style that acknowledges the importance of human factors. In terms of interpersonal relations, nurse managers can manage in such a manner that emphasizes that productivity depends on

Table 7-3 Translating Concepts of Excellence into a Personal Management Strategy

Concept*	Implications for Personal Management Strategies of Nurse Managers
Bias for action	Belief is cultivated that decisions should be made as soon as possible when the most relevant information has been assessed. Implementation of decisions pursues the path of the most immediate results.
Staying close to the consumer	When nurse managers are faced with decisions that juxtapose the needs of patients with those of the organization, the patient's interests are considered to have higher priority. Programs and services are designed and adjusted to serve patients.
Autonomy and entrepreneurship	New ideas are thoroughly examined before they are discarded. Innovation is encouraged to instill vitality. Effective nursing programs, departments, or teams are given more independence as they are able to produce results.
Productivity through people	Interpersonal relations are based on the recognition that only people produce services. The nursing staff is progressively cultivated for its commitment to performance.
Value driven	Those in charge of nursing teams, programs, or departments are those who produce the services.
Stick-to-the-knitting	Diversification of services is only undertaken when a diversification alternative relates to services in which the health care organization or nursing department has attained recognition and prominence.
Simple form, lean staff	Sufficient managerial and clinical staff are maintained to do a job correctly. Superfluous staff positions are not instituted. Nurse managers regularly audit the need for staff at management and clinical levels.
Control with participative management	Strategic nursing units, programs, and departments are responsible for direct control over operations; the highest nurse executive retains control over all operations.

*Source: In Search of Excellence by T.J. Peters and R.H. Waterman, Harper & Row Publishers, © 1982.

people. A staff or team is selected and progressively fine tuned around the idea of commitment to excellence. Leadership is assigned to those who best know how to produce excellent services.

The management of interpersonal relations and leadership will occur in some organizational structure. For many situations nurse managers will create a simple administrative structure that is lean on management positions. Even if periodic audits are needed to ensure that administration has not become too top heavy, nurse managers should contemplate the possibilities of managing through people and attaining control by the most direct methods feasible (i.e., through the staff itself).

In sum, nurse managers are in a strong position to promote excellence in performance if a proper management style is implemented. There is a significant difference between describing a management style (i.e., presenting a foundation for success) and actually implementing it. For this reason, it is important that nurse managers keep the preceding guidelines in mind when they formulate strategies and make decisions. The guidelines should help them articulate and implement a management style that produces results.

There is the potential for wide variability in interpreting the guidelines for managing. Nonetheless, the basis for effective management has always been careful forethought, selection of standards for behavior, and implementation in concert with those standards. It is up to the individual nurse manager to provide the personal effort needed to achieve a management style that is consistent with the guidelines defined above.

CONTRIBUTION OF NURSE MANAGERS TO EXCELLENCE

What is the feasible contribution of nurse managers to excellence in health care organizations? An answer to this question should recognize that the nursing staff alone does not determine excellence. Many factors facilitate or prevent excellence in health care organizations besides nurses and nurse managers. It is necessary to recognize that the strategic role of nurse managers in health care organizations has been less than extensive or visible. In view of these limitations, it is clear that nurse managers face considerable obstacles in driving their programs and organizations to excellence. Foremost is the need to promote factors that lead to excellence while minimizing factors that prevent excellence. This relationship is illustrated in Figure 7-2.

As Figure 7-2 suggests, a nurse manager's contribution to strategic management is tempered by a number of organizational and environmental factors. These factors result in maintaining the status quo and mediocrity despite best efforts to the contrary. Simultaneously a number of factors facilitate excellence, which results in progress toward changes in the structure, process, and outcomes of health care delivery. The nurse manager is positioned between these two forces.

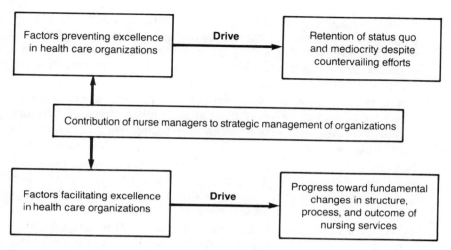

Figure 7-2 Nurse Managers' Contribution to Service Excellence

Nurse managers must produce a management style with strategies that minimize the factors preventing excellence while maximizing improvement in organizational outcomes. As long as the forces preventing excellence are allowed to dominate (because of poor management style or strategy), nurse managers are caught in a bind that is challenging at best.

Factors Preventing Excellence

There are a number of factors in the health care field that prevent attainment of excellence:

- reliance on third-party reimbursement, which has generated an attitude that most service delivery costs will be covered by some form of insurance or subsidy. Reimbursement has also stimulated the attitude that health care organizations inhabit a fail-safe environment (i.e., that fiscal solvency is guaranteed by third-party payments).
- existence of a predominant 70 percent nonprofit orientation in hospitals. Because hospitals set the tone for other health care services, there is a pervasive public belief that only minimal return on investment is appropriate in health care. Consequently, health care organizations are managed with a nonprofit attitude.
- separation of the medical staff from the line organization (i.e., administration and support services), which has produced minimal communication, a convenient point for extensive conflict, and the deletion of the

medical staff from risk sharing in organizational efforts. Clinicians (especially physicians) are outside the management control system and need to be more closely involved to the extent that they share in the risk of health care organization performance (whether in terms of profitable results or significant losses).

- lack of incentives for competing with other organizations or programs, which has caused many health care organizations to stagnate. Without competition there is little or no motivation to improve otherwise mediocre or dismal services.

- lack of sophisticated management and marketing skills, which has arisen as a result of few incentives to operate lean, efficient organizations and few incentives to compete openly. Health care organizations are unprepared in many management and marketing dimensions.

- existence of a value system that is centered on quality of care, which has removed concern for costs. Substantial lead time is needed to revise this dominant value system because of its pervasiveness.

These are the main forces that promotes mediocrity in health care organizations.

The relative impact of these factors on excellence is displayed in Table 7-4. This assessment evaluates the degree to which specific factors hinder attainment of organizational excellence. Although it is possible to argue about any specific value (i.e., low, medium, or high) in Table 7-4, the purpose is not to provide a single conclusive statement about any single factor's impact on the principles of excellence. Rather, Table 7-4 is an attempt to profile the overall influence of the factors on strategic management.

With the exception of staying close to the customer and the need to stick to the knitting, the factors in Table 7-4 have been instrumental in threatening excellence in nursing programs and health care organizations. By and large the lack of incentives for competition, cost-based reimbursement, and the nonprofit orientation in the health care field have weighed heavily on the side of promoting mediocrity. The quality of care–centered value system has also hindered some standards of excellence because it reflects a one-sided value system that limits the pursuit of excellence in other areas (e.g., cost control).

Nurse managers are unable to influence significantly some of the factors hindering organizational excellence. These factors are systemwide in nature and minimally affected by the efforts of any single nurse manager. Nevertheless, nurse managers can take responsibility for ensuring that these factors are minimized in their own programs. This means that they need to implement a management style with corresponding strategies that rebuffs the factors promoting mediocrity.

Table 7-4 Factors Preventing Excellence in Health Care Organizations

Corporate Principles for Excellence*	Extent to Which Factors Hinder Organizational Excellence					
	Reliance on Cost-Based Reimbursement	Nonprofit Orientation	Separation of Medical Staff from Line Organization	Few Incentives for Competition	Lack of Sophistication in Management and Marketing	Value System Centered on Quality of Care
Bias for action	High	High	High	High	Medium	Low
Staying close to the consumer	Low	Low	High	Low	Low	High
Autonomy and entrepreneurship	High	High	High	High	High	High
Productivity through people	Medium	Medium	Medium	High	Medium	High
Value driven	Medium	High	Medium	High	Medium	High
Stick-to-the-knitting	Low	Low	Low	Low	Low	High
Simple form, lean staff	High	High	High	Low	High	Low
Control with participative management	Low	Low	High	Low	High	High

*Source: In Search of Excellence by T.J. Peters and R.H. Waterman, Harper & Row Publishers, © 1982.

Factors Facilitating Organizational Excellence

Nurse managers should recognize that, just as there are a number of factors preventing excellence, there are factors facilitating organizational excellence that they can use to their benefit. A judicious reading of the health care context suggests that the following factors may influence organizational excellence.

* The presence of third-party reimbursement provides a financial support that protects solvency. Because this factor can create an attitude of limited concern, it also is a benefit. Failure is a low probability (all other factors considered). Third-party reimbursement not only is a fact that helps health care organizations plan for revenue inflows but also presents the benefit of supporting the financial risk (and hence the borrowing capacity for long-term debt) of most organizations.
* The rise of competition implies that health care organizations have more motivation and specific reasons for changing their status quo. Competition increases the threat of failure and hence forces all staff to reassess their commitment and productivity. This is especially true for clinical staff for whom formal arrangements have been instituted for risk sharing.
* The rising involvement of investor-owned corporations in health care has stimulated awareness among all health care organizations—public, private, and voluntary—that they must improve their performance. The impression is that, unless an organization is careful in protecting its market share, investor-owned corporations in the health field will be attracted to a competitive opportunity. Furthermore, corporate involvement has legitimized the pursuit of profit in health care. Although there still is resistance to profit, corporate involvement has fostered greater concern for financial performance.
* More health care organizations are diversifying into new service areas. Diversification is accompanied by an expanded vision of the possible. It causes health care organizations to be creative and innovative in their strategic planning. In this fashion, it promotes an infusion of new thinking that ultimately may lead to excellence.
* Health care organizations are more accepting of new organizational forms that offer significant improvements over traditional bureaucratic structures. The rise of alternative delivery modes (e.g., health maintenance organizations, preferred provider organizations, and independent practice associations) as well as joint venturing has increased the opportunities to achieve excellence in service delivery.

- A new value system is developing in the health care field that balances quality of care and cost. There is still considerable progress to be made in establishing the right combination or balance of these two end results. Nonetheless, through attention to costs the issue of quality can be reexamined and placed in better perspective. Although this balance of cost and quality causes some turmoil, progress toward equating these factors will eventually create stronger health care organizations from a financial and economic perspective.

These are the main forces that lift health care organizations above mediocrity and facilitate organizational excellence.

The relative impact of these factors on the principles of excellence is shown in Table 7-5. It should be noted that there is diversity in the precise impact of factors facilitating organizational excellence. It is apparent, however, that third-party payment, competition, and the growth of corporate involvement are the most important factors facilitating organizational excellence. Admittedly this assessment is open to interpretation, but the ratings given in Table 7-5 are an attempt to convey the general supporting factors behind principles of excellence.

Nurse managers can use these facilitating factors to promote excellence in their programs and organizations. This may mean that they develop management strategies with the full confidence that some supports exist that reinforce efforts to attain excellence. Not all these factors will be applicable at any given point in time, nor are they all equally powerful in promoting excellence. When strategies and tactics are being formulated to move an organization toward excellence, however, these compensating factors should be remembered and used to their fullest.

CONCLUSION

Nurse managers are responsible for developing strategies that lead nursing programs (and, as a result, health care organizations) toward excellent performance. There are essentially two components of this strategy formulation process: designing a personal strategy and designing programmatic or team strategies. Ideally, these two strategies should be fused as one, but organizational constraints sometimes prevent this synergy. A personal strategy that advocates excellence (or some other desirable objective) can always be pursued by nurse managers even though the organization does not provide sufficient resources to support the strategy's general development. For example, a head nurse of an obstetrics unit may personally advocate and attempt to apply a patient-oriented climate despite the fact that several

Table 7-5 Factors Facilitating Excellence in Health Care Organizations

Corporate Principles for Excellence*	Extent to Which Factors Facilitate Organizational Excellence					
	Presence of Third Party Reimbursement	Rise of Competition	Rise of Corporate Involvement	Diversification	Acceptance of Innovative Organizational Forms	Value System Balancing Quality of Care and Cost
Bias for action	High	High	High	High	High	Medium
Staying close to the consumer	Medium	High	High	High	High	Medium
Autonomy and entrepreneurship	High	High	High	High	High	Low
Productivity through people	Medium	High	High	Medium	Medium	High
Value driven	Medium	Medium	High	Low	Low	High
Stick-to-the-knitting	Medium	Medium	Medium	Low	Low	Medium
Simple form, lean staff	Medium	Medium	High	Low	Medium	Low
Control with participative management	Medium	Low	High	Low	Medium	Low

*Source: In Search of Excellence by T.J. Peters and R.H. Waterman, Harper & Row Publishers, © 1982.

obstetricians refuse to alter their attitudes toward care delivery. In time, the obstetricians (and perhaps the support nursing staff) may adopt a more enlightened perspective on patient care because of the model exemplified by the head nurse.

This chapter has outlined some of the leading ideas about competition-driven and customer-oriented strategies that are applicable to health services delivery. These strategies have helped many businesses achieve distinctive performance. There is considerable promise for the achievement of the same results in the health care field if the strategies are properly applied. These strategies represent a beginning from which nurse managers can formulate creative ideas for nursing programs and health services delivery. Above all, nurse managers are encouraged to design their own ensemble of concepts and strategies. Rote application of concepts of excellence can improve nursing services, but this approach is unlikely to evolve into a distinctive strategy. Therefore, nurse managers can expect to modify continually their personal strategies and those of their nursing programs as they strive to reach excellent and exemplary performance.

NOTES

1. T. J. Peters and R. H. Waterman, *In Search of Excellence* (New York: Harper & Row, 1982).

2. P.L. LeBreton, "Determining Creativity Strategies for a Nursing Service Department," *Nursing Administration Quarterly* 7 (Spring 1982): 1-11.

3. H.L. Smith et al., "A Retrospective on Japanese Management in Nursing," *Journal of Nursing Administration* 19 (January 1989): 27-35.

4. E.F. Schumacher, *Small Is Beautiful* (New York: Harper & Row, 1973).

5. R.R. Alward, "A Marketing Approach to Nursing Administration—Part 1," *Journal of Nursing Administration* 13 (March 1983): 9-12.

6. R.R. Alward, "A Marketing Approach to Nursing Administration—Part 2," *Journal of Nursing Administration* 13 (March 1983): 18-22.

7. D.M. Armstrong et al., "Marketing Opportunities for a Nursing Department in a Changing Economic Environment," *Nursing Administration Quarterly* 10 (Fall 1985): 1-10.

8. P.D. Warihay and D.N. Kanouse, "Playing to Win," *American Journal of Nursing* 86 (March 1986): 276-277.

9. E.K. Singleton and F.C. Nail, "Guidelines for Establishing a New Service," *Journal of Nursing Administration* 15 (October 1985): 22-26.

Chapter 8

Developing Distinctive Cultures

Nurse managers are responsible for guiding their programs and health care organizations when negotiating strategic opportunities, marketplace threats, staffing constraints, payment policy changes, and similar pressures that threaten goal accomplishment. Not every nursing program is prepared to tackle both the opportunities and the problems that it confronts. Some nursing units resist change whereas others eagerly look for new avenues to exercise skills and resources. Although nursing units vary in the skills, actions, values, mores, beliefs, behaviors, and resources that they provide to an organization, their cumulative effort describes the organization's culture. The health of this culture must be periodically monitored and a plan formulated to improve efforts at grappling with external pressures and pursuing propitious opportunities. In essence, nurse managers assist in orchestrating organizational development or evolution, which in turn increases the probability of attaining the highest standards of performance.

Traditionally, advocates of organizational development have emphasized its capabilities for minimizing internal conflicts among staff, managers, work teams, departments, divisions, and subsidiaries. Organizational development has been used to identify individual and group disagreements or conflicts that hinder operations. A broader view of organizational development's problem-solving applicability is surfacing, however. Organizational development is now being viewed as a concept with special relevance for stressful and threatening environments. It creates solutions for the internal issues and external pressures that affect an organization. With the increasingly intense, competitive environment of health care organizations, it is apparent that managers at all clinical and nonclinical levels should cooperate in building

---

For additional information about the Japanese management concepts presented in this chapter, see H.L. Smith et al., "A Retrospective on Japanese Management in Nursing," *Journal of Nursing Administration* 19 (January 1989): 27–35.

more than just efficient or effective internal performance. There is a distinct challenge to monitor continually the external environment and to remain flexible in that environment.

Organizational development is a strategic management concept that has particular relevance for contemporary health care organizations. Consequently, not only should nurse managers have a thorough understanding of the concepts underlying organization development, but they should also actively incorporate the ideas in a functional management plan. Organizational development is particularly germane to health care organizations because of the diverse constituents among staff. These factions (e.g., nurses, physicians, and managers) are often battling for control. Vestiges of these turf issues continue today and retard the ability of health care organizations to reach their full potential.

THE EVOLUTION OF ORGANIZATIONAL DEVELOPMENT

Throughout the 1970s, the goal of organizational development efforts in health care institutions was to minimize and heal internal conflicts among constituents. Health care managers attempted to maximize cohesion, to minimize conflict, and to help their organizations attain specific goals. Because of the increasingly threatening environment, it is now apparent that health care institutions must be driven toward more than just efficient or effective internal performance. There is a distinct responsibility to monitor the external environment and to remain competitive in and consonant with that environment. Hence, health care organizations require development not only in their boundaries but also in the marketplace of all health providers.

Nurse managers can play an important strategic role in forging new paths of organizational development in health care institutions. They can ameliorate the contentiousness between nursing staff and other providers or managers. Of primary importance is the nurse manager's ability to do something about the conflict between nurses (i.e., the individual clinicians) and the organization. If a health care organization is determined to resolve its problems surrounding reimbursement, competition, or economic factors, then the nursing staff must feel comfortable in its relationship with the organization. Thereafter, nurse managers can design a true collaboration among all constituents (e.g., management, nursing, medical, and ancillary staffs). Collaboration prepares health care organizations to respond optimally to many pressures. This idea is conveyed in Figure 8-1.

As Figure 8-1 suggests, organizational development began as a relatively narrow concept oriented toward problem solving in a specific organization. Early organizational development theories were not directly linked with

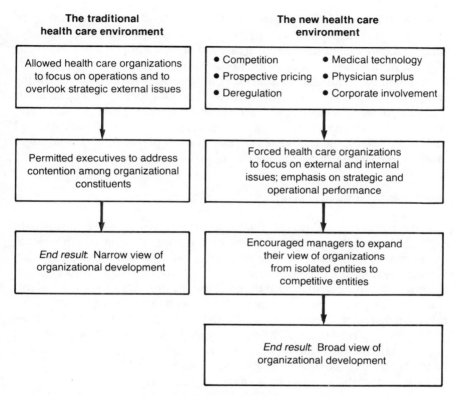

Figure 8-1 The Organizational Development Challenge and Nurse Managers

ideas about managing the external environment. Consequently, because many health care organizations inhabited relatively static or placid environments they could utilize organizational development concepts to address problems that threatened internal operations. Nevertheless, there seldom was a link between interventions used in managing the organizational culture and interventions used to manage the external environment. This culminated in a relatively narrow definition of organizational development.

The challenging environment facing health care organizations today demands a radically different and much broader perspective on organizational development. As Figure 8-1 indicates, there are many pressures outside health care organizations with the potential dramatically to affect internal operations. Management is responsible for monitoring these trends and pressures. Viable strategies must then be formulated for reducing the potential impact and for creating the optimal set of strategic responses.

As the left-hand side of Figure 8-1 suggests, the relatively static environment that preceded prospective payment and competition engendered a commensurate reaction from health care executives. The placid environment allowed health care organizations to focus on internal operational issues. Concomitantly, health care managers could overlook many external events except those with the most significant ramifications for internal operations. Strategic management was essentially limited to addressing operations and occasional environmental changes (e.g., introduction of Medicare and Medicaid, development of comprehensive health planning, and creation of professional standards review organizations).

The Traditional Environment

The result of the traditional, stable, and placid environment of health care organizations was a relatively narrow definition of what organizational development incorporated. This permitted managers to focus on conflict among organizational constituents that might otherwise adversely affect operations. In the case of hospitals, an administrator's strategy for organizational development might focus on resolving a particularly disagreeable relationship between the medical staff and the nursing staff. With relatively stable third-party payments, little overt competition, and certificate of need programs producing franchises for existing health facilities, hospital administrators could concentrate on operations. Administrators had minimal incentive to monitor, react to, or plan for strategic external issues.

The Contemporary Environment

As Figure 8-1 suggests, many pressures outside health care organizations affect internal operations. Someone must monitor these trends and pressures and formulate viable strategies for reducing their impact on the organization and for creating the optimal responses.

The organization-environment interface is primarily the responsibility of the management team. It must define the possible impact of a nursing shortage, competition, prospective pricing, deregulation, changes in medical technology, trends in physician supply, and growth of corporate involvement in the health field. The precise implications of the external factors for an organization are determined before formulating a plan of action that addresses them.

As such, the contemporary health care environment has forced many organizations to concentrate on external and internal issues. It has expanded interest in strategic and operational performance. No longer is an operations plan sufficient for survival and growth in a dynamic environment. Emphasis must also be given to external events. The end result is a dramatic redefinition of what it means to lead or manage health care organizations.

Health care managers will adjust their perspective and style in a significant way. Health sector organizations are not viewed as relatively isolated entities; now they are competitive entities. This promotes a new vision of possibilities and has also created an expanded set of responsibilities. In certain respects, a new managerial orientation is needed in the health care field today. Effective organizations and nursing programs must be driven to compete in an aggressive, regulated (in the sense of third-party payment) economy. They must also nurture a collaborative association among highly trained professionals who may have competing value systems.

The result of environmental pressures on health care organizations is a broader view of organizational development. Internal operating effectiveness must be compatible with external responses. Hence health care managers are concerned with constructing collaborative human relations in the context of lean and aggressive organizations. These organizations must be able to compete, to produce low-cost services in view of more pervasive prospective payment, to respond to new medical technology, and to react (with resiliency) to alterations in health care policy or regulations. In essence, a more comprehensive and viable posture is needed for organizational development.

Implications for Nursing

Nurse managers are discovering that many of the external changes affecting health care organizations ultimately come to rest on nursing services.[1] This has thrust nursing departments and programs into crisis situations. Nurse managers are sometimes caught in a bind because they do not or cannot control the causal factors leading to conflict, alienation, or dissatisfaction among staff nurses.[2] Furthermore, as health care organizations become embroiled in one crisis there is a tendency to encounter other crises. This produces a pessimistic climate and introduces the potential for burnout among nurse managers who are attempting to resolve or minimize the impact on their staffs.

Organizational change and the imperative for development underscore the need for an expanded vision of nurse managers, that is, for nurses who are equally comfortable in clinical and managerial situations. This challenge presents an opportunity. Nurse managers can develop a vibrant and refreshing context for nursing services. Nurse managers who are qualified for this emerging role are able to answer *yes* to the following questions:[3]

- Can you explain and interpret nursing as a clinical practice discipline in various organizational contexts? (The contexts may be planning forums, marketing programs, financial management, clinical care programs, and others.)
- Do you participate in policy and strategic planning decisions?
- Have you established the internal and external relationships that are needed to gain understanding of and support for clinical nursing practice?
- Can you reconcile clinical nursing practice with the language of business and organizations?
- Does your perspective of nursing practice enable you to separate the clinical practice from the organizational elements of support services, marketing, finance, and others that affect nursing care?
- Have you established a data base that promotes organizational understanding of nursing for decision making related to nursing practice?
- Do you have the attitude that change can be controlled, that you need qualified nurse administrators and managers working with you—people who can learn new skills and habits? Do you trust their intuition and direct their efforts where they will make the most difference?

Each of these questions is related to an expanded role for nurse managers, one that emphasizes new power and responsibility in managing. The questions also suggest that organizational development practices are appropriate for keeping up with change in the nursing and health care environments.

Another way to gain perspective on these trends is to envision nurse managers as change agents. Whether this means developing changes in clinical practice[4] or revising management practices in nursing services,[5] nurse managers can play a significant role in the evolution of the nursing profession. For example, corporate nurse managers who are responsible for long-range planning and policy issues in multi-institutional organizations have numerous opportunities to influence agreements, relationships, ventures, care monitoring, cost-quality trade-offs, and care continuity.[6] Corporate level nurse managers participate in top management decisions that determine standards, outcomes, and resource investments surrounding nursing care. As change agents, corporate nurse executives are integrated in the organizational development process.

THE BOUNDARIES OF ORGANIZATIONAL DEVELOPMENT

Perhaps the most salient definition of organizational development has been suggested by French and Bell:[7]

Organization development is a long-range effort to improve an organization's problem-solving and renewal processes, particularly through a more effective and collaborative management of organization culture—with special emphasis on the culture of formal work teams—with the assistance of a change agent, or catalyst, and the use of the theory and technology of applied behavioral science, including action research.

This definition incorporates many of the leading ideas suggested by Lippitt[8] and Argyris[9] in their complementary work as well as that of Lewin.[10] The base of organizational development is applied behavioral science and the use of survey research in organizational renewal. This is where organizational development has several recognizable strengths and inherent weaknesses.

To many people, organizational development has never really fulfilled the promise implied in the powerful work of its founders. This shortcoming may stem from excessive reliance on behavioral interventions by managers during the 1970s. The result was an obsession with the behavioral aspects of managing that downplayed other crucial perspectives (e.g., operations management, strategic management, and financial and accounting control). Managers became intoxicated with behavioral applications. Eventually, this intoxication turned into cautious adoption and, in some cases, disenchantment. Such a course of events was predictable. Overselling behavioral interventions as panaceas for many organizational problems resulted in a growing suspicion that behavioral science methods were extremely useful in some situations but inappropriate in others.

The trend toward overselling organizational development was promulgated by a healthy market for behavioral science applications. Consistent with the mood of organizations, there was rising interest in promoting the humanistic management of employees. Such concern led to the adoption of organizational development and other behavioral science ideas as fundamental mechanisms for raising productivity through employee motivation. Leadership, sensitivity training, job enrichment, job enlargement, job rotation, and similar techniques were viewed as logical means to combat behavioral problems. The techniques did not live up to the high expectations that had developed, however.

In many respects, managers' expectations had seriously grown beyond the potential benefits of organizational development that had been suggested by its theorists. When immediate results were not achieved from their investments in this method, managers turned to other, more contemporary, interventions. This tendency to move on to other tactics is not new to managing. There is often an overstatement of the end results that innovative technologies can attain. Expectations evolve beyond reasonable proportions and then are met with a serious lack of achievement. In many ways, organizational development experienced the same acceptance and rejection common to other management panaceas. In some instances, managers prudently used organizational development to the benefit of their organizations. In other cases, it became a strategy for salvation that would not succeed because it was inappropriate to underlying problems.

Successful application of organizational development ideas is contingent on understanding the most salient components of the definition offered by French and Bell. Organizational development:

- is not an ephemeral means to resolve a short-run human relations problem; it is designed to be a continuous process of renewal
- is designed to restore vitality in organizations that are confronting conflict or are unable to resolve problems; by reducing conflict and stimulating cohesion, organizational development prepares organizations for effective decision making
- is predicated on participative management by all staff; a fundamental assumption is that excessive reliance on formal structures hinders problem solving and production (or operations) in many organizations
- is most effectively implemented by impartial authorities (e.g., internal and external consultants versed in organizational development methodologies) who are able objectively to assess existing problems and methodically to institute planned change; problem-solving methodologies are based in the behavioral sciences but may incorporate interventions from other areas of management thought

Although some organizational development specialists insist that effective renewal can only be generated by outside consultants (who are therefore uncontaminated), the reality is that many large organizations have been able to use permanent staff in the consulting relationship.

RECENT TRENDS IN ORGANIZATIONAL DEVELOPMENT

Many advocates of organizational development concepts still emphasize organization culture as the primary focal point of intervention. For these individuals, organizational development must first resolve the pivotal problems of human relationships before addressing other issues such as production technology, the design of formal relationships and authority, and the control of operations. By using an iterative process of assessment, planning for objectives, providing feedback through discussion with the client, and taking directed action, the intervention specialist is able to resolve conflicts among individuals or groups and thereby to facilitate organizational functioning.

Within the last five years there has been a growing recognition among management authorities that organizational development is often more than just applied behavioral science. It is apparent that organizational development should not be limited solely to the presence or absence of effective human relationships. Instead, development of effective organization cultures has gravitated toward defining the elusive, unique qualities of distinctly high-performing organizations. Such cultures may help prevent problems and nurture conditions for desirable interpersonal relationships.

Organizational development is also being interpreted more broadly in terms of organization-environment interfaces. Thus a health care organization attains the highest standards of performance when it is in harmony with its environment. At full extension, organizational development relies not only on establishing an internal organization of cohesive units but also on promoting an ideal fit between the organization and its surrounding environment. This rationale is not difficult to understand. Even if a health care organization comprises supremely harmonious groups in which staff are satisfied and fully involved in solving service delivery problems, it may still fail.

For example, a medical group specializing in pediatric orthopedic care may comprise six physicians who, over time, become close colleagues. They are able to work in harmony with each other. When problems or disagreements occur, they are methodically resolved without continued consequence. Although this medical group is the picture of happiness, in reality it may be a financial disaster. By not adjusting to trends toward prepaid health insurance, the specialists have narrowed the patient population that they serve. Additionally, their community may be experiencing an outmigration of parents with children. The group has not kept pace with environmental changes. The loss of a patient base places the group in a serious competitive and financial predicament. At least the group will split amicably when it goes out of business; the pervasive happiness of the members with each other will guarantee that.

In conclusion, there is an evolving sense of organizational development in management today. Effective implementation means that nurse managers should pay attention to various organizational issues, including interpersonal relationships, culture, and environmental interface, among others, when preparing a culture in which people can perform at their highest levels.

THE RELATIONSHIP BETWEEN ORGANIZATIONAL DEVELOPMENT AND STRATEGIC MANAGEMENT

When organizational development is viewed as a general management approach for matching an organization with its environment as well as for instilling a functional and satisfying set of interrelationships among staff, then it begins to cross over into the area of strategic management. It is appropriate that nurse managers be sensitive to the potential for incorporating organizational development in strategic plans. The need for organizational renewal is increasingly important when health care organizations and nursing programs experience turbulent environments. Because they are confronted by a constantly changing set of pressures, it is only a matter of time before health care organizations or nursing services begin to lose their resiliency. As their culture becomes less elastic, organizations are unable to mount strategic reactions when they are most needed.

The implications of these trends for nurse managers and health care organizations are varied. As Figure 8-1 summarizes, the health care environment is laced with pressures that threaten organizational survival. For example, when a hospital encounters rising competition in the marketplace, it must mobilize resources to meet the competitive threat. This reaction seldom occurs in a vacuum, however. There may be an accompanying policy change by a third-party payer in its reimbursement guidelines. This necessitates intensive analysis to ascertain the impact of this change and to formulate methodologies for maintaining financial solvency.

With a consistent succession of similar pressures and threats to operations, there is a tendency for health care organizations to lose their vitality. They become less effective in adaptive and planned responses. In short, health care organizations such as hospitals need to generate their own renewal and to mount vigorous campaigns against threats to organizational survival.

Nurse managers who aspire to lead nursing programs to the pinnacle of the profession should be cognizant of the elasticity of their organizations. It is not a given that nursing programs or staff nurses can continually respond to threats (e.g., decreased staffing, turnover, pressures for quality assurance, and poor physician relations) without some form of regeneration. Therefore, organizational renewal through organizational development is a prerequisite of any strategic management plan.

Although the external environmental aspects of organizational development are highly relevant to health care organizations, its internal side should not be understated. Nurse managers represent one mechanism for minimizing contention between nurses and health care organizations. Because nurse managers function as a central intervention agent in combatting conflict, internal renewal efforts through organizational development may be highly applicable to strategic management plans that involve nursing. Clearly, nurse managers should contribute substantially in minimizing the conflict between nursing staff and other organizational members (e.g., managers, support staff, and physicians). Nurse managers can forge a collaborative culture and foundation from which organizational excellence is not only a possibility but a distinct, reachable reality.

Barriers to Integrating Organizational Development and Strategic Management

Nurse managers should recognize that there are a number of significant barriers to integrating organizational development with strategic management plans. Foremost is staff resistance to behavioral science's quick fixes. There has been an obsession with behavioral science applications in health care organizations to such an extent that many have lost faith in the tangible end results that are achievable through such techniques. Some behavioral science techniques have been oversold to health care organizations and nursing departments, which have subsequently discovered that applications seldom produce the prophesied outcomes. Hence nurse managers encounter resistance not only from other managers but also from staff, who have observed the failures of behavioral interventions. Admittedly, the techniques are powerful in the proper situations and have their place in the repertoire of management technology, but they are not the ultimate solution to every problem.

Nurse managers can be cognizant of this potential barrier to implementing an organizational development program. Top management echelons may be reluctant to utilize behavioral techniques because such tools have shown limited ability in the past to influence productivity directly or to resolve the issues of organization-environment interfacing. Behavioral tools are most useful in fine tuning organizational operations. Other, more traditional clinical approaches as well as functional tactics in accounting, financing, marketing, and organizing have been fruitful in generating results for health care organizations. It is unreasonable to expect that health care organizations or their staff members will let these techniques sit idle in exchange for promises. The return on investment from organizational development must be substantiated.

The problem for health care organizations and nurse managers is placing organizational behavior ideas in the proper perspective. Even the most ardent purveyors of behavioral technology are concerned about this shift toward downplaying more traditional approaches. As L. L. Cummings, a leading organizational behavioralist, notes

> Our credibility with the managerial world is damaging when [organizational behavior] comes out in executive programs as a "little of everything," as "a combination of behavioral jargon and common sense," or as "touchy-feely" without content.[11]

Nurse managers need to generate credibility. The last thing they need is to lose credibility by being perceived as selling "soft" management concepts.

Integrating Organizational Development into Nursing Programs

Enhanced understanding of a nursing program's culture is a beginning from which constructive changes can be initiated by nurse managers. Caution should be used in interpreting the culture and planning the desired direction of change, however. The challenge is well illustrated in Figure 8-2, which depicts two nursing units. It is evident that neither culture is necessarily better than the other.[12] The type of nursing services involved (e.g., intensive care and primary care), personalities of staff, interactions with medical staff, budgetary support, and similar variables determine the inherent differences between the two units. Nurse managers can see that effective management of these two units requires a unique approach in both instances.

The problem for nurse managers is to build an integral nursing services culture in which unit A and unit B are but members of a larger department. In this case the units may need encouragement to adapt their standards for working together, telling others what to do, following established standards, organizing and using time, perspective-building, and responding to change. These cultural qualities may interfere with the nursing program's effort to solidify staff in a functional team.[13] Furthermore, the differences are incompatible with shared governance. Given these limitations, organizational development provides nurse managers with a practical tool for minimizing conflict, developing a common culture, and establishing a basis on which the separate units are able to maintain their unique identities.

DIFFERENTIATING BETWEEN MACRO AND MICRO PERSPECTIVES

Nurse managers can place organizational development concepts in perspective relative to strategic management concepts by differentiating between macro and micro concerns. This valuable idea is conveyed in Figure 8-3, which illustrates variables that should be attended to in a comprehensive organizational development program. Note that neither list is exhaustive. Each captures the essence of what may be called the macro and micro perspectives.

Macro Variables

Macro variables are characterized by an organizationwide focus. In other words, the concern is issues beyond specific individuals and work groups. The emphasis is on the organization as a whole, whether it involves internal issues

UNIT A   ## UNIT B

Working Together

UNIT A	UNIT B
• See work as our work	• See work as my work or your work
• Work together	• Work independently
• Finish together	• Finish on their own
• Avoid competition	• Compete among themselves

Telling Others What To Do

UNIT A	UNIT B
• Avoid telling others what to do	• Use their authority to persuade others
• Recognize no staff nurse hierarchy	• Recognize hierarchy based on skills, knowledge, and assertiveness

Following Established Standards

UNIT A	UNIT B
• Desire to follow traditional procedures	• Desire to use their own judgment regarding procedures
• Prefer standardized guidelines	• Prefer individual decision-making

Organization and Use of Time

UNIT A	UNIT B
• Value efficiency and organizational skills	• Limit emphasis on efficiency
• Clearly identify priority activities	• Identify numerous activities as priorities

Psychological Perspective-Taking

UNIT A	UNIT B
• Attend to obvious psychological needs	• Actively look for psychosocial needs
• Show concern for a period of time	• Show concern indefinitely

Change

UNIT A	UNIT B
• Prefer the status quo	• Prefer a changing situation
• Attend certain classes	• Attend as many classes as possible

Figure 8-2 Cultural Differences between Two Nursing Units. *Source:* Reprinted from "Understanding Organizational Culture: A Key to Management Decision-Making" by H.V.E. Coeling and J.R. Wilcox, *Journal of Nursing Administration*, Vol. 18, No. 11, p. 19, with permission of J.B. Lippincott Company, © November 1988.

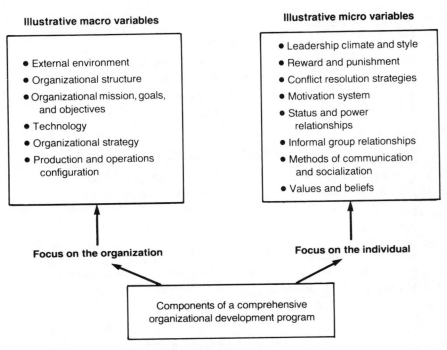

Illustrative macro variables

- External environment
- Organizational structure
- Organizational mission, goals, and objectives
- Technology
- Organizational strategy
- Production and operations configuration

Illustrative micro variables

- Leadership climate and style
- Reward and punishment
- Conflict resolution strategies
- Motivation system
- Status and power relationships
- Informal group relationships
- Methods of communication and socialization
- Values and beliefs

Focus on the organization

Focus on the individual

Components of a comprehensive organizational development program

Figure 8-3 Differentiating Macro and Micro Perspectives

(e.g., the configuration of service delivery processes) or external issues (e.g., the impact of significant environmental forces). The macro view is interested in influences that are generated by forces outside the organizational boundary. This view also recognizes that organizations are continually involved in a dynamic interplay. As the environment changes, so too should their operational and strategic responses. Hence a strategic management perspective requires nurse managers to look beyond organizational boundaries in determining limitations and possibilities facing the organization.

In addition to concern for the external environment, a number of other crucial variables involving an organizationwide perspective are displayed in Figure 8-3. For example, nurse managers who adopt such a perspective would be concerned with the form and functioning of the organizational structure, or the design of formal relationships in and among nursing units. The mission, goals, objectives, and strategy of the organization are macro-level variables. For the most part, mission, goals, and strategy are ingredients in the strategic management process. The technology used to produce services is also a macro level variable. In many respects, medical technology is directly linked to the other variables noted in Figure 8-3. In total, these macro-level variables dictate an organizationwide perspective on the part of managers.

Micro Variables

Micro-level variables are the counterparts to macro-level variables. These factors generally center around informal associations, personal relationships, coordination among small groups, and the role of the individual. In contrast to the macro perspective, the focus of micro variables is the individual. Hence a nurse manager addresses factors that promote individual commitment to the organization's efforts. A leadership climate must be created that provides direction to staff and elicits their assistance in progressing toward goals. A reward system instills a hierarchy of incentives and disincentives to elicit desired behavior from staff. When conflicts arise there must be an effective means for resolving them, otherwise nursing staff and the organization will endure an undesirable climate for providing services.

The micro-level perspective entails concern for motivating employees, the status and power hierarchy that define working relationships, interaction among groups, methods of communication and socialization, and the belief system in an organization. Each one of these factors should be incorporated in an organization's or nurse manager's plan of action. In terms of organizational development it is sufficient to emphasize the totality rather than specifics. The bottom line for micro-level variables is their emphasis on the individual.

Combining Macro and Micro Perspectives

Nurse managers should not only recognize but also concentrate on combining macro and micro variables in a comprehensive perspective. This perspective is the underlying rationale for effective organizational development as suggested in Figure 8-3. Organizational development must address both the organization and the individual to be effective. Hence there is both differentiation among and integration of valuable organizational development concepts.

Organizational development requires a skillful combination of macro- and micro-level variables. There has been a tendency, however, for disciplines to dominate or override a truly comprehensive and integrated view. The result is a separation between what may be called organizational theory (i.e., an organizationwide perspective) and organizational behavior (i.e., an individual perspective). The effective nurse manager should strive to incorporate both views in practice.

The inherent limitations of a separation between micro and macro viewpoints are accurately summarized by Cummings:[14]

> This distinction is based on two differences: unit of analysis and focus of dependent variables. [Organizational behavior] is defined as the study of individual and group behavior within organizations and the application of such knowledge. [Organizational theory] is the study of structure, processes and outcomes of the organization per se. The distinction is neither that [organizational behavior] is theoretical and concerned only with behavior nor that [organizational theory] is unique or exclusive in its attention to theory. Alternatively, the distinction can be conceived as between micro and macro perspectives on organization behavior. This removes the awkward differentiation of behavior and theory.

Cummings correctly diagnoses that several artificial differences have developed between the organizational behavior (i.e., micro) and organizational theory (i.e., macro) disciplines in their terminologies (especially the labels *theory* and *behavior*). Labeling organizational behavior as behavior and organizational theory as theory does not mean that one is more theoretical than the other or that one is more applied than the other. They both fall under the rubric of management theory. In preventing this artificial division it is better to define organizational behavior as the study of individuals and groups in organizations (a micro orientation) and to define organizational theory as the study of nonindividual management variables in an organization (a macro orientation).

The preceding definitions underscore an important difference in philosophical orientation. Organizational theory represents a macro view of organizational variables, and organizational behavior concentrates on psychological variables. The problem with totally differentiating the two views is that either can become a handicap, preventing a holistic approach to management. The need to differentiate yet simultaneously integrate organizational theory and behavior is a challenge for nurse managers.

Conflicts between the Macro and Micro Perspectives

The provocative atmosphere engendered by organizational behavior is desired by every employee and manager. We all want to be popular and well liked and to receive considerable satisfaction and recognition in our work. Nurse managers realize, however, that these niceties are more often than not a secondary goal to be pursued rather than a primary goal that ensures organizational health.

The problem with concentrating too much on a micro view instead of a macro view is not that the macro view presents a better management model or that the micro view has relatively little to offer managers. An excessive reliance on a micro perspective does not recognize the important attributes of both macro and micro disciplines. Both organizational theory and organizational behavior make important contributions to the art of managing. Therefore, nurse managers should continue to seek a meaningful differentiation and integration of the micro and macro viewpoints.

Despite the fact that organizational theory and organizational behavior are both needed in the management setting, there is a question as to which one a nurse could succeed without. Consider the micro focus of organizational behavior as it applies to a concept such as job satisfaction. The goal of job satisfaction is to motivate and satisfy nurses so that they find the health care organization a better place in which to work. Productivity, patient care, and budgetary concerns are minimized, and turnover and absenteeism are reduced. Who, however, acquires the maximum benefits from a job satisfaction program? Obviously, most benefits that are derived from a job satisfaction program are reaped by nurses. They are able to participate in decision making and to increase their autonomy and responsibility.

These trends are relevant to nurse managers. Could it be that the long-standing formula of developing an organization in response to management strategy has been sacrificed and replaced by behavioral determinism? Has individual welfare invaded the realm of the organization to the extent that organizational efficacy is now passé?

Resolving the Macro-Micro Conflict

It appears that a primary vehicle for integrating macro and micro perspectives in nursing services is the nurse manager. Harmony between macro and micro perspectives is fundamental to the continued well-being of a nursing program. In the end, failure to account adequately for the macro perspective and excessive concentration on the micro viewpoint will have nurse managers behaving in ways that could result in satisfied nurses whose departments or organizations no longer exist. Although such an exigency should cause us all to shudder, it is only a thoughtful and methodical attack on this problem that results in a more balanced approach to management.

In conclusion, the macro view and its inseparable relationship with the micro view should receive greater analysis by nurse managers. A meeting is needed between the macro and micro perspectives that will stimulate increased professional growth and personal development as well as a more realistic management approach. Integrative models and theories that combine the micro and macro disciplines should be pursued and constructed with a focus that is at least equally devoted to explaining the differences between the constructs and to underscoring their similarities.

The Nurse Manager's Role in Organizational Development

Considering the boundaries of organizational development, the alterations in the health care environment that demand attention to organizational renewal, the relationship between organizational development and strategic management, and the conceptual and practical differences between micro and macro perspectives, what is the role of nurse managers with respect to organizational development? The answer to this question is both philosophical and practical. Health care organizations need nurse managers to incorporate macro and micro perspectives in a total perspective; that is, nurse managers should understand the ingredients of the micro and macro views. Micro and macro emphases should be integrated in a general management point of view. Effective strategic management is based on a comprehensive analysis of organizational and environmental variables. To exclude or minimize one set of variables only jeopardizes the ability to attain organizational objectives.

For example, a multispecialty group practice that is planning to institute a number of satellite clinics throughout a metropolitan area must first address the macro variables associated with implementing the strategy. What form of control mechanisms will be developed to ensure that each satellite achieves predetermined productivity, profitability, and patient care goals? How will planning be coordinated among the satellites for strategic and operational issues? What sort of organizational structure will be used in each satellite? How will these subunit hierarchies fit in a total organizational structure? What marketing program will be developed to promote the total multispecialty group practice and each satellite clinic? What flexibility will a specific satellite have in establishing its own objectives and strategy as a strategic business unit relative to the master strategy and goals of the corporation? How will major capital investments in medical technology be shared among the satellite clinics? These and many other questions represent macro level issues.

Simply addressing the macro perspective, however, will not produce an effectively functioning system of satellite clinics. There are crucial micro level issues to consider in an overall strategic management plan. For example, specifically which nurses will be assigned to which clinics? At what times and on what days of the week will they be scheduled? Will the preferences and predispositions of each nurse be integrated into the total scheduling plan?

How will collaborative practice patterns be forged between physicians and nurses? What personal rewards or incentives will be allocated to each clinic that performs beyond budgeted levels? How will the rewards be distributed in each satellite clinic? How will staff, particularly the nursing staff, be integrated to maintain communication and a sense of identity? How will conflicts among nursing staff members in a clinic be resolved? What leadership style will be promoted by the group? Which individuals will be selected as leaders? What form of ethical policies and practices will be established to maintain the group's commitment to a given level of quality care? These and many other questions represent micro level issues.

Note that there are two important ingredients for efficaciously combining the micro and macro concepts in a workable whole. Philosophically, nurse managers must pursue a balance between micro level and macro level variables. An organization should lead with its strength, but excessive reliance on a set of skills or capabilities to the exclusion of others (e.g., micro as opposed to macro) ultimately threatens strategic capability. Therefore, the macro-level variables should temper the micro-level variables, and vice versa. Practically, the nurse manager should implement a plan that addresses each level.

If nurse managers adopt such a philosophy and effectively implement it in practice, they will have established the preconditions for meaningful organizational development. The most essential contribution of organizational development to health care organizations and nurses is perspective. Nurse managers must attend to organizationwide factors but not at the expense of the micro level. As we have seen, there are innumerable forces at play in the health care environment. Nevertheless, the macro level should not be addressed for its strategic value and the micro level left unattended, or vice versa.

Therefore, the nurse manager's role in organizational development is one of balance. This is easily seen in the revolution of third-party payment policies, which have produced significant organizational impacts at strategic and operating levels. Such influences should be managed prudently through internal and external responses. Organizations must be positioned strategically in the marketplace for optimum responses. This position cannot come at the expense of vital operating systems, however, especially micro variables.

For example, when Medicare's diagnosis-related group payment system was instituted, many hospitals responded at a strategic level (i.e., cost control) and gave secondary consideration to long-term operating-level ramifications (i.e., impact on the staff members). Many hospitals recognized that a quick fix for high costs was to reduce nurse staffing levels while demanding higher productivity from retained nurses. Thus the micro level was sacrificed to pursue a strategic plan. The long-term impact may be higher costs, however, because nurses are stretched to the point that higher productivity is not feasible. Nursing services offered feasible reductions with valuable savings, but a quality nursing staff that is committed to an organization is not built overnight. As a consequence, macro strategy changes need to be tempered by the needs of the micro level.

Clearly, nurse managers can contribute to a robust and effective role of organizational development in the management of health care organizations. They need to articulate strategic and operating plans with the total organization in mind. They need to balance organizational responses at both micro and macro levels. In this fashion it is possible to develop organizations that achieve broad goals while simultaneously returning satisfaction to constituents.

DISTINCTIVE CULTURAL PROTOTYPES

Seminal discoveries concerning organization cultures suggest that concerted efforts to forge a distinctive culture can lead to organizations renowned for their performance capabilities. The issue for nursing services is which cultural prototypes offer significant promise given the constraints surrounding nursing. One model has received extensive consideration in nursing to this point. Japanese management styles are a cultural prototype that is continually being advocated as consistent with the contemporary nursing context. This prototype provides a template on which organizational development efforts can be based. It is appropriate to examine this concept so that nurse managers can discern how organizational development ideas can be applied to nursing programs.

Japanese businesses have demonstrated a remarkable ability to produce high-quality goods at competitive and profitable prices. Furthermore, the rate of productivity in Japan is one of the highest for industrialized societies.[15,16] In view of these accomplishments, corporations around the world are interested in the techniques by which these results are achieved.[17–19] The popularity of Japanese management practices has reached such levels that some beleaguered corporations and managers adopt the principles as a panacea.[20,21] Despite the phenomenal success of Japanese businesses, there are numerous problems in transferring their management styles to other cultures and corporate environments.[22,23] Nonetheless, Japanese management styles continue to be respected for raising productivity and product quality when other interventions have been fruitless.

Health care organizations and their managers have expressed substantial interest in Japanese management concepts.[24,25] There have been many factors underlying this trend. First, prospective payment has constrained budgets, which in turn has reduced staffing, particularly in nursing departments. Health care organizations may be able to overcome the financial problems of prospective payment if they are able to derive higher productivity from their staff members.[26] Higher productivity is associated with lower cost and therefore represents a response to the austerity of prospective pricing. Second, malpractice litigation has stimulated great interest in quality of care. Japanese management techniques emphasize quality of product and service, hence they may be appropriate to improving patient care.[27] Third, there is a high rate of turnover among nurses. This is attributed to excessive workloads, lack of communication, and dissatisfaction with professional roles.[28,29] Japanese management styles may help provide a more meaningful work experience for health care personnel.

Administrators, like other health care managers, may envision Japanese management practices as appropriate for organizational settings.[30] Nurse managers may also view Japanese management styles as mechanisms to raise productivity and to improve patient care.[31] Such beliefs often develop from the growing discussion of these and related topics in the health care literature and among managers at their respective institutions.[32,33] In some cases this optimism is warranted, but it is essential that nurse managers understand not only the advantages but also the limitations of Japanese management practices. Furthermore, they need to know how to derive the most from Japanese management styles when these styles are adopted by their organization.[34] Communication to staff nurses and correct implementation of the concept are fundamental ingredients to their success.

Fundamental Japanese Management Concepts

Research has considered the appropriateness of Japanese management styles for industrial or production line settings. In subsequent translations and applications this fact is often overlooked.[35] Japanese management concepts, especially quality circles, have been most successful in assembly line situations.[36] Japanese management concepts may also be relevant in some less structured or less routine production or service settings, but their initial success was in industrial settings.

More evidence is needed to ascertain the efficacy of Japanese management styles in service settings such as nursing care.[37] Although there are several reports of successful implementation of quality circles in American hospitals, it should be noted that quality circles have not been totally effective in Japanese hospitals.[38-40] For nurse managers this means that the concepts should be approached cautiously. Nursing care may not reach high standards under assembly line conditions.

A literal transfer of Japanese management principles to American organizations is impractical. Therefore, an adaptation has been suggested in which the most promising qualities are incorporated in the fundamental American organizational infrastructure. The resulting hybrid has been labeled Theory Z. Table 8-1 provides an overview of terminology and concepts surrounding Japanese management, Theory Z, and American management. The traditional American approach to managing is contrasted to Theory Z along several crucial dimensions that have promoted success for Japanese corporations.

Table 8-1 Terminology and Concepts Surrounding Japanese Management

Theory Z: An adaptation of Japanese management practices to American companies. This management style combines elements of Japanese practices with American practices to create a hybrid.

	Management Style	
Characteristics	*Traditional American*	*Theory Z*
Length of employee employment	Short-term oriented	Long-term oriented
Nature of employee performance evaluation and promotion	Infrequent evaluations with rapid promotion potential	Systematic evaluation with slow promotion potential
Development of career path	Emphasis on specialization	Blend of specialization and generalization
Type of control	Formal	Informal
Locus of decision making	In the individual	In the collective group of people making up the organization
Assumption of responsibility	By the individual	By the individual
Concern for employees	Segmented	Holistic

Quality circle: A small group of employees that meets periodically to identify, analyze, resolve, and prevent problems associated with their area of work.

Example of
quality circle: A group of eight nurses meet with a head nurse to resolve continuing problems associated with medical record accuracy.

Source: Reprinted from "A Retrospective on Japanese Management in Nursing" by H.L. Smith et al., *Journal of Nursing Administration,* Vol. 19, No. 1, p. 28, with permission of J.B. Lippincott Company, © January 1989.

Theory Z recommends a metamorphosis of traditional American management practices. Employment is oriented toward the long run, with slow promotion being justified through systematic evaluation. Personnel attempt to blend specialized and generalized career paths. Control is less authoritarian and more informally applied by peers and supervisors. Decisions are made collectively. Nonetheless, individuals still assume responsibility for performance and actions. The organization strives for a holistic concern for personnel. These characteristics are theorized to produce a nurturing environment in which there is reciprocity between worker and organization. This creates a favorable climate for higher productivity and quality.

As the preceding comparison suggests, the philosophical basis for Japanese management is a substantial departure from that normally provided in the United States.[41-43] Despite the contrasts between the American and Japanese models, however, both work effectively in numerous situations, and both have their advocates. The bottom line in assessing the comparative differences is philosophy and management approach. Either model, if used to its maximum, can achieve impressive results. For example, innovation in medical technology can be supported by both organizational models. The American firm would cultivate individuals whose skills are oriented toward ingenuity. A system of rewards would provide incentives to invent the desired advancement. The Japanese firm would achieve the same level of innovation through different means. Groups would strive progressively for an innovation. Refinements of the best options would be made by other groups. The organization as a whole would be credited with producing the innovation.

If both models can produce the same end result, then why is there such interest in Japanese management principles? The inability to motivate American workers to achieve higher productivity and higher quality products has led managers to contemplate whether a new approach is warranted. For most managers the question is not whether American practices should be discarded for Japanese concepts. The main issue is to what extent American management models should incorporate Japanese principles.[44] Piecemeal borrowing may prevent attaining the total Japanese model, however. Under the incremental approach the philosophical underpinnings would be lost. The final results would be less than those achieved had the entire philosophy been implemented.[45]

A popular approach for implementing Theory Z in the work setting is to develop quality circles. Table 8-1 defines and illustrates this concept. Quality circles bring managers and nonmanagers together to solve problems in production and to identify how the production process can be improved even when problems do not exist.[46] Periodic meetings allow quality circle participants to join in the decision-making and planning processes of an organization. They gain access to an open forum with management.[47] The purpose of a quality circle is to create a better process and end product through a sharing of ideas.[48] The circles activate the participation of employees and help them experience a sense of ownership in the organization and its products or services. Quality circles remove barriers in communication between employees and management because of the close interaction that they support.

To attain the holistic integration underlying the Japanese philosophy, quality circles overlap to ensure that every aspect of production is covered. This creates a team spirit and guards against the work unit's, department's, or division's perceiving itself to be an independent unit in the organizational infrastructure. This sharing process helps cross-fertilize ideas concerning the entire production process rather than a single element of that process. The end result is the development of trust and reliance on others to fulfill responsibilities. In essence, this defines the best aspects of an effective team that is motivated toward a mutual goal.

Nursing Applications

Are Japanese management practices congruent with a nursing context? The answer to this question depends on whether an entire health care organization adopts the concept or whether a nurse manager is attempting to implement the idea in a specific nursing unit. Ideally, the Japanese management philosophy must be implemented in the organization as a whole for it to be effective. Nevertheless, there is every reason to adopt the best aspects of these principles if it means that a nursing unit or the nursing services department will function more effectively.

There is an increasing amount of information available about the use of Japanese principles in nursing situations. Table 8-2 provides a summary of recent reports, including the type of problem addressed and the end result. All these applications relied on quality circles as the adopted technique. The implication is that health care organizations are using a generalized Japanese management approach. Quality circles are being adopted to resolve specific problems. There is little evidence suggesting that other principles of Theory Z or Japanese management are applied in these situations.

It is apparent that most of the hospitals and medical centers reported in Table 8-2 are using quality circles to solve problems in nursing services. The first impression is the variability of the problem types. Quality circles are being used to manage issues ranging from communications to turnover. Second, the problems vary in their specificity from nursing care plans to general improvement in productivity. These results suggest the latitude that is available to nurse managers in applying Japanese management concepts. Table 8-2 also reports favorable end results from the use of quality circles. It

Table 8-2 Illustrative Nursing Applications of Quality Circles

Setting	Author	Problem Addressed	End Result
Medical center	Tinello–Buddle (1986)	Nursing division was planning to change from handwritten care plans to guided nursing care plans. One quality circle established.	Quality circle recommended inservice education to facilitate transition to guided care plan by staff nurses. Analysis indicated that after education 60% of all charts used guided care plan where formerly only 40% used this methodology.
Medical center	Lehman (1986)	Two quality circles established. One addressed inability of operating room personnel consistently to obtain lunch relief. Other analyzed low attendance among respiratory care personnel at departmental inservice meetings.	Operating room quality circle defined several ideas to facilitate lunch relief. Morale improved. Respiratory care quality circle recommended purchase of video cassettes to improve flexibility. Nursing staff unable to attend the inservice meetings could review the taped meetings on video cassettes at their discretion (i.e., at home or on the job).
Hospital	Burton (1986)	Analysis of employee withdrawals (i.e., employee turnover) and absenteeism among nursing staff. Ten quality circles created for 108 nurses.	Improved team building and communication led to lower absenteeism, turnover, job tension with higher job satisfaction and organizational commitment among nursing staff.
Hospital	Christen (1986)	Seven quality circles established to improve productivity and lower costs.	Budget of hospital reduced by $6 million without serious impairment of staffing levels, quality, or patient care services.
Hospital	Cornell (1984)	Quality circle established to improve communications between nursing and medical staffs.	Quality circle recommended training for nursing personnel in methods for clarifying physician test orders. Reduced number of tests duplicated and improved morale.

Source: Reprinted from "A Retrospective on Japanese Management in Nursing" by H.L. Smith et al., *Journal of Nursing Administration*, Vol. 19, No. 1, p. 30, with permission of J.B. Lippincott Company, © January 1989.

should be noted that there was considerable variation in the methodology and documentation used in concluding that quality circles have performed favorably. Nonetheless, the results are headed in the right direction as far as indicating that quality circles are worthwhile in nursing.

The successful implementation of Japanese management methodologies in nursing is contingent on several tactics. First, the concepts must be applied completely in each nursing unit. It may be ineffective to attempt Japanese management practices unless the entire nursing services department is adopting the concept. According to the basic philosophy of Japanese management, the concept should be organizationally based. In reality, this may not occur. Therefore, nurse managers might attempt to establish a skeleton of Japanese concepts solely in nursing services in anticipation that the management style will be adopted throughout their organization at a later date.

For example, nursing staff formulate quality circles. Nonnursing staff members are invited to participate when a problem pertinent to their service area is discussed. This enlightens other managers and personnel about quality circles and may spread the concept throughout the organization. Even if this transfer does not occur, nursing may be able to use quality circles to alleviate problems in the delivery of services. A more constructive spirit among nursing staff is created, which suggests that departmental members are collectively prepared to address refinements in patient care.

Second, nurse managers should be willing to tolerate the short-run costs of adopting Japanese management. These costs may include a possible stagnation or even decline of productivity as nurses familiarize themselves with the concepts. With a change of this magnitude, there is a built-in inertia. Therefore, nurse managers should not be surprised when staff are reluctant to participate at a level that is required for effective implementation of the concepts. Personnel costs associated with the adoption of quality circles may increase. Nonetheless, once nursing staff are familiar with the basic concepts and are comfortable with the new approach, they will be better able to provide input that demonstrably influences patient care and the cost of delivering services.

Third, nurse managers must share their formal authority if quality circles and the underlying philosophy of Japanese management styles are expected to work effectively. Reliance on traditional roles at supervisory and departmental leadership levels will weigh against achieving a true team culture. Even though nurse managers may be willing to discard the traditional, authority-based approach, many problems will surface in adopting a more participative approach. One tactic to prevent this problem involves retaining a nonnursing interventionist from within the organization to help leaders remain honest. This is expensive in terms of the interventionist's time and possible conflict with other job responsibilities, but it may interject objectivity where it is needed most.

A fourth suggestion for adopting Japanese management practices in nursing is to establish team-originated plans when phasing in the concept and when defining an agenda of issues to be addressed. Many health care leaders expect changes in operating policies to reach effectiveness within months. When immediate results are not produced, they grow tired of the intervention and gravitate to the next panacea. Nurse managers should underscore their long run commitment to the Japanese approach. This must be accompanied by the skillful orientation of all nursing staff and the formulation of a team-generated agenda of issues to be undertaken by the quality circles. Nurse managers should not hesitate to lengthen time horizons. It takes years, not months, to implement effectively Japanese management concepts.

Assessing the Results

The final challenge in applying Japanese management principles is assessing the effectiveness of the approach. To this point, few rigorous attempts have been made by organizations to determine the efficacy of Japanese management.[49] Nonetheless, there are many useful measures for determining whether the new management style has improved nursing services, including:

- quality of nursing care
- cost of nursing care
- employment stability
- job satisfaction and organizational commitment of staff members
- reductions in use of nursing pools
- attainment of budgets
- expressed satisfaction from patients

These and other factors normally measure the extent to which the process and outcomes of nursing care are deteriorating or improving. An additional test of Japanese management effectiveness beyond these objective measures is to determine whether staff nurses look forward to coming to work each day. Nursing staff should view the challenges and constraints in their jobs as resolvable because of the team that stands behind them.

TOWARD DISTINCTIVE CULTURES

This chapter has suggested that nurse managers can take an active role in shaping the work environment for nurses and other health care personnel. This responsibility for culture building is linked with organizational development, which represents an effort to maximize internal harmony and to address the deleterious influence of external forces. Although the theory and practice of organizational culture and development ideas are still evolving, there is compelling evidence to conclude that better-performing organizations are those that cultivate a distinct value set among staff members. These organizations are more likely to invest resources in building and maintaining healthy staff relations. Excellent organizations are also predisposed to managing external pressures (e.g., competition and regulation) that threaten organizational success.

Organizational development and organization culture are concepts with significant promise for nursing care. Nurses work in stressful environments that contain many factions (e.g., administrators, physicians, and patients) attempting to gain control. Under these conditions, strong nursing services departments and programs must rely on the self-supporting aspects of a common culture. The specific culture will vary among health care organizations and nursing programs. Some may discover success in prototypes such as Japanese management styles. Others will design and nurture their own unique cultures. The common denominator in these efforts is the nurse manager who articulates the envisioned goal and works toward achieving it in daily operations.

NOTES

1. M.J. Beyers, "Getting on Top of Organizational Change. Part 1. Process and Development," *Journal of Nursing Administration* 14 (October 1984): 32-39.

2. D.E. Hendricks, "Understanding Organizational Crisis: Opportunity for Managerial Growth," *Nursing Management* 13 (April 1982): 40-42.

3. M.J. Beyers, "Getting on Top of Organizational Change. Part 2. Trends in Nursing Service," *Journal of Nursing Administration* 14 (November 1984): 32.

4. M.C. Ahmed, "Taking Charge of Change in Hospital Nursing Practice," *American Journal of Nursing* 76 (March 1981): 540-543.

5. M. Manez, "The Untraditional Nurse Manager: Agent of Change and Changing Agent," *Hospitals* 52 (January 1978): 62-65.

6. M.J. Beyers, "Getting on Top of Organizational Change. Part 3. The Corporate Nurse Executive," *Journal of Nursing Administration* 14 (December 84): 32-37.

7. W.L. French and C.H. Bell, *Organization Development* (Englewood Cliffs, NJ: Prentice-Hall, 1973), 15.

8. G.L. Lippitt, *Organization Renewal* (New York: Appleton-Century-Crofts, 1969).

9. C. Argyris, *Management and Organizational Development: The Path from XA to YB* (New York: McGraw-Hill, 1971).

10. K. Lewin. *Field Theory in Social Science* (New York: Harper, 1951).

11. L.L. Cummings, "Toward Organizational Behavior," *Academy of Management Review* 3 (January 1978): 90.

12. H.V.E. Coeling and J.R. Wilcox, "Understanding Organizational Culture: A Key to Management Decision-Making," *Journal of Nursing Administration* 18 (November 1988): 16-23.

13. M. Jacobsen-Webb, "Team Building: Key to Executive Success," *Journal of Nursing Administration* 15 (February 1985): 16-20.

14. L.L. Cummings, "Toward Organizational Behavior," 91.

15. G.R. Ferris and J.A. Wagner, "Quality Circles in the United States: A Conceptual Revolution," *Journal of Applied Behavioral Science* 21 (1985): 155-167.

16. N. Hatvany and V. Pucik, "Japanese Management Practices and Productivity," *Organizational Dynamics* 9 (1981): 5-20.

17. H. Takeuchi, "Productivity: Learning from the Japanese," *California Management Review* 23 (1981): 5-19.

18. W.G. Ouchi, *Theory Z: How American Businesses Can Meet the Japanese Challenge* (Reading, MA: Addison-Wesley, 1981).

19. R.T. Pascale and A.G. Athos, *The Art of Japanese Management* (New York: Simon & Schuster, 1981).

20. R. Zemke, "Quality Circles Using Pooled Efforts To Promote Excellence," *Training and Development Journal* 15 (1980): 31-34.

21. D. Dewar and J.P. Beardsley, *Quality Circles* (Menlo Park, CA: International Association for Quality Circles, 1977).

22. E.J. Metz, "Caution: Quality Circles Ahead," *Training and Development Journal* 15 (1980): 71-85.

23. C.G. Burck, "What Happens When Workers Manage Themselves?" *Fortune* 104 (1981): 62-71.

24. S.M. Shortell, "Theory Z: Implications and Relevance for Health Care Management," *Health Care Management Review* 7 (1982): 7-21.

25. S.B. Goldsmith, *Theory Z Hospital Management* (Rockville, MD: Aspen, 1984).

26. R. Landsborough, "A Technique for Encouraging Employee Involvement in Improving Productivity," *Hospital and Health Services Administration Quarterly* 30 (1985): 124-134.

27. L. Cornell, "Quality Circles: A New Cure for Hospital Dysfunctions," *Hospital and Health Services Administration Quarterly* 29 (1984): 88-93.

28. A.H. Nowell and G. Nowell, "Participation Management as a Strategy for Nurse Adaptation to Hospital Unit Management Systems," *Hospital Topics* 64 (1986): 28-42.

29. G.E. Burton, "Quality Circles in a Hospital Environment," *Hospital Topics* 64 (1986): 11-17.

30. M.M. McKinney, "The Newest Miracle Drug: Quality Circles in Hospitals," *Hospital and Health Services Administration Quarterly* 29 (1984): 74-87.

31. N. Tinello-Buddle, "Quality Circles: A Management Strategy That Works," *Nursing Success Today* 3 (1986): 9-11.

32. M. Adair and K. Nygard, "Theory Z Management: Can It Work for Nursing?" *Nursing and Healthcare* 3 (1982): 489-491.

33. J.A. Wine and J.E. Baird, "Improving Nursing Management and Practice through Quality Circles," *Journal of Nursing Administration* 13 (1983): 5-10.

34. M.E. Lehman, "Quality Circles: Their Place in Health Care," *Hospital Topics* 64 (1986): 15-19.

35. J.J. Sullivan, "A Critique of Theory Z," *Academy of Management Review* 8 (1983): 132-142.

36. H. Blocker and H. Overgaard, "Japanese Quality Circles: A Managerial Response to the Productivity Problem," *International Management Review* 22 (1982): 13-16.

37. K.M. Jenkins and J. Shimada, "Quality Circles in the Service Sector," *Supervisory Management* 17 (1981): 3.

38. N. Ikegami and S.B. Goldsmith, "Quality Circles: The Myth and Reality of Hospital Management," *Health Care Management Review* 10 (1985): 45-33.

39. M. Maser, "Mount Sinai Invests in Quality Circles," *Health Services Manager* 15 (1982): 12-13.

40. J. Baird, "Quality Circles May Substantially Improve Hospital Employees' Morale," *Modern Healthcare* 11 (1981): 70-74.

41. R.J. Slothus, "Can Theory Z Work in the U.S.?" *Health Progress* 67 (1986): 6-7.

42. G. Hofstede, *Culture's Consequences: International Differences in Work-Related Values* (Beverly Hills, CA: Sage, 1980).

43. W.G. Ouchi, "Individualism and Intimacy in Industrial Society," *Technology Review* 83 (1981): 34-36.

44. S.R. Safranski et al., "Should Health Care Managers Adopt Theory Z?" *Health Progress* 67 (1986): 49-51, 73.

45. M. Brown, "An American Version of Theory Z," *Health Care Management Review* 7 (1982): 23-25.

46. E.E. Lawler and S.A. Mohrman, "Quality Circles after the Fad," *Harvard Business Review* 63 (1985): 65-71.

47. H.P. Sims and J.W. Dean, "Beyond Quality Circles: Self-Managing Teams," *Personnel* 62 (1985): 25-32.

48. J. Christen, "Problem-Solving Teams Improve Productivity, Reduce Costs," *Health Progress* 67 (1986): 74-75.

49. L.H. Aiken and C.F. Mullinix, "The Nurse Shortage: Myth or Reality?" *New England Journal of Medicine* 317 (1985): 641-646.

REFERENCES

Burton, G.E. 1986. Quality circles in a hospital environment. *Hospital Topics* 64:11-17.

Christen, J. 1986. Problem-solving teams improve productivity, reduce costs. *Health Progress* 67:74-75.

Cornell, L. 1984. Quality circles: A new cure for hospital dysfunctions. *Hospital and Health Services Administration Quarterly* 29:88-93.

Lehman, M.E. 1986. Quality circles: Their place in health care. *Hospital Topics* 64:15-19.

Tinello-Buddle, N. 1986. Quality circles: A management strategy that works. *Nursing Success Today* 3:9-11.

Chapter 9

Creating a Supportive Climate for Nursing Professionals

The quality of working life in nursing is a meaningful determinant of patient care and service delivery outcomes. Like other professionals, nurses deserve a work context that is nurturing to individual growth and helps them achieve patient care goals.[1] Nonetheless, health care organizations are not always able to provide a supportive environment.[2] For example, nursing and related medical professionals confront an inauspicious context in many health care organizations for delivering care. In acute care settings there is increasing concern for cost control. Nursing is conducted in an environment of growing austerity that potentially threatens patient care and professional satisfaction. Resource scarcity jeopardizes care delivery as a result of insufficient staffing, lack of continuity, and limited professional support.

The constraints on health care delivery ultimately influence nurses' decisions to continue in or to leave the profession. The result is a pervasive malaise among health care organizations and health professionals. Nurses discover that they lack sufficient resources to deliver patient care according to standards adopted through their professional socialization and training. Subsequently, they terminate practice or develop symptoms of stress, burn-out, absenteeism, and alienation.[3] When nurses are not satisfied in their jobs, whether in clinics, hospitals, nursing homes, or other service settings, the end result is inevitably a shortage of nurses. Without a consistent labor pool of satisfied and competent nurses, health care organizations are challenged to provide efficacious services.

For additional insight into the concepts presented in this chapter, see R.C. Burchell et al., "Physicians and the Organizational Evolution of Medicine," *Journal of the American Medical Association* 260 (August 1988): 826–831; H.L. Smith and N.F. Piland, "Managing Free Agents in Health Care Organizations: A Supervisory Challenge," *Health Care Supervisor* 8 (April 1990); and K.R. Mangelsdorf and H.L. Smith, "Toward a Cross-Cultural View of Job Satisfaction in Nursing," *Journal of Nursing Research* (in press).

ORGANIZATION CLIMATE

In the last 10 years health care organizations have expressed a growing interest in creating a climate that is conducive to nurse satisfaction and retention. Creating an enjoyable climate is a significant problem for nurse managers and health care organization development. The causal factors are numerous. A study by the *American Journal of Nursing* of approximately 3,500 nurses indicates the following sources of dissatisfaction (in rank order, with the factor causing the most dissatisfaction listed first) among those planning to leave nursing:[4]

1. help available when a patient needs extra care
2. support from nursing administrators
3. adequate salary
4. adequate nurse-patient ratio
5. sense of being an important member of the health team

Sufficient support from the health care organization (in terms of adequate staffing) and from nurse managers is a leading causal factor in nurse retention. Furthermore, these findings are consistent with those of previous studies of nurse retention in hospitals.[5,6]

The survey results clearly underscore the challenge confronting nurse managers. They can expect significant problems in designing a nursing program that is conducive to nurse satisfaction and retention. Therefore, it is appropriate to identify what concepts and objectives surround the notion of climate. Following are several key parameters of a supportive climate:

- the nature of the job context and its ability to provide a pleasant, challenging, and growth-oriented context in which nurses deliver services
- an environment that nurtures nurses' professional and personal development
- the extent to which the job context encourages nurses to reach their highest productivity, to deliver efficient services, and to maintain quality care
- the nature of interactions among nurses, nurse managers, work groups, departments, divisions, subsidiaries, and systems in health care organizations
- the degree of nurse participation in organizational decisions and functions

- the extent of commitment by nurses to a health care organization or nursing program
- the presence of reciprocity among nurses and teams in a nursing program
- the amount of stress and tension surrounding nurses' work
- the degree to which nurses feel satisfied with their tasks, supervision, remuneration, co-workers, individual and group performance, program or organizational image, physical working environment, and related factors influencing perceived satisfaction

These factors capture the essence of what nurse managers and staff nurses generally perceive as the central ingredients of organization climate. As with many evolving concepts in nursing there is uncertainty about the precise boundaries of organization climate. Consequently, it is proper to view organization climate as an evolving concept.

At the center of controversy regarding what organization climate does or does not incorporate is the recent popularity of organization culture. Health care organizations and nursing programs are intoxicated with searches for excellence in patient care.[7] Excellence is one aspect of culture. Broadly defined, organization culture involves the specific developmental stage of an organization's modes, means, and ends of action. When people talk about an organization's culture they are referring to the values, mentality, goals, methods of working toward ends, and style in which work is accomplished. Hence organization culture is a more encompassing term (involving values) than organization climate. Organization climate describes the work environment. Culture involves many factors, such as climate, beliefs, and goals.

To many nurse managers the issue appears to be simply one of semantics. To others, however, the issue involves seeking clarification before simply assuming a definition of organizational development, climate, and culture. The definitional boundaries are shifting among these terms, and it is easy to misinterpret another's intentions. That the boundaries are shifting in health care is not all that bad. It implies that the health professions are gradually reaching new understandings about the elusive nature and personality of organizations.

The concept of developing patient-centered nursing programs with a satisfying work setting for nurses is central to health care strategies.[8] Patient outcomes are inevitably linked with nurse morale.[9] As a result, nurses are differentiating relatively insensitive organizations from enlightened organizations. The former attract few nurses to work for them over an extended period. The latter are exemplars. Other nursing programs attempt to emulate them, and nurses will accept some personal sacrifices to enter their ranks.[10]

Managing Organization Climate

Given all their other responsibilities, it is little wonder that nurse managers seldom develop specific plans pertaining to organization climate. Nonetheless, there are ample pressures suggesting the need for action to the contrary. Stress,[11] the need for collaborative relations with physicians,[12,13] excessive expectations for nonnursing functions,[14] salaries,[15] and constraints on motivators[16] are a few factors suggesting the need for greater attention to the climate of nursing programs. The continual unexpected problems that arise in the course of clinical practice, however, cause nurse managers to focus on immediate crises rather than long-run operations. Crises both large and small inevitably distract nurse managers from planning alternative configurations for the environment that they and their staff members share. These crises include both problems and opportunities. For example, a shortage of supplies may produce the same disruption as a sudden opportunity to purchase from a competitor. Often, events cannot be forecasted. As a result, nurse managers are unable to allocate sufficient time to refining the organization or the nursing climate. They are too busy making 1–minute decisions.[17,18]

Failure to adjust the organization or nursing climate periodically can produce new crises. Nurse managers are then forced into allocating time to resolving problems rather than to preventing them. For example, nursing personnel may be highly upset about nursing standards and the inability of a health care organization to provide resources to maintain sufficient staffing.[19] Alternatively, staff may be particularly upset about pay, vacation, retirement benefits, cleanliness of the work environment, or other identifiable factors expressed directly to the nurse manager. Unless input is deliberately facilitated, nursing personnel may not openly express their views (because nurse managers have not created mechanisms for them to do so).[20] Consequently, staff express their disenchantment in (not so) subtle ways such as absenteeism, turnover, grievances, low productivity, poor-quality care, inattention to detail in service delivery, or the creation of waste in the service delivery process. These messages may take time for nurse managers to recognize unless an effective control system identifies the discrepancies and communicates them to nursing management.

In time, nursing management begins to sense that everything is not entirely well with the climate established for nursing personnel. It is the process of recognizing that the climate is dysfunctional that creates problems for nurse managers, however. By the time they realize that the nursing program or organization climate is unsatisfactory, it is usually too late to implement sufficient corrections before valued staff terminate. The problems have become so firmly established that a major crisis unfolds. At this point nurse managers experience the uncomfortable realization that it is not easy to create an effective nursing climate. It does not simply develop overnight. It takes a long time for a nursing program (and perhaps longer for a health care organization) to earn trust and respect from nursing personnel once that trust and respect have been lost. Throwing money at nursing staff only generates superficial solutions. Remaining causal factors seldom evaporate.

Considering these thoughts, it should be apparent to nurse managers that they need to be more deliberate in managing the organization climate surrounding nursing staff. This is precisely what has happened for many health care organizations that are experiencing high nurse turnover. Because it may cost more than $8,000 to recruit a nurse, health care organizations are realizing that it is more cost effective to retain current staff.[21] This problem in turnover is particularly insidious in large health care organizations because a long time is needed by many of these institutions to recognize and relate to the underlying problems. By then it may be too late. Partly, the answer lies in adopting nursing program structures that are flexible and nonbureaucratic and that facilitate communication. Partly, the answer lies in incorporating nursing program climate as a high priority in the daily process of managing. An additional answer is for nurse managers to assess periodically their climate to ascertain problems, the potential for problems, and mechanisms that can prevent further problems.

Periodic Assessments

Nursing research has made a number of remarkable strides in developing and applying instruments that are useful in assessing dimensions of the organization climate.[22] The work has established a benchmark from which to measure organization climate.[23,24] There is a growing profile of indices for these scores that allow nurse managers to compare their nursing programs with those of other organizations.[25,26] By moving from the abstract to the measurable, nursing research has created methodologies that can be periodically applied in determining the strengths and weaknesses of a nursing program's climate. With the use of survey data, specific interventions can be formulated that improve the existing climate.[27]

In view of the availability of tested and validated assessment tools, it is surprising that more nursing programs do not employ them for periodic use. In some respects it may be that nursing programs are reluctant to discover how their organization climate scores relative to that of other organizations. There may be a suspicion that the organization will not score well. This lack of confidence is not a prudent reason for not using such instruments. If a nursing program's climate is less than healthy, nurse managers want to know about it so that they can devise interventions that rectify underlying problems.[28] Nursing and health care organizations need to progress further in their thinking.

Periodic assessments or management audits should not be viewed negatively; rather, they should be viewed as an opportunity for constructive action. Such techniques and audits can confirm exceptional performance or a superlative nursing climate just as well as they can indicate poor performance. It is this positive perspective that nurse managers need to incorporate in their own practice. The prospects for improving a nursing program's climate are contingent on defining its present state. Periodic audits may confirm that actions are producing intended results. Alternatively, audits may suggest that factors outside the control of nurse managers (e.g., existing organizational policies) are responsible for the negative findings. When viewed from this perspective, nurse managers can be more confident that audits are ultimately a means to improve the climate of their nursing units, teams, departments, and programs.

Although various organization climate assessment instruments are found in the literature, several crucial dimensions normally should receive attention from nurse managers.[29] At the heart of organization climate is the ability to measure:

- organizational commitment
- job satisfaction
- job tension or stress
- absenteeism
- turnover
- esteem

These dimensions describe the esprit de corps or spirit of nurses toward their job context. Several of these key dimensions deserve further examination.

Organizational Commitment

Organizational commitment is the extent to which staff feel an allegiance to an organization. A high level of commitment is a preferred characteristic in health care organizations. In an organization of committed staff members, the prospects for attaining goals are improved. There is an intangible quality associated with high organizational commitment. Staff are willing to make sacrifices that they would not make for other programs or organizations. They may be willing to accept lower rates of pay, to strive toward seemingly impossible service goals and deadlines, to provide superb services in relatively spartan surroundings with dated equipment, and to remain with a program despite lucrative offers from local competitors. In short, when nursing staff are committed to an organization, the prospects are that much higher that nursing services will achieve impressive results. It is also likely that nurse retention will improve.[30]

Job Satisfaction

Job satisfaction is another vital aspect of organization climate that nurse managers can associate with high program performance. There is a rich literature on job satisfaction in nursing. As with organizational commitment, research suggests that when nurses express high levels of satisfaction they are more productive and provide higher quality care. Therefore, nurse managers are interested in formulating environments in which these end results can be attained. Nonetheless, some disagreement exists about the precise strategies that should be used to derive high job satisfaction. Results are conflicting. The by-product is that a number of theories overlap.

There is a growing number of studies on job satisfaction in nursing. Table 9-1 provides an overview of illustrative studies that have been completed since 1980. Judging by the number of studies, it is apparent that nurses' job satisfaction is an important research topic. Hospitals, nursing homes, clinics, and government health agencies need high productivity and quality patient care from nurses. Establishing a context in which nurses are satisfied with their jobs is one strategy for achieving these end results.

Several patterns are evident in Table 9-1. First, job satisfaction research is international in scope. The studies cited in Table 9-1 were conducted in Canada (British Columbia), Ireland, Australia (Melbourne), and the United States. Job satisfaction research is not limited to a few countries where nursing is struggling with various constraints. Many countries are concerned about the nursing environment. The specific research emphasis on variables related to job satisfaction (e.g., the association with primary nursing, retention and turnover, organizational hierarchy, and the like) varied among studies. Despite these variations, the common denominator is nurses' satisfaction with their work context.

Second, most of the studies cited in Table 9-1 involved hospitals as the primary study site. This pattern may imply that hospitals are more sensitive than other health care organizations to job satisfaction issues involving nursing staff. Also, hospitals provide a convenient site for field research, they are accessible, and they are the prevalent employer of nurses. Furthermore, hospitals offer a study site in which organization and management variables are relatively controllable.

Third, there is considerable variation in sample size among the hospitals and nurses studied in Table 9-1. The smallest sample was 37 nurses, and the

Table 9-1 Illustrative Studies of Job Satisfaction among Nurses since 1980

Author(s)	Description of Work	Sample	Results
Bush (1988)	Analyzed the relationship of job satisfaction to powerlessness and locus of control. Hypothesized that nurses expressing the inability to control events around them and feelings of powerlessness will be dissatisfied with their jobs.	145 nurses from six U.S. hospitals.	Both powerlessness and feelings of being unable to control events are associated with job dissatisfaction. Powerlessness is the primary explanatory variable.
Stewart-Dedmon (1988)	Explored differences in job satisfaction among recent graduates of nursing programs in relation to selected job characteristics and type of nursing education.	216 graduates from three schools of nursing in the United States.	Baccalaureate nurses express lower job satisfaction than nurses from an associate degree program or diploma program.
Dolan (1987)	Examined the relationship between job satisfaction and personal burn-out. Hypothesized an inverse relationship between the two variables.	90 female nurses from hospitals in Dublin, Ireland.	Low job satisfaction is associated with high burn-out. The work environment has a deleterious effect on job satisfaction and promotes burn-out.
Metcalf (1986)	A system of patient allocation is predicted to improve job satisfaction and quality of working life. Analyzed the differences in job satisfaction between nurses incorporated in a patient allocation system and those in a task-centered system.	54 nursing auxiliaries, nurses, and midwives in an Irish maternity hospital.	Limited confirmation that the system of patient allocation influenced job satisfaction. Results may have been affected by study site and sample size.
Lemler and Leach (1986)	Investigated turnover and job satisfaction. Prior research suggests that turnover is higher where job satisfaction is low.	74 nurses at a U.S. hospital.	Nurses were not leaving their jobs because of the normal factors associated with dissatisfaction (e.g., staffing, pay). Nurses who quit were more satisfied than dissatisfied. Research instrumentation and total personnel outlook may explain turnover.

Table 9-1 continued

Author(s)	Description of Work	Sample	Results
Simpson (1985)	Analyzed the association between job satisfaction and job level in organizational hierarchy. High-level jobs are expected to raise job satisfaction.	497 nurses from five hospitals in British Columbia.	Mixed results were found for the association between satisfaction and organizational level. High levels of dissatisfaction were reported for all nurses.
Weisman and Nathanson (1985)	Proposed that client satisfaction is contingent on staff job satisfaction.	344 family planning and community health nurses in Maryland.	Staff job satisfaction is associated with greater client satisfaction, but certain moderating variables (e.g., percentage of nurses with teenaged children, ability to set policies) influence the association.
Duxbury, Armstrong, Drew, and Henly (1984)	Leadership style variations in consideration and initiating structure are predicted to influence job satisfaction and burn-out.	283 registered nurses in staff nurse positions in 14 neonatal intensive care units in the United States.	Head nurse consideration (i.e., concern for personal needs) is clearly related to job satisfaction and to burn-out to a lesser degree.
Sellick, Russell, and Beckmann (1983)	Primary nursing is viewed as a mechanism to improve client and staff satisfaction as a result of individualized care and autonomy to plan and implement care.	37 nurses in a medical-surgical hospital in Melbourne, Australia.	Mixed results indicated lack of conclusive evidence for a firm association between staff satisfaction and primary nursing care.
Carlsen and Malley (1981)	Studied the relationship of job satisfaction with team nursing compared to primary nursing. Primary nursing is predicted to produce higher job satisfaction.	115 primary-system nurses were compared with 65 team-system nurses from a U.S. hospital.	Primary-system nurses reported more opportunity for accountability and related factors of job satisfaction.
Weisman, Alexander, and Chase (1980)	Examined variations in job satisfaction relative to individual characteristics, structural attributes of nursing units, attributes of the job, and perceptions of the job and unit.	5-month study of two panels of 594 nurses and 386 nurses at two U.S. hospitals.	Nurses' perceptions of their jobs and work units are the most important determinants of job satisfaction.

largest was 980 nurses. The unit of analysis that deserves attention, however, is not necessarily the number of nurses participating in a study but the number of organizations. The actual number of hospitals involved in the research was small. In effect, the research has limited external validity. Neither health care organizations nor nurses are adequately represented in job satisfaction studies. Additionally, the work environment in one hospital or health agency is assumed to be representative of that in other hospitals or health care organizations. The numerous variables differentiating among organizations may vitiate this premise.

Fourth, job satisfaction has been studied as both an independent and a dependent variable. It has been associated with:

- nursing philosophy (e.g., team-centered nursing or primary nursing)
- nurses' feelings, attitudes, and behavior (e.g., powerlessness, burn–out, stress, turnover, and absenteeism)
- client or patient satisfaction
- leadership styles
- job characteristics

The association between nursing philosophy and job satisfaction is a central focus of the research. Mixed results were obtained in the studies by Metcalf[31] and Sellick, Russell, and Beckmann,[32] whereas one study by Carlsen and Malley reported favorable job satisfaction associated with a primary nursing system.[33] This emphasis on nursing philosophy is a departure from previous studies, which have investigated quality of working life factors,[34,35] measurement techniques,[36,37] or turnover issues.[38,39]

Fifth, job satisfaction research has been carried out with inconsistent methodologies. There is wide variation in study populations as well as research instrumentation. Despite these differences, a remarkable similarity in results has been attained. Greater confidence could be placed in the findings if consistent measures of job satisfaction were utilized. Additionally, attention should be devoted to sampling. Often, different groups of nurses are compared, such as licensed practical nurses, registered nurses, nurse executives, nurse practitioners, and nurse specialists. Prior education (i.e., degree) and job level may significantly alter comparability of samples.[40,41]

The overall impression from Table 9-1 is that many variables influence or are associated with nurses' job satisfaction. The type of nursing philosophy (e.g., patient centered or team centered) may affect job satisfaction. Structural characteristics of a job including pay, level in the organizational hierarchy, control, role tension, and organizational stress are believed to affect job satisfaction.[42-45] In sum, a multivariate model is needed to explain variations in perceived job satisfaction among nurses.

Turnover

Few nursing management problems were as apparent in the 1980s as nurse retention and turnover.[46] A shortage of nurses has been compounded by numerous factors, resulting in significant challenges for health care organizations and nurse managers.[47-49] The problem is made even more difficult when turnover occurs among nursing administrators.[50] Some research studies have suggested that job satisfaction is associated with retention.[51] Consequently, nurse managers are examining various strategies for raising satisfaction and retention.[52,53] Successful efforts recognize the interaction of numerous variables, such as those portrayed in Figure 9-1.

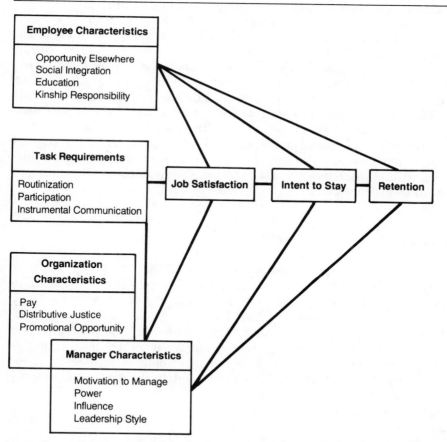

Figure 9-1 A Model of Retention in Nursing. *Source:* Reprinted from "Manager Impact on Retention of Hospital Staff: Part 1" by R.L. Taunton, S.D. Krampetz, and C.Q. Woods, *Journal of Nursing Administration*, Vol. 19, No. 3, p. 15, with permission of J.B. Lippincott Company, © March 1989.

This model suggests that four categories of variables affect nurses' job satisfaction and hence their intention to stay, which leads to retention.[54] Nurse manager characteristics (e.g., motivation to manage, power, influence, capability, leadership style, and experience) and organizational characteristics (e.g., incentive systems, remuneration, equity, career ladders, size, and decentralization of authority) affect task requirements of nursing positions and job satisfaction. Health care organizations and nurse managers are able to influence task requirements. They are able to expand (e.g., enrich nursing jobs through monitoring tasks, encourage participative decision making, or jointly establish challenging work goals) or contract (e.g., centralize decisions, underscore routine tasks, or dictate nursing objectives) the nature of nursing roles. These actions are causally linked to job satisfaction.

Despite the potential areas through which nurse managers and health care organizations influence nurses' job satisfaction, there is still an important uncontrollable variable shown in Figure 9-1: employee characteristics. Nurses have their own personalities, goals, experiences, familiar responsibilities, professional socialization, and market opportunities, all of which influence job satisfaction and retention. Turnover is directly linked to these personal predispositions. Nurse managers can only control the variables under their command. They can seek to attract and hire nurses whose values are consonant with those of the nursing program and health care organization. Beyond this action they can also establish an organization climate (by altering organization characteristics, task requirements, and their own management style) that supports staff.

Strategies for Improving Climate

After nurse managers have determined that their nursing program or organization climate is less than desirable, they must devise strategies to promote its potential well-being. Numerous strategies are available. Many concentrate on motivation and reward strategies. At this point it is appropriate to analyze briefly three strategies that have received widespread attention for their promise in improving organization climate. These three strategies are merely representative of the hundreds of options available to nurse managers. The art of managing is to select carefully the right strategy for the right situation.

Job Design

One strategy that has been recommended for improving nursing program or organization climate is job design. It consists of three ingredients:

1. *Job enlargement.* Nurses are assigned more tasks to improve the challenge of their job and to reduce boredom. For example, instead of just performing triage, a nurse may be delegated the responsibility of defining a treatment plan and schedule for patient follow-up. This instills variety in the task and relieves the boredom of repeating a single task.

2. *Job enrichment.* Nurses are incorporated into decision-making processes of the nursing department and are assigned more meaningful tasks. By sharing decisions about the service delivery process, their work tasks acquire more meaning. They are no longer simply repeating tasks but are active in and appreciative of the complexity surrounding health care services. For example, a licensed practical nurse at a clinic may log in patients and then assign them to examination rooms. Under a job enrichment strategy, he or she might participate in determining which patients will be scheduled for return visits during the following week and which will be scheduled for another week because of an excessively busy schedule. The job includes more tasks that require decision-making discretion.

3. *Job rotation.* Nurses periodically rotate in assignment in completing the various tasks that are included in a service. In this strategy, nurses come to know, appreciate, and complete all the tasks in a specific service. Variety prevents boredom. Additionally, there is greater flexibility because more nurses are capable of filling in at any specific point if illness or absenteeism occurs. Bottlenecks can be prevented. For example, a nurse executive in a consulting firm may be required to write proposals, to present the proposals to clients, to undertake the proposed analysis, to write up the analysis, to present the results to clients, and to undertake the follow-up. After rotating through each of these tasks, spending perhaps 4 months on each task or a combination of tasks, the nurse executive can fill in at any point in the process as necessary. Furthermore, by purposefully scheduling rotation it is unlikely that the nurse executive will be bored with any assignment.

The premise underlying job enlargement, job enrichment, and job rotation is that job variety and flexibility in assignments leads to fewer bored and more satisfied personnel. Under these conditions there is a high probability that the nursing program or organization climate will be improved.

Highly satisfied nurses are more likely to display this satisfaction in ways that generate a positive internal organizational environment. Does this necessarily lead to a desirable organization climate, however? The answer to this question is maybe. Satisfaction among nurses with their job assignments is a baseline that must be created before improving further on the organization climate. It should not be assumed, however, that simply by adjusting job design organization climate will reach the point where no further action must be taken. There are many other aspects of climate, such as commitment to excellence, loyalty, ethics, patient orientation, tolerance for sacrifice, team support, and related dimensions, that ultimately determine the personality and nature of the workplace. Job design alone cannot produce a favorable nursing climate.

Autonomous Teams

Autonomous work teams represent another strategy for improving organization climate. Under this strategy the dysfunctional effects of large-scale organization are reduced by grouping nurses into teams, which allows them to interact meaningfully with others. Large-scale health care organizations are notorious for creating feelings of unimportance among staff. Individual contributions appear to occur in a vacuum. By relying on teams, a nursing program creates an environment in which nurses know and share with other staff members. This is not to suggest that team members will always appreciate other team members, but the impersonality of the large organization will be reduced. The prospects for creating a sharing and nurturing environment for individual nurses are improved. The individual is less likely to perceive that a personal contribution or problem exists in a vacuum or void. Autonomous teams thereby instill a sense of contribution, membership, and self-worth that contributes to a productive nursing climate.

Quality Circles

Quality circles represent another approach that is seen as a cure-all for organizational ills. Although quality circles are primarily a problem-solving technique for service delivery, it has also been suggested that use of quality circles can improve organization climate. By bringing nurse managers and staff together in a forum in which authority has few privileges and communication is encouraged, quality circles may ultimately improve the organization climate. There is a diminished probability that staff nurses will perceive a division between themselves and management ranks as a result of sharing in the quality circle. The informal setting may allow nursing staff to express complaints and thereby serves as a valve to let off tension.

MANAGING ORGANIZATIONAL AVERSION

Nurse managers have had to contend with a series of intense changes during the last decade. Revisions in reimbursement policy, aggressive competition, multi-institutional system development, expanding corporate influence, diversification and joint ventures, and a more enlightened patient constituency illustrate the challenges confronting nursing programs and the health care field in recent years. A central tendency underlying these pressures is the development of large-scale or multi-institutional systems.[55] Although large–scale organizations provide distinct advantages for achieving economies of scale, they also have a number of disadvantages that may affect nurses. Concern about the dysfunctions that accompany large-scale health care organizations is most noticeable among clinicians (e.g., physicians and nurses).[56,57] Nurse managers may also have observed a spirit of uneasiness among staff members about the power and control of health care organizations. The implications of this trend are crucial. If nurses become distracted, they are less able to provide quality care or to maintain their productivity.

Harmony between nursing personnel and a health care organization can be disrupted by any number of factors, including compensation, performance expectations, lack of participation in decision making, and deficient leadership, to name a few. Many of the characteristics surrounding large-scale health care organizations affect harmony and create a sensitive interface with staff nurses. This disruption is fundamentally a problem of organizational aversion. In the problem's most basic form, staff are reluctant to make a sincere commitment to an organization or its goals.[58,59] Nurses may hesitate to cooperate with their programs and managers because they sense an inherent struggle.

The potential for organizational aversion among nurses is a problem because it threatens productivity, efficiency, and quality of care. If nurses do not sanction organizational efforts, they may render their work units and departments less effective in achieving goals. In turn, this may hinder health care organizations from addressing environmental constraints such as prospective payment, competition, or corporate takeover threats. Therefore, the desire of nurses to work in a supportive organization ultimately translates to a responsibility for nurse managers to provide the proper milieu.[60] Nurse managers need to circumvent the pressures that create conflicts between nurses and organizations. In short, they must manage the contentiousness that generates a feeling of organizational aversion among their staff members.

Organizational Aversion and Its Causal Attributes

In its most basic form, organizational aversion concerns the interrelationship of nurses and organizations. Exhibit 9-1 provides an overview of the concepts, symptoms, and determinants of organizational aversion. Specifi-

Exhibit 9-1 Concepts, Symptoms, and Determinants of Organizational Aversion

Organizational aversion: An adverse reaction by nurses to growing organizational control over their lives and work. At its extreme, staff may feel that they are unable to contribute in significant ways to an organization. They perceive that their role is inconsequential in the delivery of services.

Symptoms of organizational aversion

- Cynicism or pessimism about organizational values, operations, and issues
- Disagreement with the goals established for nursing units, departments, and the organization
- Hesitancy to cooperate with other personnel or departments outside nursing services
- Resistance to proposed changes
- Emphasis on self-interest rather than team effort

Determinants of organizational aversion

- Exclusion of nursing personnel from participation in or contribution to strategy formulation and objective-setting processes
- Limited channels of communication from nurses to top management
- Upward flow of information without reciprocity from top management
- Introduction of major organizational changes (e.g., staff reductions) without preparing staff
- Concentration of power and control in top management
- Utilization of organizational methods to promote growth in service delivery
- Revision of goals to emphasize efficiency, profitability, and market share at the expense of patients and nurses

cally, it refers to the schism that can develop between nurses and their employees. Nursing staff members recognize their limited impact on strategic decisions and plans.[61] They are omitted from strategic level planning that determines how health care organizations operate, under what policies, with guidance from which strategic objectives, and with what degree of resource support to implement plans. In essence, nurses may see themselves as making a relatively limited contribution to organizations. Additionally, they may perceive that they are treated as inconsequential in the larger service delivery process.

Organizational aversion has many similarities to patterns of alienation. Therefore, nurse managers should anticipate the presence of the symptoms outlined in Exhibit 9-1. They should suspect organizational aversion when nurses hesitate to cooperate with personnel in other departments. Organizational aversion should also be anticipated when staff are consistently cynical or express pessimism about organizational operations, goals, and values. In sum, there is a general climate of disagreement and resistance to efforts that are organizationally based.

The determinants of organizational aversion suggest that nurses are somewhat powerless to alter the basic relationship between themselves and their employer. Staff may be unable to correct significant problems in service delivery despite their obviousness. Few channels are available to nursing leaders or top management to express concern. In some cases, there is no reaction from top management because of the lack of subsequent communication or the low priority assigned to a problem, or because input is simply ignored. In short, nurses feel devalued and that their concerns exist in a vacuum. Meanwhile, the importance of the organization grows as an inverse function of the importance of nursing staff.

Nurse managers are caught in the middle of this conflict. They can either ignore the problem or address the symptoms and causal factors. Inaction will mean an escalating problem that may erupt with severe consequences (e.g., high absenteeism, high turnover, or union activity). Under more fortunate circumstances, top management will recognize the problem and administer organizationwide solutions. Alternatively, nurse managers can attack the problem by creating a better climate for staff members and patients or clients. To formulate an effective treatment program, nurse managers should understand the causal factors underlying organizational aversion.

Organizational Intensity in Health Care

Although organizational aversion has always been present in the health care field, its intensity has been minimal because of the prevailing cost-based reimbursement systems and the nonprofit orientation of health care providers. Health care was delivered through low-stress, resource-rich, nonsystematized institutions whose mission was primarily patient service. This tradition has been replaced by an entrepreneurial, competitive, and multi-institutional industry that pursues a diverse set of goals.

Central to the changing context of the health care field are new organization cultures that are centered around efficiency, economies of scale, and return on investment.[62] This may produce a less gratifying organization culture for several reasons. First, profit has become a legitimate organizational goal. Inevitably quality of care and profit (or efficiency) clash, but neither organizations nor health care professionals have been able to determine the extent to which quality should be traded off for profit or efficiency and vice versa. As a result, health care organizations are blindly trying to achieve both without understanding the consequences of mutually conflicting goals. Inevitably, nursing staff experience the brunt of this conflict.

Second, multi-institutional systems have expanded in health care.[63] Systems of care, as well as systems comprising smaller systems, have proliferated in the health care environment. Multi-institutional alliances, arrangements, and systems are developing among formerly autonomous providers. The end result is that nursing staff members find themselves at the bottom of a complex organizational structure. Their institutions represent only one unit in a larger system of institutions. Power is no longer locally based but centralized in corporate offices (possibly in another state) and invested in individuals whose names, faces, ideals, or agendas are not well known.

Third, control of health care organizations is concentrated in the hands of professional managers whose frame of reference is organizational well-being.[64] These managers are responsible for chains or systems of organizations. They may be sympathetic to the plight of any single institution, but their allegiance is to the system as a whole. This orientation may directly conflict with that of the nursing staff. The inherent altruism of health care delivery is being replaced by a new set of goals that nurses have little voice in establishing. Consistent with this change, nurses are viewed as productive resources. There is an attempt to derive the maximum productivity from a given investment in these resources.

Fourth, diversification has increased among health care providers.[65] The outcome of diversifying for many organizations is a loss of identity. The scope of strategy has been broadened to the point that virtually any link to health services makes an opportunity a legitimate strategic option. Many health care organizations are experimenting in services in which they lack a competitive advantage. Furthermore, diversification has diluted the sense of what health care organizations are all about. This trend has several ramifications for nurses. Staff observe that new groups of personnel are being added who do not necessarily hold the same values as the dominant culture. Nurses also recognize that the expendability of any service area has increased because virtually anything goes.

In sum, organizational aversion has become prominent as a result of the growth of organizational forces in health care. The prognosis is that the intensity of organizational influence will expand as health care providers wrestle with the complex pressures that are present in the health care sector. The implications for nurses are numerous, but they basically distill to one realization. There are likely to be numerous conflicts between nurses and organizations in the foreseeable future. Nurse managers will be confronted with this conflict unless their institutions establish specific plans and actions for remedying the forces of contention.

The Organizational Imperative

The trend toward increased organizational influence in society has been termed the "organizational imperative."[66] According to this view organizations are dominating many aspects of life, but particularly the production of goods and services. This theory culminates in the dominance of organizations, to which nurses have an inherent aversion. Nurse managers provide the most feasible option for overcoming this aversion. The excesses of organization can be tempered at the operating level when nurses are treated with dignity and when their worth as individuals is underscored.

Conflicts between Nurse and Organizational Goals

Organizational aversion reaches significant proportions when the goals of nurses and the goals of organizations separate from each other.[67] Nurses are motivated to join organizations for reasons other than just to be employed and to earn compensation. They may be attracted to a particular health care organization because it has a reputation for high-quality care, exceptional customer or patient service, a renowned nursing staff, opportunities for staff growth, profit sharing, or other salient features. Staff are disappointed to discover that such attractive aspects of the organization are gradually being replaced with other, less attractive ones.

As health care organizations become increasingly concerned with goals that emphasize the bottom line of financial statements, the opportunities for disparity between organizational and individual goals increase. Nurses are left with few choices other than to terminate their affiliation or to respond in counterproductive ways. Even nonprofit health care organizations are beginning to mimic their for-profit counterparts. They are more reluctant to practice under financially constrained operations, as they did in the past. Nonprofit organizations must emulate for-profit organizations if they intend to survive financially. Consequently, most health care organizations are cultivating a climate in which organizational aversion is possible.

The reorientation of organizational goals is alarming to nursing staff members who have not adopted, and do not have the incentives to adopt, a new philosophy for health care delivery. Furthermore, nurses, who have traditionally held little power or prestige in organizations, are witnessing a continued deterioration of their status. In the end many nurses are left with a sense of frustration in their profession and in their organizations. Once part of a noble endeavor, nurses are discovering that they are viewed as employees in manufacturing sectors. Service delivery is scrutinized for the consumption of resources and production of revenue. Nurses are crucial but expendable units of production.

The lack of harmony between individual goals and organizational goals is more than just a disquieting disconformity. At the same time that health care organizations are adopting new goals, they are also asking nurses to work even harder in the conversion. For example, nurses are directly confronting the demands of resource-constrained organizations.[68] The easiest way to trim costs in the short run is to decrease expensive nurse staffing. This places a greater burden on remaining nurses to provide high-quality and nurturing care to patients because they care for too many patients. Simultaneously, health care institutions are requesting more assistance in meeting cost-control goals. It is little wonder that, squeezed to the limit, nurses have difficulty in joining the drive to greater austerity. Such tactics may not be consistent with their view of how services or care should be delivered. Moreover, they recognize that the next level of staffing cuts may slash their positions. Under these circumstances, it is understandable why nurses are not embracing organizational goals.

Management theory and research suggest that the best organizations formulate a culture in which personnel share the same values, beliefs, attitudes, and goals.[69,70] When these cultures are working at their optimum, remarkable gains can be made in productivity, quality, costs, and profit. Organizational aversion implies a relationship that is counterproductive to an effective culture. Therefore, health care organizations and nurse managers need to address the disconformity that exists in expressed goals. For health care organizations and nurse managers, organizational aversion is an impediment to a productive organization culture. They must invoke tactics that address goal conflict.

Methods for Minimizing Organizational Aversion

As Figure 9-2 suggests, increasing organizational intensity in health care plus the prevailing trends in organizational climates create the need for an agenda that minimizes organizational aversion. The most frequently mentioned remedy is to encourage accommodation between organization and nurses.[71] Both organizations and nursing staff members need to appreciate each other's goals and values if they intend to create an effective service delivery environment.

How can the concept of accommodation be implemented in an effective manner? Available research suggests that three strategies have promise for reaching a mutual understanding and collaborative relationship between organizations and employees.[72] Organizations and nurse managers have the responsibility to initiate these strategies because they have the power to revise their infrastructure and service delivery process. In contrast, nurses have relatively little power to initiate change, especially when it involves a fundamental difference in goals. As a result, nurse managers must take the lead in resolving differences. A prudent plan to minimize organizational aversion should center around anticipation, diagnosis, and treatment.

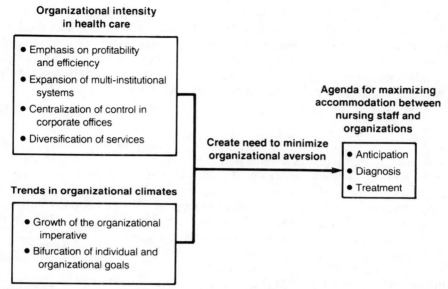

Figure 9-2 Determinants of Organizational Aversion and Methods for Minimizing Its Impact on Nurses

---

Anticipation

Nursing programs need to be more sensitive to the implications of their decisions, plans, and changes relative to nurses. Ultimately, it is nursing staff members who implement change. Nevertheless, nurses tend to avoid change. In many cases, the prospect of undertaking change is far more traumatic than the actual magnitude of the change. Therefore, nurse managers need to anticipate and minimize the dysfunctional consequences resulting from operational changes in their respective clinical departments. Anticipation may be as simple as soliciting input from staff members before a change is introduced. Nurses might be asked to recommend methods that will minimize the adverse impact felt by patients and themselves. If nurse managers would seek this input before planning and implementing changes, it is possible that much greater commitment would be elicited from staff members before alterations began. If they do not seek the input, then the decisions or actions may be viewed as unilateral and hence organizationally centered.

In other situations anticipation may by implemented by keeping nurses informed of pending decisions or plans and of the rationale for such actions. The key is to expand communications to prevent the possibility of miscommunication or misinterpretation. For example, nurse managers can brief staff on the progress of new projects so that staff can understand why certain events are happening and what direction will be taken in the future. The communication should not be one sided. Staff should be encouraged to analyze what a specific change implies for departmental, team, or unit operations. Recommendations can also be solicited regarding how to improve the change. It is through this mutual sharing that miscommunication is avoided and commitment elicited.

Diagnosis

Organizational aversion is easily detected if nurse managers remain alert to its potential outbreak among staff members. Nurse managers are often hesitant to probe too far when they first discover dissatisfaction among staff members, however. They may perceive that nurses do not want any intrusions. Alternatively, they may not know how to resolve problems and hence are reluctant to pursue the matter further. By maintaining these attitudes, nurse managers do not improve the situation and risk compounding problems. In short, it is difficult to detect and treat problems unless the extent of the issue is clarified. By prudent assessment and incorporation of findings in a plan of action, nurse managers may be able to minimize the growth of organizational aversion.

For example, nurse managers might ascertain the extent to which staff members share the same values as the organization. Through personal discussions and group meetings, a profile of nurses' values in a unit or team can be established. In other cases, nurse managers may utilize survey instruments to assess attitudes. When this information is compiled, a better understanding of variances between organizational values and individual, group, team, unit, or departmental values is established. Knowing the scope and magnitude of the difference facilitates planning to manage the difference. Diagnosis identifies the problem and helps clarify what interventions are needed, and for whom, in creating a more healthy organizational environment for nursing staff.

Treatment

Unless nurse managers initiate corrective action, organizational aversion may continue to hamper nurse performance. At issue is which treatment methodologies to utilize. It should be recognized that no panacea or quick fix has much promise of resolving the fundamental problem. Instead, a reasonable treatment plan considers the causal factors of organization aversion and responds accordingly. In many cases this means that nurse managers will be challenged to build confidence among staff members that a balance can be attained between personal aspirations and organizational goals. Commitment can be elicited by creating opportunities for investment on the part of staff members. When they have meaningful input into unit or department changes, they are more likely to perceive that the resulting program reflects their goals.

Not every nurse perceives the need to participate in determining how organizational changes will take place. Some may wish to avoid the issue altogether. Nurse managers should anticipate this response. The process of participation acquires a sense of purpose among those nurses who do participate. When nurses are judiciously approached to provide their thoughts about specific issues, it becomes easier for them to offer suggestions even though they may normally be hesitant to do so. In this manner, organizational aversion loses its power because nursing staff have an active role in direction setting. Trust and understanding begin to bridge the gap between individual and organizational values.

Another approach in treating organizational aversion is to restructure the delivery process around teams. The purpose of team building is to erase the rigid formality that characterizes bureaucratic organizations. This is not to imply that efficiency that accompanies bureaucracy is undesired. Rather, excessive efficiency may prevent the attainment of broader goals, such as effectiveness. Redesigning work units to form collaborative teams or quality circles can forge a spirit of cooperation. Then, as part of a collaborative team rather than a formal work unit, nursing staff are better able to instill their values into the work process.

Implications for Nurse Managers

From many perspectives it appears that health care organizations are beginning to serve their own interests instead of those of nurses. Despite this conflict, it is obvious that organizations and nurses need each other. Organizations cannot deliver high-quality and low-cost services unless they have committed nurses. Conversely, nurses need an environment for work that supports their basic value system and dignity; otherwise they become averse to their job setting. Organizational aversion is a significant issue for nurse managers because of their strategic location and ability to implement remedial strategies that reduce the underlying tension. Through anticipation, diagnosis, and treatment, nurse managers can improve the opportunities for their staff members to contribute to the evolving goals of organizations.

MANAGING FREE AGENTS AND NURSING CLIMATE

Nurse managers are responsible for developing teamwork in their units, programs, and departments. Books such as *Theory Z*,[73] *In Search of*

Excellence,[74] *The Art of Japanese Management,*[75] and *A Passion for Excellence*[76] have reinforced the role of corporate cultures in improving organizational performance. Strategies for achieving powerful organization cultures are popular topics among executives. However fruitful this thinking, nurses who are not interested in contributing to the organization culture are often overlooked. It is presumptuous to think that every nurse will enthusiastically embrace the responsibilities and effort of forging the culture.

The nurses who are most likely to present a problem in culture building are those who behave as free agents. They are not overly interested in joining an organization's culture. Some are not seeking long-term employment with an organization. They may have other job options. They focus on personal goals instead of organizational goals. Nonetheless, organizations need their services. Considering this predicament, nurse managers should be alert to the anomaly known as the free agent. They must understand organizational culture goals and free agent goals as well as the unique perspectives of each. Such fundamentals are crucial for managing nurses who behave as free agents.

The Free Agent Concept

In the organizational sense, a free agent is any nurse who is unwilling to make a strong commitment to a health care organization's mission, goals, policies, culture, and strategies for achieving goals. The primary distinguishing characteristic of nurses who behave as free agents is the reluctance to make an organizational commitment. A free agent may develop a low or moderate level of commitment,[77] but such individuals are not champions of their organization. They can achieve personal and professional goals in many organizations. Hence there is limited incentive to be highly committed to any one organization.

Powerful organization cultures rely on high staff commitment. If a sufficient number of nurses do not actively support the organization's goals, policies, and strategies, then the desired culture may not evolve. Free agents are weak links in the culture-building process. They will not personally sacrifice to reinforce the culture. They may not hinder the evolution of a culture, but they are not reliable for maintaining its momentum. Beyond this hesitancy to make an organizational commitment, free agents share several characteristics.

Free agents have a narrow view of organization-individual reciprocity. They have a strong sense of self-interest that overrides their concern for an organization. For example, a nurse may be concerned about the quality of care that he or she delivers and the contribution made to the organization's final product. Although this concern is tangible, it does not outweigh the nurse's allegiance to self. If another health care provider offers a $2-per-hour pay increase, the nurse will probably take the new job. This may disrupt the staffing schedule of the present employer, a fact that concerns the nurse but does not prevent termination.

Free agents view all organizations as nearly equal despite management's efforts to create distinct cultures. For example, many nurses encounter virtually the same treatment—wages, schedule, benefits, perquisites, and working conditions—from all employers. These variables may differ among employers, but the magnitude of the differences is insufficient to distinguish one organization from another. Therefore, nursing service jobs in hospitals, nursing homes, or clinics may have few distinctive advantages. The free agent nurse tends to view these employers as relatively equal.

Because free agents have a limited organizational commitment, they are willing to change affiliations. In extremes, they will exit a profession if circumstances are not personally rewarding. For example, an RN discovers that local community hospitals offer the same scheduling opportunities, salary and benefits, approach to patient care, medical staff relations, and career advancement opportunities. There are minimal penalties for changing jobs because marginal differences exist in organizational benefits and climate. Additionally, the RN discovers that hospital medical staffs comprise virtually the same physicians with whom it is impossible to work. Consequently, the free agent may quit nursing altogether or seek employment in other health services organizations (e.g., a nursing home or a private medical practice).

Free agents may manifest short-run loyalty to an organization, but such tendencies should not be interpreted as an indelible commitment. The job is only a momentary event in a lifetime. For example, a nurse manager may remain loyal by conscientiously managing staff productivity and care quality. As a loyal nurse manager, group performance goals must be achieved. Although this perceived responsibility guides managerial behavior, it does not bind the nurse to the organization. When a more attractive director of nursing position becomes available in another hospital, the nurse manager cuts the ties of loyalty.

Some free agents are more committed to their profession than they are to an organization. They are interested in the skills and knowledge associated with the nursing profession, are identified by those virtues, and are able to fulfill profession expectations under many organizational circumstances. The profession breeds autonomy from organizations. For example, a professor in a nursing school can conduct research and teach at many colleges and universities. Alternatively, some of these professional activities can also be completed at a private research institution or in industry.

Many nurses, including free agents, become less committed to an organization when they perceive a lack of reciprocity from their employer. For example, an RN discovers that exceptionally high risks for nursing malpractice are occurring because a hospital is understaffed. In this case free agents perceive that they are investing more in the organization than the organization is investing in them.

Managing the Free Agent Phenomenon

The problem of free agents is experienced in many health care organizations. This phenomenon could become more prevalent as societal values change and as the role of health care is reassessed. The disturbing realization is that, just when health care organizations and nursing programs recognize the importance of cultures, obstacles to this goal become apparent. At some point nurse managers may begin to question whether cultures of excellence are really attainable.

Nurse managers could benefit from a broader understanding of free agents' characteristics, behavior, and values when formulating strategies. Ultimately, insight into free agents' attributes and motivations can facilitate how they are managed in a nursing department, program, or unit. The salient point for nurse managers is that some nurses, particularly those exhibiting free agent characteristics, cannot be persuaded to invest in a specific corporate culture. In many health care organizations free agents are responsible for affecting services and thus the quality of care, profitability, and effectiveness of goal attainment.

If nurses are unwilling to make a high organizational commitment, it will be difficult to forge a powerful culture. This problem has serious ramifications when free agents have direct contact with patients. Most nursing staff may pursue excellence; free agents may not. More troubling still, the patient-organization transaction may be handled by a free agent. The intended culture remains partially hidden. Consider the temporary nurse who is employed for a 2-month period and who holds a limited interest in excellence. The organization can expend great effort in providing efficient nursing or patient care equipment, spotless and comfortable facilities, the finest supplies, high-profile marketing, sophisticated orientation and training for nurses, competitive wages, and skilled supervision, but at some point the patient and nurse must interact.

The nurse is pivotal in conveying the corporate culture. If the nurse is a free agent, there is a reasonable possibility that the organization's intent may never reach the patient. Granted, not all nurses are free agents. Many perceive themselves to be part of a larger culture that is seeking excellence in health care delivery. Nevertheless, how many temporary nurses are merely marking time until other job opportunities become available or until their personal plans begin to mature? How many could be working down the street at another hospital? Given these considerations, a difficult challenge confronts nurse managers who seek to build cultures and climates of excellence.

Management Strategies

How can nurse managers respond to the free agent phenomenon? First, they should not assume that there is safety in numbers. For example, a nursing program may be founded on the belief that nurses who are making a conscientious commitment to quality care greatly outnumber free agents. This difference in numbers may be true. Nonetheless, poor-quality care has a powerful negative influence on patient attitudes. Once this negative attitude is established, it is difficult to alter. Nurses play an extremely important role in generating service quality. Free agents can produce serious consequences, whether intentional or not.

Recognizing that even a few free agents can create havoc, nurse managers should reassess their control over patient service or care quality. They should anticipate disasters that could occur, create mechanisms by which the program responds to patients' perceptions of poor service or care quality produced by free agents, analyze service delivery to ascertain where weaknesses exist, and determine the points at which free agents can adversely influence patients.

Second, nurse managers should reexamine nurse recruitment and selection processes. When a culture is being built, nurses should be recruited and selected who have values that are consistent with the intended culture. Personnel evaluation is sufficiently sophisticated to measure personality differences and to facilitate selections on the basis of a desired culture. Two steps must be completed. The values and beliefs characterizing the envisioned culture are defined, and then the corresponding attributes held by applicants and needed by the culture are specified. The goal is to match individual and organization. In sum, a higher investment in human resource management promotes recruitment and selection of the proper candidates.

Third, nurse managers can adjust the incentive systems that are available to free agents. This strategy requires a decision about the additional expenditures necessary to minimize the free agent phenomenon. Ultimately this may mean that salaries or benefits are raised, but analysis of incentives should extend beyond pay. The entire spectrum of benefits, working conditions, and incentives should be assessed. (The objective is to determine when the additional costs of retaining free agents exceed the benefits.) Admittedly, this strategy may create high economic costs in resolving the free agent problem. These costs could be too excessive for some health care organizations to tolerate.

Pay deficiency is not the primary factor that determines whether nurses are free agents. It may be convenient to explain the free agent phenomenon in economic or labor market terms, but free agents prevail because of factors other than pay. Even when pay levels are exceptionally high, free agents exist. Furthermore, free agents cannot be explained solely on the basis of labor market dynamics. For example, RNs have numerous job opportunities in various professional settings. There is a wide continuum of professional wages and salaries. Despite these degrees of freedom, some RNs are unable to make commitments to health care organizations. They become free agents and drop out of the RN labor pool.

Fourth, nurse managers can settle for powerful subcultures in their total organization. This strategy recognizes that large organizations comprise many individuals. The expectation that each nurse will adopt and support a common value system may be too idealistic. Nurse managers should recognize that cultures devoted to excellence remain an ideal rather than a reality. The evolution to a more powerful culture could take decades. As a result, it may be feasible to reach consensus at specific levels of the organizational hierarchy. Progressive refinement of the culture and adherence to an ideal model could eventually produce the desired results.

Toward Distinctive Nursing Cultures and Climates

Free agents are typically the nurses whom health care organizations least expect to represent a constraint when creating a powerful culture. They may have minimal ability to influence organizational goals. Often, they can be replaced at limited expense. Nonetheless, they represent a distinct threat to cultures. Free agents make it difficult to achieve the ideal cultures that so many nurse managers and health care organizations believe are necessary in the current competitive environment.

Several promising strategies have been identified above for managing free agents. The first step is recognizing that a problem exists. On this basis, a plan of action can be formulated. As with most organizational problems, there is no one best way to resolve the dilemma presented by free agents. In fact, some health care organizations can reverse the algorithm by capitalizing on free agents in their ranks. This approach will become less viable as organizations begin to pursue a specific culture. In the final analysis, the best advice is to proceed cautiously when managing the free agent–organization culture interface.

NOTES

1. C. Weisman and C.A. Nathanson, "Professional Satisfaction and Client Outcomes: A Comparative Organizational Analysis," *Medical Care* 23 (September 1985): 1179.

2. J.R. Hackman and J.L. Suttle, *Improving Life at Work* (Santa Monica, CA: Goodyear, 1977).

3. F.T. Helmer and P. McKnight, "One More Time—Solutions to the Nursing Shortage," *Journal of Nursing Administration* 18 (November 1988): 7-15.

4. F.L. Huey and S. Hartley, "What Keeps Nurses in Nursing," *American Journal of Nursing* 88 (February 1988): 181-188.

5. E.E. Mann and K.J. Jefferson, "Retaining Staff: Using Turnover Indices and Surveys," *Journal of Nursing Administration* 18 (July/August 1988): 17-23.

6. M.L. Duxbury and G.D. Armstrong, "Calculating Nurse Turnover Indices," *Journal of Nursing Administration* 12 (March 1982): 18-24.

7. P. Scherer, "Hospitals That Attract (and Keep) Nurses," *American Journal of Nursing* 88 (January 1988): 34-40.

8. R.D. Hays and K. White, "Professional Satisfaction and Client Outcomes," *Medical Care* 25 (March 1987): 259-264.

9. C.E. Loveridge, "Contingency Theory: Explaining Staff Nurse Retention," *Journal of Nursing Administration* 18 (June 1988): 22-25.

10. L.L. Wall, "Plan Development for a Nurse Recruitment-Retention Program," *Journal of Nursing Administration* 18 (February 1988): 20-26.

11. P.A. Gray-Toft and J.G. Anderson, "Organizational Stress in the Hospital: Development of a Model for Diagnosis and Prediction," *Health Services Research* 19 (February 1985): 753-774.

12. C. Ziegfeld and S. Jones, "An Innovative Strategy to Facilitate Nurse-Physician Interaction," *Journal of Continuing Education in Nursing* 18 (March/April 1987): 47-50.

13. C. Miller, "Shaping a Collaborative Practice Environment," *Nursing Administration Quarterly* 11 (Summer 1987): 24-26.

14. K. Davis, "Non-Nursing Functions," *American Journal of Nursing* 82 (December 1982): 1857-1860.

15. N.P. Greenleaf and M. Stevenson, "Economic Beliefs and Nurses' Wages: Sorting Fact from Fantasy," *Nursing Forum* 21 (February 1984): 53-62.

16. E. Sanger, J. Richardson, and E. Larson, "What Satisfies Nurses Enough To Keep Them?" *Nursing Management* 16 (September 1985): 43-46.

17. R.S. Ferri, "In Search of the Excellent One-Minute Megatrend . . . Or How To Tolerate the Five-Minute Burden," *American Journal of Nursing* 87 (January 1987): 109-110.

18. M.A. Grantham, R.C. MacKay, and C.M. Allison, "Job Satisfaction and Interruptions in the Planned Time of Nursing Managers," *Journal of Nursing Administration* 15 (May 1985): 7-8.

19. W.B. Young, "Who Sets Nursing Standards: The Nursing Profession or the Employment Setting?" *Nursing Administration Quarterly* 12 (Winter 1988): 78-86.

20. D.D. Pointer, D.W. Strum, and C.C. Scalzi, "Strengthening the Top-Level Management Team," *Journal of Nursing Administration* 11 (February 1981): 45-48.

21. A.S. Henshaw, C.H. Smeltzer, and J.R. Atwood, "Innovative Retention Strategies for Nursing Staff," *Journal of Nursing Administration* 17 (June 1987): 8-15.

22. C.S. Weisman, C.S. Alexander, and G.A. Chase, "Job Satisfaction among Hospital Nurses: A Longitudinal Study," *Health Services Research* 15 (April 1980): 341-364.

23. D. Slavitt et al., "Measuring Nurses' Job Satisfaction," *Hospital and Health Services Administration* 24 (Summer 1979): 62-76.

24. R.H. Carlsen and J.D. Malley, "Job Satisfaction of Staff Registered Nurses in Primary and Team Nursing Delivery Systems," *Research in Nursing and Health* 4 (1981): 251-260.

25. K. Simpson, "Job Satisfaction or Dissatisfaction Reported by Registered Nurses," *Nursing Administration Quarterly* 9 (Spring 1985): 64-73.

26. N. Dolan, "The Relationship between Burnout and Job Satisfaction in Nurses," *Journal of Advanced Nursing* 12 (1987): 3-12.

27. C.A. Metcalf, "Job Satisfaction and Organizational Change in a Maternity Hospital," *International Journal of Nursing Studies* 23 (1986): 285-298.

28. R.R. Roedel and P.C. Nystrom, "Nursing Jobs and Satisfaction," *Nursing Management* 19 (February 1988): 34-38.

29. M.L. Duxbury et al., "Head Nurse Leadership Style with Staff Nurse Burnout and Job Satisfaction in Neonatal Intensive Care Units," *Nursing Research* 33 (March/April 1984): 97-101.

30. K. Kerfoot, "Retention: What's It All About?" *Nursing Economics* 6 (January/February 1988): 42-43.

31. Metcalf, "Job Satisfaction and Organizational Change in a Maternity Hospital," 285.

32. K.J. Sellick, S. Russell, and J.L. Beckmann, "Primary Nursing: An Evaluation of Its Effects on Patient Perception of Care and Staff Satisfaction," *International Journal of Nursing Studies* 20 (1983): 265-273.

33. Carlsen and Malley, "Job Satisfaction of Staff Registered Nurses in Primary and Team Nursing Delivery Systems," 251-260.

34. A.P. Brief, "Turnover among Hospital Nurses: A Suggested Model," *Journal of Nursing Administration* 6 (1976): 55-58.

35. H.L. Smith, "Nurses' Quality of Working Life in an HMO: A Comparative Study," *Nursing Research* 30 (1981): 54-58.

36. F. Munson and S. Heda, "An Instrument for Measuring Nursing Satisfaction," *Nursing Research* 23 (1974): 159-166.

37. Slavitt et al., "Measuring Nurses' Job Satisfaction," 64.

38. G.A. Nichols, "Job Satisfaction and Nurses' Intentions To Remain with or Leave an Organization," *Nursing Research* 20 (1971): 218.

39. M. Kramer, *Reality Shock: Why Nurses Leave Nursing* (Saint Louis, MO: Mosby, 1987).

40. Simpson, "Job Satisfaction or Dissatisfaction Reported by Registered Nurses," 67.

41. M. Stewart-Dedmon, "Job Satisfaction of New Graduates," *Western Journal of Nursing Research* 10 (1988): 66-72.

42. J.P. Bush, "Job Satisfaction, Powerlessness, and Locus of Control," *Western Journal of Nursing Research* 10 (1988): 718-731.

43. S.F. Lemler and A.K. Leach, "The Effect of Job Satisfaction on Retention," *Nursing Management* 17 (1986): 66-68.

44. Duxbury et al., "Head Nurse Leadership Style," 99.

45. K.L. Ruffing, H.L. Smith, and R. Rogers, "Factors That Encourage Nurses To Remain in Nursing," *Nursing Forum* 21 (1984): 78-85.

46. P.A. Prescott and S.A. Bowen, "Controlling Nursing Turnover," *Nursing Management* 18 (1986): 60-66.

47. L.H. Aiken and C.F. Mullinix, "The Nurse Shortage: Myth or Reality?" *New England Journal of Medicine* 317 (1987): 641-646.

48. J.K. Inglehart, "Problems Facing the Nursing Profession," *New England Journal of Medicine* 317 (1987): 646-651.

49. National League for Nursing, "Summary Report on American Nurse Career Pattern Study: Baccalaureate Degree Nurses Ten Years after Graduation," *Journal of Advanced Nursing* 4 (1979): 687-692.

50. D.R. Sredl, "Administrative Turnover," *Nursing Management* 13 (November 1982): 24-30.

51. Lemler and Leach, "The Effect of Job Satisfaction on Retention," 66.

52. Henshaw, Smeltzer, and Atwood, "Innovative Retention Strategies for Nursing Staff," 10.

53. Dolan, "The Relationship between Burnout and Job Satisfaction in Nurses," 7.

54. R.L. Taunton, S.D. Krampetz, and C.Q. Woods, "Manager Impact on Retention of Hospital Staff: Part 1," *Journal of Nursing Administration* 19 (March 1989): 14-19.

55. A.S. Relman, "The New Medicine-Industrial Complex," *New England Journal of Medicine* 303 (1980): 963-970.

56. S.M. Shortell, "The Medical Staff of the Future: Replanting the Garden," *Frontiers of Health Services Management* 1 (1985): 3-48.

57. J.E. Kralewski et al., "The Physician Rebellion," *New England Journal of Medicine* 316 (1985): 339-342.

58. R.T. Mowday, L.W. Porter, and R.M. Steers, *Employee-Organization Linkages: The Psychology of Commitment, Absenteeism and Turnover* (New York: Academic Press, 1982).

59. C. Argyris, *Integrating the Individual and the Organization* (New York: Wiley, 1964).

60. S.A. Culbert and J.J. McDonough, *The Invisible War: Pursuing Self Interests at Work* (New York: Wiley, 1980).

61. A.L. Hillman et al., "Managing the Medical-Industrial Complex," *New England Journal of Medicine* 315 (1986): 511-513.

62. B.H. Gray, "Overview: Origins and Trends," *Bulletin of the New York Academy of Medicine* 61 (1985): 7-22.

63. M.D. Fottler et al., "Multi-institutional Arrangements in Health Care: Review, Analysis, and a Proposal for Future Research," *Academy of Management Review* 7 (1982): 67-69.

64. J.B. Quintana, W.J. Duncan, and H.W. Houser, "Hospital Governance and the Corporate Revolution," *Health Care Management Review* 10 (1985): 63-71.

65. J.D. Goldsmith, "Competition: How Will It Affect Hospitals," *Healthcare Financial Management* 36 (1982): 64-74.

66. W.G. Scott and D.K. Hart, *Organizational America* (Boston: Houghton Mifflin, 1979).

67. L.R. James and A.P. Jones, "Organizational Climate: A Review of Theory and Research," *Psychological Bulletin* 81 (1974): 1096-1112.

68. Inglehart, "Problems Facing the Nursing Profession," 646.

69. T.J. Peters and R.H. Waterman, *In Search of Excellence* (New York: Warner, 1982).

70. V. Sathe, *Culture and Related Corporate Realities* (Homewood, IL: Irwin, 1985).

71. E.A. Simendinger and W. Pasmore, "Developing Partnerships between Physicians and Health Care Executives," *Hospital and Health Services Administration Quarterly* 29 (1984): 21-35.

72. S. Wright and A. Wright, "A Cooperative Organizational Form for Hospitals," *Health Care Management Review* 9 (1984): 7-19.

73. W.G. Ouchi, *Theory Z: How American Business Can Meet the Japanese Challenge* (Reading, MA: Addison-Wesley, 1981).

74. Peters and Waterman, *In Search of Excellence.*

75. R.T. Pascale and A.G. Athos, *The Art of Japanese Management: Applications for American Executives* (New York: Warner, 1981).

76. T.J. Peters and N. Austin, *A Passion for Excellence* (New York: Random House, 1985).

77. D.M. Randall, "Commitment and the Organization: The Organization Man Revisited," *Academy of Management Review* 12 (1987): 460-471.

REFERENCES

Bush, J.P. 1988. Job Satisfaction, powerlessness, and locus of control. *Western Journal of Nursing Research* 10:718-731.

Carlsen, R.H., and J.D. Malley. 1981. Job satisfaction of staff registered nurses in primary and team nursing delivery systems. *Research in Nursing and Health* 4:251-260.

Dolan, N. 1987. The relationship between burnout and job satisfaction in nurses. *Journal of Advanced Nursing* 12:3-12.

Duxbury, M.L., et al. 1984. Head nurse leadership style with staff nurse burnout and job satisfaction in neonatal intensive care units. *Nursing Research* 33:97-101.

Lemler, S.F., and A.K. Leach. 1986. The effect of job satisfaction on retention. *Nursing Management* 17:66-68.

Metcalf, C.A. 1986. Job satisfaction and organizational change in a maternity hospital. *International Journal of Nursing Studies* 23:285-298.

Selleck, K.J., S. Russell, and J.L. Beckmann. 1983. Primary nursing: An evaluation of its effects on patient perception of care and staff satisfaction. *International Journal of Nursing Studies* 20:265-273.

Simpson, K. 1985. Job satisfaction or dissatisfaction reported by registered nurses. *Nursing Administration Quarterly* 9:64-73.

Stewart-Dedmon, M. 1988. Job satisfaction of new graduates. *Western Journal of Nursing Research* 10:66-72.

Weisman, C.S., C.S. Alexander, and G.A. Chase. 1980. Job satisfaction among hospital nurses: A longitudinal study. *Health Services Research* 15:341-364.

Weisman, C., and C.A. Nathanson. 1985. Professional satisfaction and client outcomes: A comparative organizational analysis. *Medical Care* 23:1179.

Chapter 10

Establishing a Managerial Profile

Why are nurse managers a crucial link in the survival plan for nursing and health care organizations? Is it reasonable for nurse managers to expect to resolve many of the problems that are facing the profession? What sort of managerial profile is needed for nurse managers to function more effectively as intermediaries between nurses and organizations? What is needed for nurse managers to succeed in the future when in the past they have faced many obstacles and constraints? The purpose of this chapter is to answer these questions. Arguments for and against the expanded leadership role of nurse managers are considered. The rationale is multifaceted. As a result, nurse managers can be viewed as more than a short-run panacea for resolving the problems and constraints that are facing health care. They represent a viable long-run option for improving the prospects of the nursing profession and the health services delivery system.

THE CHANGING MANAGERIAL ROLE

There is a growing recognition that the views of health care administrators (and the organizations that they represent) and those of nurses (and the organizations in which they are employed) contrast in various ways.[1] Fundamentally, this is a result of different values, training, experience, and professional socialization. Nurses derive their power from professional expertise, and managers derive their power through delegation of authority. Nurses are interested in patient care processes and their implications for the individual patient. Managers tend to focus on outcomes in an aggregate sense (e.g., in terms of cases served, average costs, budgets attained, or revenues per visit). Managers also are committed to organizational goals. Nurses tend to emphasize personal and professional goals. These disparities existed in a competitive and cost-based reimbursement environment in which health care organizations did not battle for survival, but they are intolerable in a health care system in which mutual sacrifices and sharing are needed from nurses and health care organizations.

A changing role confronts nurse managers. Now more than ever, nurse managers are responsible for balancing organizational and nursing needs. To the extent that nurse managers achieve a harmonious balance, they will gain not only the respect of their staff members but also the respect of nonnursing managers as well. It is a matter of a better integration of nursing in an organizational context, which presents an entire range of new expectations and constraints.

As several nursing authorities have underscored, nurse managers must create a climate or culture in which nursing thrives while organizational objectives are achieved (e.g., costs are controlled; patient care is maintained; and staff, patients, and providers are satisfied).[2,3] In many respects, this orientation is a radical departure from the nursing leadership problems that existed throughout the 1970s and 1980s.[4] In other respects, however, the nursing manager's role has not changed. There is the prevailing question of how power will be exercised and responsibility shared to the benefit of nursing staff and the health care organizations for which they work.

Although the changing role of nurse managers is directly associated with significant alterations that are currently affecting health delivery, there are many antecedents from nursing's past that are also operating. Nursing has a long history of uncertainty about exactly how nursing administrators should be educated and what their managerial orientation should encompass.[5,6] Recently, there has been a shift in nurse executives' education toward a concentration on some area of administration.[7] The prognosis is that managerial preparation will increasingly be needed for effectively addressing nursing career problems,[8] the nursing shortage,[9] job enrichment,[10] turnover and satisfaction,[11] and structural relationships,[12] among many other difficult issues that are facing nurse managers. As a recent study of 350 nurse executives by the American Organization of Nurse Executives suggests, the challenge of this environment is the primary reason why many nurses are now seeking nurse executive positions.[13] Many are also discovering that they are expected to produce as well as manage, however.[14]

THE PROMISE OF NURSE MANAGERS

The rationale for and promise of nurse managers are intertwined with the values and needs of the nursing profession, the corporate infrastructure, and the health system's evolution (Figure 10-1).

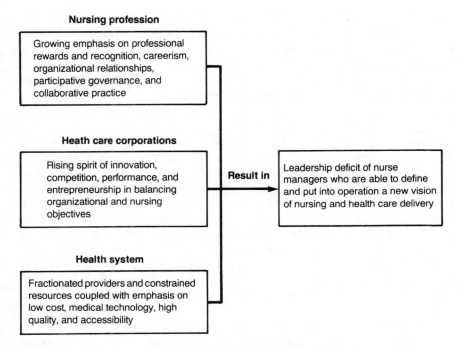

Nursing profession

Growing emphasis on professional rewards and recognition, careerism, organizational relationships, participative governance, and collaborative practice

Heath care corporations

Rising spirit of innovation, competition, performance, and entrepreneurship in balancing organizational and nursing objectives

Result in

Leadership deficit of nurse managers who are able to define and put into operation a new vision of nursing and health care delivery

Health system

Fractionated providers and constrained resources coupled with emphasis on low cost, medical technology, high quality, and accessibility

Figure 10-1 Health System Changes Producing a Leadership Deficit in Nursing

From the perspective of the nursing profession, it is apparent that extensive changes confront nurses, their value system, their patterns of practice, their professional and personal expectations, and their functional relationships. The result is a profession in transition without clear leadership. Although staff nurses are emphasizing professional rewards, career ladders, meaningful organizational relationships, participative governance, and collaborative practice, countervailing pressures are limiting the feasibility of achieving these interests. Nurse managers play a pivotal role in balancing nursing and organizational objectives.[15]

From the perspective of corporations, the issues raised in the nursing profession have always been important but seldom have been addressed directly. The management structure and governance of most health care corporations have been decidedly nonnursing in composition. This is caused by (1) nurses' compelling interest in clinical practice, (2) the lack of managerial skills development by key nurse managers, (3) a nursing profession value system that has not concerned itself with administrative issues or the power base inherent in nursing, and (4) a belief among health care managers that nurses are best utilized in clinical practice. All these factors have generated and perpetuated the assumption that nurses should not be sought for managerial and executive positions.

As prospective payment and competition have driven the health system toward more innovative, competitive, performance-oriented, and entrepreneurial patterns, it has become apparent that nurses should take a much more active managerial role.[16] Nurses ultimately determine whether patients, clients, or customers are satisfied with the care delivered by health care organizations and programs. Admittedly, physicians may have greater power than nurses in controlling satisfaction with treatment and diagnosis, but the nurse functions as an effective intermediary (i.e., between patients and health care organizations or providers such as physicians) and as an organizational representative. Nurses are also the primary people who are responsible for implementing physician orders; hence they are especially important in controlling resource allocations. These factors suggest that nurses should be integrated in the managerial infrastructure not just in token positions but in ways that facilitate nursing input and contribute to distinctive nursing performance. Many nurses are discovering that they are inexorably immersed in managerial and executive issues that were previously left to nonmedical managers.

Finally, the rationale for nurse managers is related to alterations in the health system. There has been progressive fractionation of the power base in health care. For example, the American Medical Association and its members formerly held extensive control over the health system. Physicians controlled strategic decisions such as facility construction, program expansion, equipment acquisition, scope of service, and other strategy-level issues. Much of this power has been lost, and the prospects are for continued erosion of the power base formerly held by physicians. In its place is a power base that is more evenly distributed among clinicians (i.e., nurses and physicians) and managers. Nurses have yet to utilize this new-found asset, however.

Pressures to contain health services use, a growing emphasis by the public on preventive health care, restructuring of medial practice to increase productivity, substitution of physician-based care with low-cost services by nursing and physician assistants, proliferation of medical technology, and rising interest in providing accessible services (consistent with competitive programs) result in an unsettling context. Nurses are immersed in this change. Whether their interests will be conveyed and respected is contingent on the abilities of their representatives.

Accompanying the fractionated health system is the need for effective leadership provided by nurse managers. As Figure 10-1 suggests, this leadership must define and put into operation a new vision of nursing in health care. That vision must acknowledge past traditions, values, and relationships, but it must also be less conservative, more economic and market driven, centered around organizational methods, and relieved of constraining protocols and traditional role perceptions. Constructive evolution of the nursing profession implies a reordering of priorities in nursing leadership but not such radical change that the system cannot accept or tolerate the progress. For these reasons, it is appropriate that nurse managers provide new leadership in the health system.

The future health care system will still be organizationally oriented and dominated, but nurses will encounter new opportunities to serve in organizational leadership capacities alongside those in clinical positions. As a result, the issue of who controls nursing and ancillary staff will become ever more controversial. Nurses can be most effectively managed by their peers. The best option therefore appears to be leadership from nurse managers who have acquired education, training, and experience in management concepts and skills. These leaders must be more than just token representatives; they must provide distinctive guidance for nursing and the health system.

Some nurse managers will occupy important managerial positions (e.g., department heads, program directors, or directors of nursing). Others will progressively attain even more powerful positions that allow them to affect the strategic directions of health care organizations and the health system. As key managers in line or staff positions and through participation in organizational governance (e.g., as board members), nurse managers will articulate how the health system evolves. In this process they will acquire sufficient organizational power to alter the structure and functioning of the health system.

The health system has become organizationally oriented with the expansion of corporations, multi-institutional arrangements, and managed reimbursement. Increasingly, health care organizations and corporate systems are discovering the importance of selecting the most capable managers at all levels. Nursing is no different. In this respect, health care organizations are beginning to emulate business corporations in terms of the investments made in choosing key managers. Businesses have found that managerial skills provide the foundation for success in highly competitive settings. A corporation may be able to maintain stability for a period of time without quality leadership, but growth will eventually be retarded or strategic errors made that jeopardize long-run organizational survival.

In view of these tendencies, corporations are aware that selecting capable leaders throughout the organizational hierarchy is essential for future corporate performance. Management staff determine where the firm is going (i.e., its mission) and how it will get there (i.e., its strategy). Implementation of the strategy also depends on managers. Furthermore, creation of strategic visions is now seen as a bottom-up process rather than a top-down and centralized exercise by the chief executive officer. Determination of vision remains the purview of top management, but strategy formulation increasingly requires involvement from managers throughout the organization.

THE MERITS OF NURSE MANAGERS

Figure 10-2 illustrates several valuable explanations of why nurse managers represent a promising choice for leading health care organizations and the nursing profession. Any one or a combination of these reasons may be sufficient incentive for organizations to develop their nurse managers.

Trust from Nurses

Realistically, nurse managers are an excellent choice for leadership positions in health care organizations because nurses trust and take direction best from their peers. What is true for many professionals, such as lawyers, accountants, educators, dentists, and physicians, holds true for nurses as well. The best way to develop effective leadership is to select a leader who already is trusted by those who will perform under the leader. Trust is not the only requirement for effective leadership, but it is a valuable precondition for eliciting desired responses from subordinates.

As highly educated professionals, nurses are predisposed to respect someone who has equivalent credentials. Nurse managers are positioned excep-

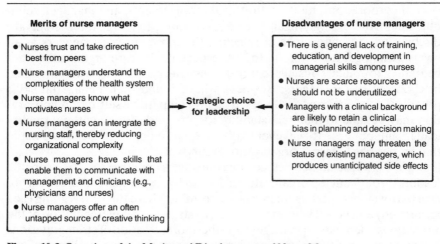

Figure 10-2 Overview of the Merits and Disadvantages of Nurse Managers

tionally to serve in leadership roles because they have already attained respect and trust. Both nurses and nonnurses (e.g., support staff and other managers) respect the training of nurse managers, and nurse managers can play on this respect and confidence to their greatest advantage. Clinicians will be less suspicious and more trusting of nurse managers. This trust can be used to its utmost when nurse managers are proposing significant strategic changes, resolving conflicts among nursing staff or between nursing staff and nonclinical staff, or eliciting commitment to decisions.

In sum, nurse managers represent a logical choice for leadership positions in the future as a result of the trust and respect that they command from other nurses. Because the health care system will always depend on nurses as long as they are the professionals who are licensed to deliver nursing care, it is reasonable to expect that health care organizations will take this factor into account in the selection of leaders. Trust is essential to any leader. Nurse managers have a unique ability to generate trust and respect.

Comprehension of Health System Complexities

A second reason why nurse managers can play a leading role in health care organizations involves their understanding of health system complexities. Nurses are highly conscious of trends that shape the health field. Why does an understanding of the complexities of the health system merit particular consideration when selecting nurse managers for leadership positions? The answer to this question is related to the nature of managerial functions and organizational behavior. A major conclusion from business research conducted since the 1960s is that corporate executives are primarily responsible for managing the interface between the organization and its environment. Organizations must respond to their environment if they expect to thrive.

For example, hospitals that were alert to certificate of need (CON) legislation trends prepared their organizational responses to accord with impending regulation before legislation was enacted. This attention to environmental trends and timely decision making helped them initiate facility construction projects and thereby avoid excessive costs associated with the CON review process, especially high construction costs due to delays in the review process. In short, sensitivity to environmental factors determined organizational success in responding to regulation.

Although nurses are educated to assist in identifying and curing specific diseases, they are also trained in a biological systems view. Hence they possess a fundamental philosophy about interrelationships among variables. They are analytically educated to put diagnostic evidence into an understandable whole when preparing for patient care and rehabilitation. This skill is a perfect precondition for a leadership perspective. By supplementing this perspective with knowledge about strategic management skills such as planning, decision making, and entrepreneurial foresight, nurse managers become well prepared for leadership positions in health care organizations.

Ability To Motivate Nurses

Nurse managers are commendable choices for leadership positions in the health care system because they know what motivates other nurses.[17] They have been educated with, have practiced with, and have cooperated with other nurses, so that they know what motivates them. Obviously, individuals differ. Some wish to keep the values underlying their personality private. Nevertheless, if nurse managers interact with enough colleagues they eventually are able to profile nurses according to basic values. The indoctrination of nursing training also stabilizes value differences. The result is consistency among nurses about the values surrounding medical care delivery.

Nurse managers make good leaders because they know how other nurses think and what they value.[18] Although only a moderate percentage of personnel in most health care organizations are nurses, the presence of nurses is important because they make decisions that affect medical care expenditures. Therefore, the basis for good organizational performance is addressing the motivations of nurses. By understanding these values and constructing appropriate reward systems there is an excellent probability that better performance will be attained, whether in terms of higher quality of care or lower cost of care.

Because nurse managers know the motivations of other nurses, they are better prepared to articulate sophisticated performance evaluation systems and compensation plans. The impact of any single nurse on total organizational performance should be minimized. Nurse managers may have a distinct advantage in being able to provide leadership through an effective control and reward system. A nurse manager has a decided advantage over non-nurses in articulating performance incentives, defining tolerable systems of personal performance evaluation, and attaining nursing staff support of the proposed programs.

Ability To Manage Nursing Staff

Nurse managers are effective agents for working with the nursing staff. Staff nurses will increasingly need a representative whom they can trust because many of the pressures that are forcing financial restructuring of the health system also have a direct effect on services provided by nurses. This is a serious situation because the relationship among nursing staff, medical staff, and management staff in most health care institutions is less than agreeable. Hospitals amply illustrate this point. The history of hospital–nursing staff relations has often been adversarial. Many nursing staff members perceive that hospitals view nurses only as an essential prerequisite for organizational survival. This attitude has forced hospitals to rethink their investments in service delivery. Hospitals have grown increasingly hesitant to succumb to the requests of an unreasonable nursing staff. The supply and demand in the labor economics of the nursing profession prevent excessive retaliation, however. Hospitals are forced to retain good relations with the nursing staff despite the acrimony that may surface over resource allocations.

These pressures point to one inevitable conclusion. The overlooked issue of nursing staff relations must eventually receive attention from health care organizations. The primary questions are "How will these relations be improved?" and "Who will be most responsible for introducing change or negotiating improved relations?" There have been few advocates on either the management side or the nursing staff side who can cross over and attain compromise. Therefore, nurse managers hold substantial promise for resolving one of the most difficult problems facing health care organizations.

Dual Set of Skills

Nurse managers have skills that are mutually admired by management and nursing staff. Accompanying these skills is a familiarity with both managerial and nursing (or clinical) terminology. This asset is important because nurse managers can communicate in a common language with both managers and nurses. It is not the terminology itself that is so important but the concepts underlying the terminology and what the concepts convey philosophically. In other words, nurse managers are prepared to understand the needs of managers and nursing staff. Through better understanding comes a propensity to identify workable solutions that promote compromise and agreement instead of conflict and problem continuation.

The organizational implications of smooth nursing staff–management relations from this dual set of skills are impressive:

- nurses are more easily integrated with the rest of the organization, thereby producing more efficient operations
- the dichotomy of nursing staff authority and managerial line authority is minimized, thereby producing more opportunities for productive interaction rather than reaction

- the nursing staff can provide insight into operations and planning for the organization; as health care organizations are now operated, the nursing staff may not have an active role in this regard
- the nursing staff is encouraged to promote the organization in the community and when serving clients; essentially, the nursing staff can provide valuable marketing assistance in extensive word-of-mouth advertising and explicit actions

These and other benefits suggest that nurse managers should be strongly considered a strategic advantage for leadership positions.

Source of Creative Thinking

Nurse managers offer a fruitful source of creative ideas for many organizations. Despite their training and exposure to policy issues in the health care field, the nursing staff can be one of the least used sources of innovative thinking in health care organizations.[19] This results from several factors:

- nurses seldom are encouraged by management to share their good ideas; there are no conduits by which this can be achieved
- without an expectation that nurses have valuable ideas to share, managers seldom think of asking them for their input
- strategic planning (in which creativity is vitally needed) proceeds with representation primarily from management staff; nurses are incorporated minimally in strategic planning processes
- there are few, if any, rewards for sharing creative ideas; in fact, the opposite—criticism—occurs because creative ideas may be viewed as radical departures from the status quo
- nurses are involved in producing services in which they see immediate and tangible benefits from their efforts; participation in strategic planning produces tangible end results only over the long run

Considering these and similar reasons, nurses have little motivation for sharing creative ideas.

A significant question is to what degree health care organizations are losing valuable ideas that should be considered in long-run planning or strategy formulation. If one extrapolates the total professional network held by any single nurse over the entire nursing staff, it becomes clear that the nursing staff is an incredible reserve of new ideas. Any single nursing staff member has an extensive collegial network. There are ties to nurses throughout the community and across the nation. As a result of professional training, the network extends to internships, professional societies, and universities.

At any given moment, a nurse uses a minor percentage of information from the professional network. From a practical standpoint, nurses have no other choice because they are immersed in delivering care and cannot afford to maintain active contact with the professional network. Even if a nurse wanted to massage the network, it would be difficult to do so in terms of the time required. Thus messages and creative ideas are received sporadically and with no apparent method. When this randomness is spread over a large nursing staff, an incredibly rich source of information is not being utilized.

Can nurse managers tap the creative ideas and professional network of staff nurses? The answer to this question depends on the extent to which the organization is interested in receiving good ideas. Nurse managers should provide a valuable conduit for the ideas of nursing staff members. They are nurses themselves and hence know what mechanisms to employ in soliciting input. They can acquire the trust of nurses. They are alert to blocking tactics because they have probably used the same tactics themselves to avoid requests from the organization. From all these perspectives, nurse managers are a valuable asset for directing nurse input of creative ideas into the organization.

THE DISADVANTAGES OF NURSE MANAGERS

Balanced against the arguments as to why nurse managers should be managing key positions in the health system are a number of counterclaims (Figure 10-2). Many of these countervailing arguments are compelling. By assessing the pros and cons of expanded nurse manager roles, health care organizations will be better prepared to establish a strategic choice for leadership and a foundation for an organization culture that is devoted to excellence. Not every health care organization should automatically adopt an expanded role for nurse managers. There are a number of factors that suggest that such wholesale adoption could cause problems.

Lack of Managerial Education

One of the most cogent reasons why the health system should not support expanded roles for nurse managers relates to their lack of education in and development of managerial skills.[20] Few nurses who enter management or administrative positions have extensive, formal training in management skills. This does not suggest that all administrative or managerial positions require specialized business administration training. Some positions do require the skills; others do not. If nurse managers are interested in improving personal performance, however, their actions should be related to a conceptual or theoretical framework that provides the best possibility for success. Theory alone is not enough. There should also be a curriculum of skills accompanying the theory as a means for attaining the ends proposed by the theory.[21]

How can nurses acquire the skills necessary to prepare them for managerial level positions? Nurses must recognize that simply holding a nursing degree is no guarantee that they are qualified to fill managerial positions. Skills must be cultivated beforehand. The alternatives to acquiring training are numerous and readily accessible and include:

- formal degree programs in management at the undergraduate or, preferably, graduate level
- management development programs that educate participants in all functional areas
- professional association programs in continuing education
- internal organizational programs in management development
- self-study incorporating university and executive development courses

Executive development programs seldom address the more quantitative sides of managing, but these are precisely the skill areas that nurse managers need most.[22] It is too easy to conclude that information processing, accounting, or financial techniques can be completed by line managers who are extensively trained in these functional areas.

Nurses who wish to assume managerial positions must search for opportunities to gain experience and education that contribute to their professional growth. Taking part in truly worthwhile responsibilities (to gain experience) and programs (for education) requires substantial investments of time. Even after prerequisites are attained, nurses realize that the developmental process is never ending. It is a quest that requires continued investment. Some nurses may be willing to undertake such efforts, especially because they have already invested heavily in their nursing careers.

Scarcity of Nursing Resources

Another reason why nurses should not seek managerial positions in the health system relates to the undersupply of nursing resources. For years the U.S. health care system has fought a battle of scarcity of resources. It is apparent that not enough registered nurses are electing to continue in practice. Although advocates for nurse managers can point out that the number of nurses actually entering management positions is small compared with the total number of nurses, there still is the recognition that the health system has fought a battle to increase the number of nurses who are engaged in clinical practice. To transform them into managers appears to obviate this effort.

A Clinical Bias

A third argument against nurse managers relates to a potential clinical bias in their decisions. It can be argued that managers educated in the business, administrative, and management sciences are better prepared to make the businesslike decisions that are needed in the health care field.[23] They have cultivated a perspective that allows them to focus on organizational issues. This viewpoint is derived from exposure to the following topics during education:

- decision trees, probability, and expected values
- decision criteria (e.g., minimax and maximax)
- linear and integer programming
- systems analysis
- break-even analysis
- computer and systems modeling
- statistical applications in quality control
- techniques for evaluating rate of return (e.g., average rate of return, payback, net present worth, and so forth)
- capital budgeting methods
- cost-effectiveness analysis

These are only a few of the techniques to which managers are exposed in the best business school programs. The intent of these techniques is to facilitate decision making in a wide variety of situations ranging from certainty to uncertainty.

Unless nurses acquire additional education in managerial decision-making techniques, they may be unprepared to leave behind their clinical bias and thereby to achieve desired objectivity in management decisions. It is not that nurses are any less objective in their approach to decision making than other managers. They are predisposed to a clinical bias because of their nursing education. The press of daily decision making provides plenty of incentive to become immersed in operating details, which drives decision makers into ad hoc and reactionary responses.

By not becoming thoroughly familiar with the best technology available from management science, nurse managers may not be prepared to address the trade-offs between clinical and organizational issues. Even more troublesome, they have not established a basis for carrying this frame of reference over into daily activities. They are more attuned to the clinical side of operations. A good illustration is the problem of nurse staffing. Nursing education predisposes the nurse manager to do everything possible to provide the highest quality of care. This demands the best nursing care feasible and suggests that more nursing hours per patient will attain this patient care goal. Higher nursing hours per patient raises the cost of care. Consequently, nurse managers face the dilemma of simultaneously advocating clinical (i.e., nursing hours) and managerial (i.e., lowered costs) objectives.

The clinical education of nurses creates a bias toward patient care issues. This is a vital orientation, but one that may be an obstacle to organizations attempting to drive down the cost of care. Superfluous nursing hours are expensive. There is a need to cut nursing costs to a minimum. The nurse manager may recognize this but may also be unable to implement the idea optimally because of prior professional socialization. Furthermore, the nurse manager may simply not know what to do to achieve the desired goal.

Threats to Existing Managers

Another reason why nurse managers should not be advocated in the health system relates to the impact on existing managers. There may be unanticipated consequences for the management infrastructure.

- By instituting a policy of developing nurse managers, an organization explicitly alters the career ladder for managers who do not have a nursing degree.
- Managers who are not chosen for promotions because nurse managers have been chosen instead may engage in sabotage. People pursue self-interests in an organizational context. When that self-interest is blocked, there is an increasing probability that retaliation will occur.
- The organization may be directed away from a hard-nosed approach to managing operations toward a strategy that emphasizes patient care. It may be difficult for nurse managers to abandon their patient care roots.

For every action there is a reaction. This fundamental law of science applies in organizations as well as in physics. If the top echelon of health care organizations supports the proliferation of nurses in management positions, there may be a reaction somewhere in the organizations (e.g., among ancillary services department heads who perceive that they are losing power). The challenge is to anticipate this reaction and to prevent it before it occurs.

THE POTENTIAL FOR NURSE MANAGERS

On balance, there are many good arguments both for and against nurse managers. Nevertheless, the sum of these arguments suggests that there is considerable promise for expanded roles of nurse managers in health care. The problem is to minimize the dysfunctional factors that may be associated with their contribution. This can be achieved through the following means:[24]

- educate nurse managers so that they are on par with other managers and executives in expertise
- instill incentive and reward systems that encourage nurse managers to make objective, organization-oriented decisions; tie performance to diverse organizational goals, particularly economic goals, to temper the temptation to concentrate on patient care (or other special emphases)
- maintain a competitive career ladder such that end results, rather than training or predispositions, determine who will or will not fill managerial positions

These are only a few of the actions that can be taken to prevent the criticisms normally associated with clinician involvement in management.

Rather than dwelling on why nurse managers should not expand their roles, it is constructive to focus on their potential contribution (Figure 10-3). Nurse managers have exceptional promise for improving management in health care organizations. They are knowledgeable about health organization operations. They are analytical in perspective, systems oriented and decisive (as a result of their clinical education), and able to elicit trust and confidence from health professionals.

The point of Figure 10-3 is that nurse managers have exceptional promise for contributing to the management requirements of health care organizations.[25] As a result, they should be able to provide leadership as health care organizations confront many of the diverse environmental pressures that are shaping the industry. Whether it is changes in reimbursement policy, corporate growth, regulation, fiscal pressures, changes in medical technology, or public expectations and values that demand new performance from health care organizations or the problems presented by professional career ladders, nurse managers appear to be well prepared to address the ambiguities of these pressures.

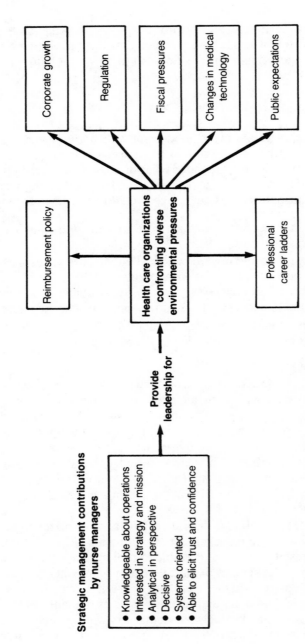

Figure 10-3 The Potential Contribution of Nurse Managers to Health Care Organizations

Identifying Crucial Skills for Nurse Managers

In the management field, a consensus has gradually been forming that there is no single best set of skills (and hence education or development) that should be taught to aspiring managers. In fact, developments in systems theory and contingency views of managing suggest that there is no single best way to manage.[26] Each situation requires a unique management style and set of skills for effective performance. Therefore, managers attempt to control relevant variables in specific settings to influence performance.

For example, a medical laboratory manager might concentrate on managing the acquisition and maintenance of equipment (because of such equipment's ability to raise productivity), scheduling of personnel to match demand for tests with productive capacity, rewarding and retaining personnel who are not only productive but also commit a minimum of errors, and structuring work to heighten productivity while instilling checks on the accuracy of testing. The laboratory manager may devote less attention to integrating the laboratory with other functions in the overall organization, identifying methods for diversifying services, planning cost containment, initiating participative decision making in the structure of the laboratory, and contributing to the market mix of the overall organization. The point of this illustration is that the laboratory manager can devote considerable attention, time, and resources to some factors and minimal time to other factors.

In contrast, the stockbroker who is in charge of 30 associates will undertake an extraordinary effort to manage many of the variables that the laboratory manager has suboptimized. The stockbroker is concerned with smoothly integrating all operating functions in the agency (i.e., economic forecasting, client service, financial consulting services, maintenance of the agency's portfolio, and so forth); identifying alternatives by which the agency can logically and profitably diversify its services (e.g., into other financial services, life insurance, and investment counseling); devising methods for helping associates raise productivity while maximizing the return to the agency; implementing decentralized decision making and quality circles to maximize the organic (as opposed to bureaucratic) nature of human relations in the agency; and marketing the agency's services through an expanded advertising program.

The dual illustrations of managing the medical laboratory and stockbroker agency underscore that the appropriate management response in different settings is unique. No single set of skills is appropriate for every management or executive position. As W. Allen Wallis, former Dean of the University of Chicago School of Business and Chancellor of the University of Rochester, indicates, managers of the future do not need instruction in what to do or how to do it.[27] They need exposure to broad concepts that will stand the test of time. Specific skills and knowledge can be acquired in each job context as conditions dictate their acquisition.

These thoughts are important when considering the set of skills and concepts required by nurse managers. It is clear that no one set of specific skills will help them manage every situation. Instead, nurse managers need to develop methods of thinking that are simultaneously based on nursing, patient care, and business principles. They need to develop a posture toward managerial responsibilities that addresses day-to-day operations. It follows that the specific functional requirements differ for administrative, managerial, and executive leadership positions.

The variations in functional requirements for nurse managers are illustrated in Table 10-1. Chief nursing officers, associate and assistant chief nursing officers, and head nurses are compared according to conceptual, human, and technical skills. It is suggested that matching skill requirements (held by nurse managers) with position demands can result in highly effective managerial performance.[28-30]

Chief nursing officer positions require individuals who are capable of thinking at conceptual or abstract levels in terms of priorities and trade-offs among objectives. Conceptual thinking supports the decision-making demands that confront chief nursing officers. Less important than conceptual skills but still significant are skill requirements in human factors (e.g.,

Table 10-1 Variations in Skill Levels among Nurse Managers

	Skill Level		
Skill	Chief Nursing Officer	Associate or Assistant Chief Nursing Officer	Head Nurse
Conceptual (thinking in abstract terms about priorities and trade-offs among objectives, probabilities, and patterns)	Very high	High	Moderately high
Human (leadership ability and intergroup relations)	High	High	High
Technical (capability in nursing practice)	Low	Moderate	High

Source: Adapted from "A Management Progression System for Nurse Administrators, Part 2" by M.F. Fralic and A. O'Connor, *Journal of Nursing Administration*, Vol. 13, No. 5, pp. 32–38, with permission of J.B. Lippincott Company, © May 1983.

leadership ability and intergroup relations). Less relevant for chief nursing officers are technical nursing skills, although they do need a high level of technical managerial skill.

These skill requirements are easily contrasted with those of head nurse positions. Head nurses have close supervisory interactions with staff nurses. Consequently, they must be able to perform the tasks required of staff nurses to monitor, control, and evaluate staff performance. Ability to mentor hinges on their understanding of and ability to undertake nursing care. Head nurse interaction with line nurses mandates a high degree of skill in human relations. Unlike the chief nursing officers, however, head nurses need fewer conceptual skills. In sum, Table 10-1 underscores that skill competencies and requirements are contingent on the managerial position.

Differentiating Administrators from Managers

Administration is centered around large-scale organization and is most prevalent in (although not exclusive to) bureaucratic organizations such as government agencies. Despite a change of emphasis in bureaucratic administration over the last several decades toward concern for effectiveness, the basic difference between administration and management remains.[31,32] Administration and supervision imply a relatively passive approach to overseeing operations of a program, department, or organization. It suggests that the person in charge is attempting to achieve smooth or efficient operations within given resource allocations. Consequently, the administrator usually does not develop a strategic vision or articulate new goals. The administrative role is basically one of ensuring the highest level of operational efficiency.

In contrast, management implies a much more dynamic and proactive approach to running operations.[33] It suggests that managers are concerned not only with achieving efficient operations but also with ensuring that effective performance is attained (however effectiveness may be defined). The manager may be actively involved in defining a vision of which goals and objectives the program, department, or organization will pursue. The manager will react to resource allocations in an organization by negotiating, arguing, politicking, or other means to acquire a larger allotment. These characteristics of administrators and managers are depicted in Figure 10-4.

The primary difference between administrators and managers in nursing is best captured by the concept of scope of responsibility.[34] Administrators are basically maintenance oriented; that is, they focus on existing operations.[35] Administrators usually are minimally involved in defining a vision for the nursing program.[36] Managers, in comparison, are involved in setting direction and objectives for nursing services. They utilize a general management

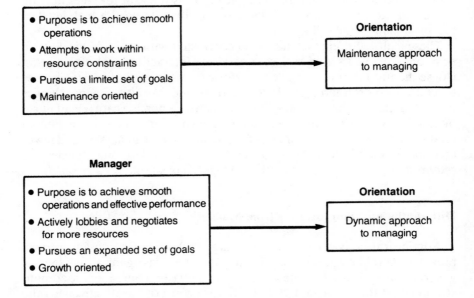

Administrator

- Purpose is to achieve smooth operations
- Attempts to work within resource constraints
- Pursues a limited set of goals
- Maintenance oriented

Orientation

Maintenance approach to managing

Manager

- Purpose is to achieve smooth operations and effective performance
- Actively lobbies and negotiates for more resources
- Pursues an expanded set of goals
- Growth oriented

Orientation

Dynamic approach to managing

Figure 10-4 Key Differences between Administrators and Managers

perspective.[37] They aggressively pursue more resources to support an expanded vision or purpose for their work team, department, division, or organization.

Differentiating Managers from Executives

Just as there is a difference between administrators and managers, so too is there a contrast between managers and executives. This contrast is largely the result of basic entrepreneurial activities, the growth of large-scale organizations, the separation of ownership and control, the development of strategic management theory, and the differentiation of operational responsibilities from key leadership responsibilities. These differences between managers and executives are depicted in Figure 10-5.

The primary feature that differentiates managers from executives is the extent of their authority to formulate organizational vision. Managers hold a limited strategic vision for their program, department, or organization because they are extremely involved in controlling current operations. They have restricted time, freedom, and prerogative to determine where an

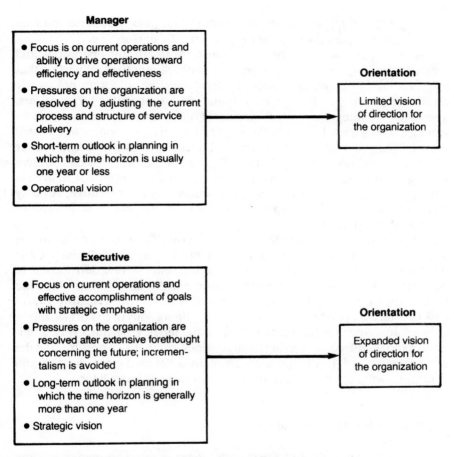

Figure 10-5 Key Differences between Managers and Executives

organization is headed over the long run.[38] On the other hand, executives are more interested in forming a strategic vision of where a program, department, division, or organization is headed and in elucidating the conceptual steps that are required to arrive at that point. As a result, executives have an expanded vision for organizations.[39]

Managers are oriented toward current operations. Consequently, their effort is directed to operations management, or fine tuning of operations. This is generally reflected in a short-run outlook in planning. Goals and objectives are primarily set for a period that is consistent with the current budgeting cycle. The culmination of this operations orientation is a limited vision of where an organization is headed. Less effort is devoted to conceptualizing which direction the organization should pursue because so much effort is given to how the organization is currently performing.

Executives are normally oriented toward both current operations and long-run strategy.[40] The executive attends to operations to make certain that efficiency and effectiveness goals are achieved. Executives do not overly dwell on current operations, however; that is a responsibility for managers. The executive integrates a focus on current operations with an emphasis on strategy. This is clearly seen in the need to formulate responses to external pressures (e.g., heightened competition). Executives move deliberately after they have envisioned the big picture. Thus market changes or competitive aggression are insular events that must be placed in perspective. Changes in strategy, structure, or process may be introduced by the executive, but only after the future is taken into consideration. In this way, a disjointed or incremental approach is avoided.

Executives maintain an outlook of the long run. Their planning horizon is seldom less than 1 year. They concern themselves with events outside the organization and the manner in which those events will be detrimental to operations. The result is an expanded vision of the direction in which the organization is headed. Executives temper this vision with a healthy awareness of internal operations. The abilities and limitations of the organization are well analyzed. Therefore, executives avoid moving too quickly or ambitiously and thereby endangering fiscal solvency, competitive posture, and the general essence of the organization. Executives define the organization and determine what the organization will resemble many years hence.

Implications for Nurse Managers

As the preceding discussion suggests, there is more to managing than appears at first glance. There is an entire hierarchy of managerial roles that has surfaced in nursing administration alone. It is probable that the diversity of these roles will increase in the future. In each of the primary roles defined above there are numerous gradients of skill requirements. For example, chief nursing officers, associate and assistant chief nursing officers, and head nurses need different skills because of variations in their delegated responsibilities. These variations account for the fact that some managers are delegated extensive autonomy to define the direction of their department or division. Others are primarily responsible for operations. These distinctions are illustrated for decisions made in selected areas by the three levels of nurse managers in Table 10-2.[41]

It is difficult to identify and categorize precisely the skills that are associated with managerial roles in nursing. This does not mean that managerial

Table 10-2   Variations in Decisions by Nursing Managers

Decision Area	Chief Nursing Officer	Associate or Assistant Chief Nursing Officer	Head Nurse
Environmental interface			
Economic forces	• changes in hospital financing systems • cost controls exerted on hospitals • economic conditions in local business and industry • patterns of workers returning to the work force	• impact of cost-control measures on the work of the service • impact of cost-control measures on patterns of patient care • possible alternative responses to potential decline in resources available for patient care	• impact of cost-control measures on the work of the nursing unit • impact of cost-control measures on patterns of patient care • possible unit-level responses to potential decline in resources available for patient care
Mission, purpose, and goals			
Organizational	• participation in the development of institutionwide goals and strategies	• interpretation of organization's mission, purpose, and goals	• interpretation of organization's mission, purpose, and goals
Divisional	• development of nursing division goals incorporating the organization's goals and objectives	• participation in the development of nursing division goals and objectives	• participation in the development of nursing division goals and objectives
Unit philosophy	• reflection of the nursing division philosophy in individualized unit-level philosophy statements	• establish philosophy statements for each unit in the service that conform with and support the nursing division philosophy	• establish unit-level philosophy statement that conforms with the nursing division philosophy

continues

Table 10-2   continued

Decision Area	Chief Nursing Officer	Associate or Assistant Chief Nursing Officer	Head Nurse
Objectives	• goals and objectives statements for each unit reflective of the unique work of each patient care unit	• establish goals and objective statements for each unit in the service that contribute to divisional goals and reflect the unique work of the unit	• establish unit-level goals and objectives that contribute to divisional goals while reflecting the unique work of the unit
Organizational design			
Preparation of staff	• selection of key managers who are appropriately experienced and prepared	• selection of head nurses and other key nursing personnel who are appropriately experienced and prepared	• identification and selection of appropriately prepared nursing personnel to accomplish the work of the unit
	• standards and qualifications for all levels of personnel in the nursing division	• standards and qualifications for all levels of personnel in the service	
Managerial strategies			
Position descriptions	• system to provide for the definition and delineation of the work of each position in the nursing division by using organizational guidelines	• system to provide for the definition and delineation of the work of each position in the service by using organizational and divisional guidelines	• clarification or adaptation of divisional position description to reflect the specialized work of the unit

Source: Reprinted from "A Management Progression System for Nurse Administrators, Part 1" by M.F. Fralic and A. O'Connor, *Journal of Nursing Administration*, Vol. 13, No. 4, p. 12, with permission of J.B. Lippincott Company, © April 1983.

roles are impossible to distinguish, however, as Tables 10-1 and 10-2 illustrate. There are several dimensions that differentiate among the types of skills that nurse managers must utilize. These differences are useful in understanding the variability among roles. These differences also imply that what it means to manage today is becoming increasingly complex. There is no common stereotype of a nurse manager that encompasses the administrative, managerial, and executive roles. Managing is a complex task that is ever changing.

Prognosis for Nurse Manager Roles in the Future

In the future, the level of distinction among nurse manager positions will probably increase. The tendency for external environmental forces to influence managing continues. As health care corporations become more complex, nurse manager roles will increase in sophistication. Nonetheless, the functions of managers will remain the same. Recognizing that management functions are likely to remain the same, it is appropriate for aspiring nurse managers to gain specific knowledge and skills in these functions. The functional knowledge and skills can be invoked as the role requires.

NOTES

1. B.N. Carlson and C.P. McLaughlin, "Managers and Nurses: Understanding Both Worlds," *Nurse Practitioner* 10 (October 1985): 51-54.

2. M.A. Poulin, "Future Directions for Nursing Administration," *Journal of Nursing Administration* 14 (March 1984): 37-41.

3. D. England, "The Strengths and Weaknesses in Nursing Service Administration," *Nursing Outlook* 28 (September 1980): 551-556.

4. J.M. Zorn, "Nursing Leadership for the 70s and 80s," *Journal of Nursing Administration* 7 (October 1977): 33-35.

5. R.B. Fine, "The Supply and Demand of Nursing Administrators," *Nursing and Health Care* 4 (January 1983): 10-15.

6. R.R. Alward, "Nursing Administration in Crisis," *Nursing Forum* 19 (1980): 242-253.

7. B. McCormick, "Nurse Executives Most Often Picked from Hospital Staff," *Hospitals* 60 (November 1986): 91.

8. K.W. Vestal, "Nursing Careers: Challenges for the Nursing Administrator," *Nursing Clinics of North America* 18 (September 1983): 473-479.

9. H. Benedikter, "Nurse Administrator's Role Grows as Staff Problems Continue," *Hospitals* 58 (April 1984): 154-158.

10. J.L. Garvey and S. Rottet, "Expanding the Hospital Nursing Role: An Administrative Account," *Journal of Nursing Administration* 12 (December 1982): 30-34.

11. P.F. Johnston, "Head Nurses as Middle Managers," *Journal of Nursing Administration* 13 (November 1983): 22-26.

12. "Nursing or Administration: Which Is Better?" *American Operating Room Nurses Journal* 29 (May 1979): 1130-1135.

13. B. McCormick, "Nurse Executives Seek Advancement," *Hospitals* 60 (October 1986): 138.

14. C.M. Freund, "The Tenure of Directors of Nursing," *Journal of Nursing Administration* 15 (February 1985): 11-15.

15. F.H. Howarth, "A Holistic View of Middle Management," *Nursing Outlook* 30 (November/December 1982): 522-526.

16. L.C. Hodges, R. Knapp, and J. Cooper, "Head Nurses: Their Practice and Education," *Journal of Nursing Administration* 17 (December 1987): 39-44.

17. K. Moore et al., "Nurse Executive Effectiveness," *Journal of Nursing Administration* 18 (December 1988): 23-27.

18. C.M. Freund, "Director of Nursing Effectiveness," *Journal of Nursing Administration* 15 (June 1985): 25-30.

19. C.K. Golightly, "Head Nurses' Activities and Supervisors' Expectations: A Nurse Executive Responds," *Journal of Nursing Administration* 13 (June 1983): 31-33.

20. L. Friss, "Nursing Administration: The Problem or Solution?" *Nursing Management* 18 (August 1987): 84-85.

21. M.M. Hansen, "Preparing for High-Level Nursing Administration Positions," *Critical Care Quarterly* 5 (June 1982): 7-15.

22. M.E. Stokinger, "Nursing vs. Nonnursing Preparation," *American Journal of Nursing* 80 (June 1980): 1129.

23. P.S. Nugent, "Management and Modes of Thought," *Journal of Nursing Administration* 12 (February 1982): 19-25.

24. N. Ertl, "Choosing Successful Managers," *Journal of Nursing Administration* 14 (April 1984): 27-33.

25. M.F. Fralic, "The Effective Nurse Executive's Blueprint for Success," *Journal of Nursing Administration* 18 (June 1986): 9-12.

26. M.J. Cutler, "Nursing Leadership and Management: A Historical Perspective," *Nursing Administration Quarterly* 3 (1979): 7-19.

27. W.A. Wallis, "Educating Future Managers," in *Managers in the Year 2000*, ed. W.H. Newman (Englewood Cliffs, NJ: Prentice-Hall, 1978), 105-106.

28. M.F. Fralic and A. O'Connor, "A Management Progression System for Nurse Administrators, Part 1," *Journal of Nursing Administration* 13 (April 1983): 9-13.

29. M.F. Fralic and A. O'Connor, "A Management Progression System for Nurse Administrators, Part 2," *Journal of Nursing Administration* 13 (May 1983): 32-38.

30. M.F. Fralic and A. O'Connor, "A Management Progression System for Nurse Administrators, Part 3," *Journal of Nursing Administration* 13 (June 1983): 7-12.

31. F.A. Kramer, ed., *Perspectives on Public Bureaucracy* (Cambridge, MA: Winthrop, 1977).

32. L. Gulick and L. Urwick, eds., *Papers on the Science of Administration* (New York: Institute of Public Administration, Columbia University, 1937).

33. H. Koontz, C. O'Donnell, and H. Weihrich, *Management* (New York: McGraw-Hill, 1984).

34. M.L. McClure, "The Administrative Component of the Nurse Administrator's Role," *Nursing Administration Quarterly* 3 (Spring 1979): 1-12.

35. J. Nyberg, "The Role of the Nursing Administrator in Practice," *Nursing Administration Quarterly* 6 (Summer 1982): 67-73.

36. L.B. Williams and D.W. Cancian, "A Clinical Nurse Specialist in a Line Management Position," *Journal of Nursing Administration* 15 (January 1985): 20-26.

37. J. Blake and D. Towell, "Developing Effective Management for the General Nursing Service," *Journal of Advanced Nursing* 7 (1982): 309-317.

38. R.S. Dunne, S.A. Ehrlich, and B.S. Mitchell, "A Middle Management Development Program for Middle Level Nurse Managers," *Journal of Nursing Administration* 18 (May 1988): 11-16.

39. B.M. Kooker, "The Corporate Images of a Nurse Executive," *Nursing Management* 17 (February 1986): 52-55.

40. M.A. Poulin, "The Nurse Executive Role: A Structural and Functional Analysis," *Journal of Nursing Administration* 14 (February 1984): 9-14.

41. Fralic and O'Connor, "A Management Progression System for Nurse Administrators, Part 1," 9-11.

Index